Local Governance in India
Experiences after the Constitutional Amendments

Local Governance in India

Experiences after the Constitutional Amendments

Edited by

E. Venkatesu

KALPAZ

ISBN: 978-93-5128-202-0

Price: ₹ 1125

First Published, 2016

Published by

Kalpaz Publications
C-30, Satyawati Nagar,
Delhi – 110052
E-mail: kalpaz@hotmail.com
Ph.: 9212142040

Printed at: G. Print Process, Delhi

Cataloging in Publication Data—DK
Courtesy: D.K. Agencies (P) Ltd. <docinfo@dkagencies.com>

National Seminar on 'Democratic Decentralisation in India Two Decades of Constitutional Amendments: Experiments, Issues and Challenges' (2013 : Department of Political Science, University of Hyderabad)
Local governance in India : experiences after constitutional amendments / [editor], E. Venkatesu.
pages cm
Papers presented in a National Seminar on 'Democratic Decentralisation in India Two Decades of Constitutional Amendments: Experiments, Issues and Challenges' organized by Department of Political Science, University of Hyderabad, on April 25-26, 2013.
Includes bibliographical references.
ISBN 9789351282020

1. Local government—India—Congresses. 2. Local government—Law and legislation—India—Congresses. 3. Decentralization in government—India—Congresses. I. Veṅkaṭēśu, I., 1969- editor. II. University of Hyderabad. Department of Political Science, organizer. III. Title.

JS7008.V46 2013 DDC 320.80954 23

Contents

Foreword

—Professor P. Durgaprasad*

'Good governance is the lifeline of any vibrant democracy. Decentralised planning and community-driven development comprise the core of grass root management, especially in the context of growth with justice and inclusive development'.

There is growing demand from the state governments and local bodies as well for nurturing key components of democracy, human rights and governance. Measurement of basic outcomes, effects and game changing impacts of democracy and governance is enabling real time decision-making by the elected representatives of PRIs, and officials of the rural development delivery systems.

Functional use of indicators and calibrated indexing of welfare, gender and socio-economic progress is conspicuous in a significant number of papers of this edited volume. The criticality of well-articulated debate, robust policies and dynamic action plans is forcefully driven home by Asia-Pacific and pan-Indian papers in particular.

The plethora of governance indicators that are used by State Governments, development agencies, NGOs, CBOs, Media, Academic Institutions and the Private Sector is highlighted with illustrations with specific reference to welfare programmes like the PDS in particular. The expected development outcomes and indicators are used to inform the users regarding allocation of public funds, advocacy, academic research and business investment in the context of public-public and public-private partnerships.

The book makes a significant contribution to development thinking by outlining specific drivers of development transformation and by suggesting future policy priorities that could help sustain the new impetus to inclusive growth.

---

* Chairman and CEO, National Council of Rural Institutes, Ministry of HRD, GoI, Hyderabad.

A key message that emanates from the empirical evidence in the book is that economic growth alone does not automatically translate into human development. Pro-poor policies and significant investments in people's capabilities via literacy, education, skill development, employment, health, and nutrition are seen as harbingers of good governance and prime movers of rural change.

That infrastructural development and cutting edge convergence of development institutions like the PRIs and rural development programmes such as the MGNREGS, is key to sustained social change is succinctly brought out by the book editors. Environmental problems and promotion too, are seen as strategic components of ecological balance and climate change. The point of rural-urban continuum and the need for urban governance is articulated in tune with the current emphasis on balanced growth.

The point that 'the letter and spirit of the 73rd Constitutional Amendment is the seed-bed of sustained change' is imaginatively captured by the writers with illustrations of models of self-governance including the intent and import of PESA.

Evidently, a great deal of effort has gone into the making of this book with high contemporary relevance and application for micro-planning and decentralised development. The consequences of social stratification and administrative biases and incompetence would inevitably provide room for conflict and negative energy. This is timely caution by the paper writers for the development fraternity. Conflicts and negative assertions constitute a magnified version of the divisions within us. Problem resolution and conflict management episodes are highlighted in the discussions on Panchayats and local governance. In this context, I am reminded of Shiv Khera's articulation on 'problem-resolution' when he said "if you want to resolve a problem, you should become a part of the problem resolution... and if you are not, then, you are the problem." I find this premise and strategy quite promising, as I had tried it out successfully in my own institutional management context.

Policy-makers, development practitioners, and scholars working on public systems and good governance will find this meticulously edited book immensely useful.

Preface

*—Professor I. Ramabrahmam**

According to the conceptual framework of the principle of subsidiarity, the process of governance is devolving of the functions from bottom to top. The citizen, as an individual, alone may not be able to perform all the functions, which are essential for the fulfilling of basic needs, therefore, some of them will be given to the community. Again, the community may also not be able to discharge all the functions that have been assigned by the citizens, so that certain functions will be devolved to the local governance institutions. Similarly, the local governance institutions also devolve functions, which are beyond its capacity to perform. The process of evolving decentralised governance from the bottom to top results in the formation of national level government.

Another way of looking at the process of decentralised governance is the principal agent framework. According to principal agent theory, the centralised nation-states requires an agency to perform its functions at the local level with certain mandatory powers and responsibilities. In the context of principal agent framework, the institutions, functions and responsibilities, durability and time span are designed by the principal is also known as the central government. The fundamental crux of the framework is nothing but top down approach.

When any dispassionate observer who looks at the functioning of local governance in India would be struck by blend of the principle of subsidiarity and the principal agent theory. When you look at it from the historical and *Gandhian* perspective, one can find the characteristic features of the former conceptual framework. If you look at it from the *Ambedkar* and contemporary perspective, one will have to come to a conclusion that the democratic decentralisation process is imbibed with later theoretical framework.

---

* Dept. of Political Science, University of Hyderabad, Gachibowli, Hyderabad.

The institution of local governance also known as *Panchayati Raj* has got long historical legacy of having originated and growing in India itself. The indigenous institution of local governance has got Constitutional statues through 73rd and 74th Amendments in 1992-93. Retrospectively, the research on the status of local governance for the last about two and half decades reveals that the focus was on the historical account, *Gandhian* notion of *Gram Swaraj* and empowerment of women and marginalised social groups. On these aspects, hardly there is any social science department in the universities and research institutions without dissertation/thesis on Panchayati Raj institutions in India. One of the major limitation of these studies is that having neither strong theoretical ground nor sufficient empirical data to draw the perceptions of various categories in the system.

The empirical evidences indicate that there are diversified perceptions on the institution of local governance in the country, for instance, the political parties look at them as ground for the political activities, the Members of Legislative Assembly at state and national level have been making them as the basis for their electoral politics and the bureaucrat feels that these are institutional arrangements for the top down implementation of the developmental initiatives. Another important observation is that in the context of using of the decentralised institutions by the multiple players for different purposes the institutional conflicts have been emerging.

The institutional conflicts by nature multi-dimensional such as local bodies versus bureaucracy, formal institutions of Constitution versus informal institutions and parallel institutions and the local body institutions versus the members of state and national legislative assemblies. In this process of various kinds of conflicts at the functioning of grassroots level institutions, the Constitutional spirit of planning for economic development and social justice is missing.

The present volume is the mirror reflection of the functioning of local bodies in India, it is also, in a sense, an independent evaluation of the emerging experiences, issues, restraints, constraints and gaps since 1990s. Broadly, the issues and constraints are relating to the Constitutional provisions of local governance and state government political will in the form of State Panchayati Raj Act provisions. The subject of devolving of functions, functionaries and funds (3Fs) is the will of the federal units of the governance. But, the measuring of the level of devolution, while using devolution index (The State of the Panchayats, A Mid-Term Review and

Appraisal, 22 November 2006, Volume – III, Ministry of Panchayati Raj, Government of India. pp. 677-691), found that the functioning of these institutions are not uniform for the entire country. Few states have effectively devolved 3Fs, some states are medium and the highest number of states could not adhere to the guiding provisions of the Amendment Acts.

As a result of the weak functioning of decentralised institutions, the issues of poor participatory planning, diverting of funds, absence of convergence, community monitoring, transparency and accountability have been cropping up. The historical, socio-economic, cultural and political background of the elected public representatives of local governance is also a very big constraint in exercising the public sphere for discharging of the mandatory Constitutional obligation towards civil society for the newly elected representatives especially on the ground of gender, caste and tribe.

Despite having several constraints in the functioning of local governance, it is inevitable upon these institutions to be the instrument for deepening of democracy, economic development and conflict resolution of the present and future world.

Acknowledgements

The volume is based on the presentations, which were made in the national seminar on 'Democratic Decentralisation in India Two Decades of Constitutional Amendments: Experiences, Issues and Challenges'. For conducting the seminar, the Indian Council of Social Science Research and University of Hyderabad under University Potential for Excellence provided the financial support and these two institutions are fully acknowledged for their co-operation. Decentralisation Community Solution Exchange of India (UNDP) and University of Hyderabad are also conveyed thanks for widespread campaign about the seminar through their websites.

I am thankful to department of Political Science, University of Hyderabad for providing logistic facilities to conduct the seminar, specifically to G. Hara Gopal, Shanta Sinha, Ramabrahmam, Arun Kumar Patnaik, Sudarsanam, K. C. Suri and other faculty members. The volume could not be materialised without contributions of the participants in the seminar and subsequent revision of the papers, that's why they are all fully deserve for a rich gratitude. In terms of making all the arrangements for the conducting the seminar, the research scholars such as Ramesh Kumar, Umar, A K Salman, Sakru Naik, Umamaheswar Rao, Y Suresh, B Ajad Chandrasekhar and others put a lot of efforts for which it would be appropriate to appreciate them.

It would be appropriate to convey my thanks and regards to those people who have inspired me to work on Democratic Decentralisation and Rural Development. They includes V Ramachandran, B N Yugandhar, B K Sinha, Sudheer Krishna, K Raju, T Vijay Kumar, Hrusikesh Panda (all are belongs to Indian Administrative Service), S K Singh, Y Venkat Reddy, K Murali, T Vijay Kumar, K Pallavi, Y N S Choudhary, Rajendra Prasad, Narayana Reddy, P Dasthagiri, Maruthi and P Madanna.

It may be something gap in the book if I can't convey my regards to Gyan Publishing House for bring out the compiled volume. Last but not the least is to my wife G Varalakshmi, daughter Harshitha and son Srivikas.

The contributors are responsible for any mistakes.

—E. Venkatesu

March, 2016, Hyderabad

Introduction

—E. Venkatesu

For the last three decades, local/decentralisation governance has emerged as a global phenomenon irrespective of the nature of political regimes whether they are democratic, autocratic, monarchical, military etc. In the contemporary world, all forms of government has been possessing the element of decentralisation. The post-colonial society like India opted for the democratic decentralisation, both in rural and urban areas, through making it as part of the Constitution. The Constitutional provisions, which are dealing with the decentralisation process, reveals that the Indian model of democratic decentralisation has got multi-dimensional character in terms of the accommodation of social groups, planning, generation of the resources, transparency, accountability, community participation etc.

In order to capture the changing character of local governance attempts have been going on in several parts of the country in the form of seminars, workshops, conferences, symposiums and trainings by the Universities, training and research institutions, non-governmental organisations etc. Present Volume is also the output of a seminar. Broadly, it deals with two aspects at a larger context. One is the existence and functioning of local governance in Asia and the Pacific in general and two, India's experiences in specific with focus on urban and rural areas in terms of institutional arrangements, devolution process, empowerment of the lower castes, women and minorities through reservations in local bodies, the process of service delivery, transparency and accountability, the emerging institutional conflicts at various levels and finally the experiences over a period of more than two decades.

The chapter one by S. K. Singh covered the nature and character of local governance institutions and their functioning in some of the Asia and the Pacific countries with reference to Bangladesh, Fiji, Indonesia, Iran, Malaysia, Pakistan, Philippines and Sri Lanka. In the chapter two

Shankari Murali discussed about the urban local governance while tracing out historical roots, present status and need to strengthen it. Chapter three focuses on the inter-play of the elected public representatives, government officials and community through committee system in the urban areas. It has examined the issue of community participation in the urban areas of Maharashtra and Kerala. It has also brought out the limitations for the participation of community in the urban areas. Harsha deals with the structural and functional aspects of the local governance in Assam with reference to Panchayats and autonomous councils.

Kondala Rao examines the issue of reservations for backward classes in undivided Andhra Pradesh. He has highlighted the frequent controversies and politicisation of the reservations of backward classes. Sreeramulu in his chapter highlighted the political participation and their limitations of backward classes on the basis of the field work that was conducted in Andhra Pradesh. Abdul Mateen examine the participation of religious minorities in the local governance of West Bengal. He has concluded that, despite long history of decentralisation, the religious minorities are lagging behind the other communities. ShriramYarankar highlighted the emerging leadership from the women category due to reservation policy and constraints upon them in the functioning. He also brought into the light several measures for the empowerment of women leadership in the local bodies.

Mahi Pal in his chapter on Panchayat Extension to Fifth Scheduled Areas made an attempt to understand the issues in its implementation. He traces the issues in implementation of state government political will and conformative State Panchayati Raj Acts. Jadhav Pratap Singh looks at the question of self-rule in the light of PESA and FRA, while referring to Tribal areas in Adilabad district of Telangana.

E. Venkatesu attempted to study the changing role of Panchayati Raj Institutions in the implementation of rural development programmes, particularly in the context of MGNREGA. He found that the provisions of Constitution and guidelines issued by Ministry of Rural Development for the implementation of MGNREGA that PRIs has got the role of planning, convergence and transparency and accountability in the implementation of rural development programmes. Ramabrahmam and Kiran Kumar chapter on Public Distribution System through e-Governance is the documentation of the policy initiation for the electronic governance mechanism for the improvement of Public Distribution System to reach out the real beneficiary. The government of Telangana proactively responded to the emerging trend applying the latest technology for the welfare programmes like Public Distribution. The finding is that there has been a lot of improvement in the delivery of goods and services to the citizen through e-governance initiatives. Mehar Puri explained the decentralised delivery of Health Services in Uttarakhand apart from partnership with the private sector and subsequent emerging issues. Umar Jalees Moniri has tried to suggest a PPP mode at the decentralised level to govern climate and environment on the basis of experiences of different environmental movements in India.

Aditi Rane in her chapter on Panchayati Raj Institutions in Goa and emerging constraints for the participation of community, criticised the emerging institutional conflicts at multiple levels such as political and bureaucratic executives on the one hand and local governance institution and members of legislative assembly at state and national level. K. Murali brought out the failure of the social accountability, which is an in-built institutionalised mechanism in the designing of MGNREGA from the field experiences of undivided Andhra Pradesh. The chapter on Transparency and Accountability Mechanism in Panchayats and Autonomous Councils: A comparative study in Assamby Harsha is a venture into the most cardinal issue in local governance which is accountability and transparency. In the light of theories of decentralisation, he takes up a comparative study of transparency and accountability mechanisms of Panchayats and Autonomous Council of Assam. Based on the comparative study, it has come up with recommendations to streamline transparency and accountability mechanism and reinvigorate local governance. The final chapter by Ch. Balaramulu is on the issues and challenges that have been emerging for the last two decades in India's experiment for democratic decentralisation. He cites several factors, such as instability of government at the national level, rise of regional political parties, and emergence of new middle class from new social groups and new economic policy, for the initiation of policy framework to decentralise the governance. But he also criticise the issues in the devolution of funds, functions and functionaries, participation of the people, management of natural resource management, resource envelop through centrally sponsored schemes and parallel institutions.

It is understood from the experiences of the functioning of local governance in different parts of the country that there is uniformity in terms of institutional designing to a large extent, but their performance is depending upon the political will of the state government and given socio-economic structure at the local level. The community at the local level needs to be prepared to assert the local governance. It is possible through reversing the present top down model of decentralisation into bottom up citizen centric and inclusive governance for the assertion and effective delivery of the services.

List of Contributors

(1) **Aditi M. Rane**

Assistant Professor, Government Degree Collage, Goa.

(2) **Ch. Bala Ramulu**

Professor (Retd.), Department of Public Administration, Kakatiya University, Warangal, Telangana. Former National Fellow, ICSSR, New Delhi and at present UGC Emeritus Fellow.

(3) **E. Venkatesu**

Assistant Professor, Department of Political Science, University of Hyderabad, Hyderabad, Telangana.

(4) **Gooru Sreeramulu**

Professor, Department of Political Science, Gulbarga University, Gulbarga.

(5) **Gowd Kiran Kumar**

Research Fellow, Department of Political Science, University of Hyderabad, Hyderabad, Telangana.

(6) **Harsha, S.**

Assistant Professor, Department of Political Science, Assam University, Silchar, Assam.

(7) **I. Ramabrahmam**

Professor, Department of Political Science, University of Hyderabad.

(8) **Jadhav Prathap Singh**

Research Fellow, Department of Political Science, University of Hyderabad, Hyderabad, Telangana.

(9) **Janmejay Sahu**

Research Fellow, Department of Political Science, University of Hyderabad, Hyderabad, Telangana.

(10) **K. Kondala Rao**

Advocate, Andhra Pradesh High Court, Hyderabad.

(11) **K. Murali**

Assistant Professor, Tata Institute of Social Sciences, Mumbai.

(12) **Mahi Pal**

Director, Ministry of Rural Development, Government of India.

(13) **Mehar Puri**

Research Scholar, Tata Institute of Social Science, Mumbai.

(14) **Shankari Murli**

Research Fellow, Institute for Social and Economic Change (ISEC), Bangalore, Karnataka.

(15) **ShriramYerankar**

Head, Department of Political Science, Jijamata Mahavidyalaya, Buldana, Maharashtra.

(16) **Sk. Abdul Matin**

Research Fellow, Centre for Political Studies, JNU, New Delhi.

(17) **S. K. Singh**

Former Director (Trainings), Centre for Integrated Rural Development in Asia and the Pacific (CIRDAP), Dhaka, Bangladesh.

(18) **Smita Waingankar**

Research Fellow, Tata Institute of Social Sciences, Mumbai.

(19) **Umar Jalees Moniri**

Research Fellow, Department of Political Science, University of Hyderabad, Hyderabad, Telangana.

(20) **Yacoub Zachariah Kuruvilla**

Research Fellow, Tata Institute of Social Sciences, Mumbai.

1

Local Governance in Selected Asia-the Pacific Countries

—S K Singh

The Context

It is an attempt to highlights the prevailing decentralised system in select Asia-Pacific countries so that it can be critically analysed to ascertain where Indian system stands with in comparison to countries from this region and what are the best practices that can be considered suitable for India and what India can offer to them. In fact, the dynamic nature of public policy require critical inputs which are pragmatic, and contain comparative perspectives and analytical views emerging from cross-fertilisation of ideas and thoughts from various experiences and experiments available in different countries in the region.

For the stated objective, it will briefly touching upon the structure, composition and functions of local government system in Bangladesh, Fiji, Indonesia, Iran, Malaysia, Pakistan, Philippines and Sri Lanka. Covering so many countries drawn from South Asia, South East Asia, West Asia and one from the Pacific region is stupendous task. However, in this paper an attempt has been made to provide status and innovations, and diverse decentralised system being practiced by these countries in service delivery efforts and dealing with rural development and poverty alleviation. Undoubtedly, the paper suffers from severe limitations. The paper is based on secondary sources of information taken from documents, reports, etc. available in English, which are at variance, uneven and inadequate. Most of these countries have official reports in their country's language, not in English. So, it is very difficult to extract information. Nevertheless, an attempt has been made to provide a broad picture that may be useful.

Undoubtedly, several countries in the Asia-Pacific region have initiated decentralisation process as an important strategy and approach for development. Each country has its own plans for decentralisation and achievements have also been different. Among them, some decentralisation programmes have been more successful as compared to others. The approach, form and content in these countries vary since there are differences in their history, administration, social system, cultural values, economic and political regime. However, decentralisation embraces a variety of concepts which need to be carefully analysed in country specific context.

The Theme

It is necessary to underscore conceptual underpinnings of decentralised development within the gamut of the wider development agenda in order to understand and appreciate the efforts and strategy adopted by these countries. In the last three decades, a wave of decentralisation swept across the globe in public sector governance and as a development strategy. Regardless of political regime, many countries of the Asia-Pacific region have embarked on some form of decentralisation reforms with diverse motives and approaches. However, the basic premise has been to move decision-making for local public services closer to the people, increase efficiency, and encourage effective participation and greater private sector contribution, among others. More so, there were manifold country specific factors that lead to decentralisation of the system. For some countries, the motivation for decentralisation came from internal political and economic transformation, ethnic and regional conflicts, fiscal crisis, need to improve public delivery, enhance participation, etc. Nevertheless, the quest was to achieve the right balance, i.e., appropriate division of powers among different layers of the government. The major catalyst could be political considerations and external influences through globalisation and the information revolution. These may have profound influences on the division of power within the country.

Conceptually, as it has been widely used and available in literature, decentralisation stands for the transfer of power, authority and responsibility of public functions from the central government to intermediate and local governments. It may include quasi-independent government organisations or even private sectors. In other words, it is a process of dispersing decision-making authority down to the lower tier/ unit of governance. This is a multifaceted and complex concept. It embraces a variety of themes. Different types of decentralisation show different characteristics, policy implications and conditions for success. Typologies of decentralisation are broadly three types in the public sector-political decentralisation, administrative decentralisation and fiscal decentralisation. More importantly, decentralisation depends upon the 'principles of subsidiarity'. According to this principle, what is suitably performed at lower level unit should not be assigned to higher level unit. It is presumed that due to proximity with people, lower level units can provide better delivery of services than higher level units. People will have easy access to that lower level unit as well. Hence, problems can best be solved in the subsystem where they arise. Nevertheless, the concept has both legal and political dimension and relevance in many countries. A proper devolution of powers on the basis of subsidiarity will make decentralisation effective and meaningful.

The overall evidences available from these countries confirm that under appropriate conditions it play an important role in broadening and increasing participation in political, economic and social activities and better accountability can result from democratic decentralisation. A better decentralisation can have positive implications on flourishing local economy and democracy. It buttresses policy advocacy, particularly for those countries where decentralisation is still dominated by bureaucratic governance and political rhetoric and rigmaroles. It has also facilitated re-defining role of governments and strengthening the administrative and financial capacities of local government. It will ultimately lead to pro-poor development, and its substantive benefits cannot be underestimated. Furthermore, decentralised approach to rural development has shown result in improving the living conditions of the poor, protect the interest of the people, and ensures accountability and openness.

Country-wise Decentralised Local Governance

A panoramic view of Decentralised System of Governance has been discussed below to get an idea about the legal frame, structure, composition and functional domain of the existing local government institutions in these countries. It also provides basic components of, and level of decentralisation. Interestingly, these countries represent a laboratory having variety of local government system. These institutions are at variance and have different levels of development.

A brief country-wise description of administrative arrangement of decentralised governance is presented here to understand the existing situation, particularly in terms of functional domain and responsibilities entrusted to them.

Bangladesh

The local government system in Bangladesh has a long history with ups and downs. It can be traced with British colonial period to administrative set up of Pakistan and then independent Bangladesh. The country has unitary form of government and for administrative purposes it is divided into Divisions and Districts. There are seven Divisions and 64 Districts. Below the District, the administrative units are Upa-Zillas and below that are Union Parishads. There are 483 Upa-Zillas (average population – 2.5 Lakhs) and 4498 Union Parishads (average population 270,000) and each Union Parishad consists of several contiguous villages. The total number of villages is 87,319.

Presently, there are two sets of local government covering urban and rural areas. The Constitution of Bangladesh, Chapter III, Article 59(1) envisages establishment of Local government in each administrative unit of the Republic, composed of persons elected in accordance with the law.

The rural local government at the district level is Zilla Parishad; at the Upa-Zilla (Thana) level is Upa-Zilla Parishad and the lowest tier is Union Parishad. In the urban areas the local government are Pourashava (Municipalities) and City Corporations. Besides, in the hilly terrain are there is Hill District Local Government Council.

The present status of rural local government is that the Union Parishad and Upa-Zillas are constituted whereas the district level body called Zilla Parishad is in dormancy. For development purposes Upa-Zilla is considered to be the main unit and it has strong bureaucratic set up where most of the line departments have their units, which functions in coordination with Upa-Zilla Parishad. The Upa-Zilla has one Chairman and two Vice-Chairmen having one male and another female, directly elected by the people. The Upa-Zilla has development functions and coordinates with others departments. Below the Upa-Zilla Parishad, the grassroots unit is Union Parishad which comprises 12 members elected by the people from wards. These wards are carved out on the basis of population; each union is divided into nine wards to elect one representative. Three seats are reserved for women. One reserved ward for women comprises three general wards, i.e., larger unit than general ward. The Chairperson is directly elected by the people. The duration of the Union Parishad is five years period. Political parties are not allowed to contest election; however, candidates may be card holder of some political party. Union Parishad has civic responsibilities, police, revenue and developmental functions and judicial responsibilities. As per provisions, government may transfer certain programmes and responsibilities to the Upa-Zillas, if desired. They are also engaged in rural development work, if assigned by the government.

According to existing constitutional provisions, at the Zilla (District) level, there will be a council. A Zilla Parishad should consist of a chairman, 15 members and five reserved seats for women members. The chairman and the members are supposed to be elected by an electoral college. In fact, elections to this level have never been held and district level bodies were never constituted, apparently because of legal complications and political reasons thinking that this is not an appropriate level for such bodies.

The Urban Local Bodies are -Pourashavas for smaller municipalities and City Corporations for the six largest cities. The heads of city corporations are called mayors and for Pourashavas are called chairman. Elected member from each ward is called commissioner. Mayors and chairmen are directly elected every five years; and all ward commissioners are also directly selected every five years. They are responsible for all civic services. Some seats are reserved for women.

For Hill Track Area, separate Acts are enacted. The Hill District Parishads have been established to give representation to the tribes living in the Hill District Areas. Each Parishad has a designated number of tribal members as well as a Chairperson and non-tribal members. The tribal seats are further divided according to the number and proportion of tribes in the Hill District. The members are elected by the people. The Chairperson is elected from amongst the tribal members. The electoral procedures for the Hill District Parishads are determined by the government.

Fiji

Fiji is located in the South Pacific Ocean and has some 330 islands; only about 100 of these are inhabited with a multi-ethnic population composition. Fiji gained Independence in 1970 and became a Dominion within the Commonwealth, with a Governor-General representing the British Queen and a Prime Minister as the head of the government. It is a multi-cultural and pluralistic country with a multiplicity of languages, religions and ways of living. The indigenous people are known as i-taukei which means the owners of the land. It was declared a republic in 1987 after two military coups d'état. A new Constitution, formulated in 1990, was implemented in 1992. This Constitution provided for a President as Head of State and a Prime Minister as the head of government. In accordance with that Constitution, a Constitution Review Commission (CRC) undertook a comprehensive review through an extensive system of public consultations. A revised Constitution, which is based on the recommendations of the CRC, which addresses many of the shortcomings of the previous one, was adopted in July 1997.

At sub-national level, governmental and administrative activities are undertaken through four distinct systems: the Government Administration, the Fijian Administration for matters concerning exclusively native affairs, the Municipal Administration and Rural Local Authorities. It has long history of Local Government system starting from colonial period. The Fiji administration is divided into four administrative Divisions and below is 15 Provinces. Each province has several Tikina and below is villages. Each Division has a Division Council headed by Divisional Commissioner; each Province has Provincial Council headed by ROKO; each Tikina Council is headed by BULI; and Village Council is headed by TURAGA NI KORO (village headman). It has two types of local government systems, that is, urban local government and rural local government constituted under the provisions of Local Government Act of 1972.

In urban areas, under the provisions of the Local Government Act, Municipalities are operating in two major cities whereas eight Township Boards are operating in small city areas. These bodies are elected by the eligible population residing within proclaimed boundaries. The Ministry of Local Government, Housing and the Environment have overall responsibility over municipal government. The Act provides for the Constitution of a council for the government of each municipality. Legally each council is a body corporate with perpetual succession and a common seal. The Electoral Commission decides on the number of councillors that constitutes a council as well as the number of councillors from each ward. This Commission also conducts the municipal elections. However, these were suspended after the military coup in 1987 until 1993 during which period the Minister appointed the councillors under a decree of 1988. Every person of or over the age of twenty-one years who is a citizen of Fiji and who is the occupier or owner of land or house within the municipality is eligible to be enrolled as an elector. A councillor may hold office for a period of three years and is eligible for re-election.

A Mayor who is elected annually by the council from among the councillors heads each council.

The rural development administrative set up comprises of Village Committee for Fijians and Settlement for non-Fijians. At the district level, a District Development Committee and above Divisional Development Committee is established to advice and decide on all development works within their jurisdiction. For development of rural areas, in 2009, an Integrated Rural Development (IRD) programme has been introduced by the government. Rural local authority functions under the Local Government Act and other legislation, local authorities are entrusted with responsibilities that include issues concerning public health, town planning, sub-division of land, roads and traffic, markets, purity of foods and licensing of businesses, including shops, restaurants and hotels.

Rural local authorities cover large areas outside towns and deal with varying amounts of urban development within their boundaries. In addition to their main function as public health authorities, they undertake a variety of functions usually undertaken by urban local authorities such as building control, town planning and garbage disposal, arranging dislodging of septic tanks and issuing business licenses.

Absence of elections at the national government due to military coup in December 2006, local governments or municipalities are also currently operating without elections, and consequently, special administrators are appointed by the Ministry of Local Government, Squatter Resettlement and Housing under Section 9A (1) & (2) (revised Act, 2005) of Act. Therefore, democratic content is absent, but participatory approach is being practice.

Indonesia

The Constitution of Indonesia (called Undang-undang Dasar, 1945) provides for Presidential form of Government with unitary system. The President is directly elected by the people for five years. The country has bicameral parliament, known as Majelis Permusyawaratan Rakyat (MPR; People Consultative Assembly). It consists of members of Dewan Perwakilan Rakyat (DPR; House of People Representative or Parliament) and Dewan Perwakilan Daerah (DPD; Regional Representative). Members of the Parliament are also elected by the people.

The Constitution provides for establishment of Local Government system in the country through 1945 proclamation with local autonomy as basic premise of governance. The provisions have undergone several changes in 1948, 1957, 1959, 1974 and 1999. The last amended Decentralisation policy, 1999 was implemented in January, 2000 and has several implications on the government system, particularly emanating from the two laws - Law No. 22 on Regional Government and Law No. 25 on Financial Balance between Central Government and Regional Government. Under the law of local autonomy, local government is given authority that is realised by the regulating, allocating and utilising national resources as well as fiscal balance between central and local government in accordance to democratic principle, public participation, equality, and justice as well as local potentials and diversity. The Law no. 22/1999 stipulates territorial division into autonomous Provincial Regions, Regency Regions and Municipal Regions. A region has full authority in the field of governance and complete autonomy is given to regency/city. The Head of Region is responsible to DPRD (Local Parliament) and DPRD can propose dismissal of Head of the Region to central government. This law also has provision for village governance and its machinery like village head and Village Representative Board.

As per administrative divisions, there are 30 Provincial Regions and 416 Local Regions, which aredivided into 92 Pemerintah *Kota* (City Governments) and 324 *Pemerintah Kabupaten* (District Governments). Based on new laws, the form and structure of local administration consists of Dewan Perwakilan Rakyat Daerah (DPRD; Provincial/Local Parliament) as the legislative body, and local government as the executive body. The DPRD is elected for five years and has wider authority. Local government consists of a Head of Regionand local apparatus. The decentralisation policy does not have hierarchical links between provincial and city/district levels rather the law stipulates that city/districts are autonomous regions. However, there are multiple forms of coordination, cooperation and partnership between them. The provincial level of government is headed by a Governor who is elected by local parliament. The city/district level of government is headed by a Mayor for the city and a Regent for the district elected by local parliament.

According to the decentralisation law, the local government has been assigned all development sectors in the region, except international affairs, defence, judiciary, monetary and fiscal policies, and other authorities governed in the laws (assigned to Central Government). Provincial government is empowered with matters across local governments.

The local legislative body has the authority to establish local regulations, local revenues, and expenditure budgets; to conduct investigation; to express opinion and considerations, as well as to facilitate and follow up the aspirations of its citizens. The local legislative body is also empowered to ask for information from the Head of Region regarding policy drafts and implementation, as well as on matters that requires legal action. Furthermore, the local legislative body can conduct investigations, including collection of information on public opinions. Thus, there is paradigm shift from a "strong executive system" to a "strong legislative system." The legislative body is assisted by a Secretariat.

As per provisions under Article 7-11 of the Law no. 22/1999, a Region has the authority to manage the interest and aspirations of the local citizens. Some regions may enforce such regulations to involve people in development planning and/or the preparation of local regulations. The more intense public participation and higher awareness will increase public demands for their involvement in every development process, and transparency of governance. If required, one Region may cooperate with another on issues like management of natural and human resources and heritage.

Hence, a regency and municipality become more self-sufficient and intervention from central or provincial government does not exist. The only form of intervention by the central government could be relating to training and investigation in an effort to enforce the laws. Therefore, local governments can make policies and development programmes for their regions. This shift of authority from central to local government automatically brings the policy-makers closer to the people. However, the policy formulated by local government should not be contradictory to the policies of higher level of government. It essentially calls for the involvement of all stakeholders in the region including government, private sector and the community to control the issuance of new local regulations.

Thus, it can be summarised that the local government has freedom and responsible to choose and determine matters according to local needs depending upon the parameters of financial ability.

Despite strong autonomous local government, there are some challenges. Due to autonomy and wide powers, local bodies are not in a position to formulate policies since earlier it was done by the central government. These bodies lack professionalism. Therefore, there is need for capacity building of local government functionaries covering various aspects of governance. In view of local independence, local bodies sometimes behave independently whereas there are occasion when they need cooperation from other region local government. Moreover, responsibilities have increased but financial position is not compatible with assigned work, and therefore, local bodies have to depend upon grants from central government. For development work they have to mobilise their own resources.

Iran

After Islamic Revolution in Iran, a new constitution was introduced for the administration of the country. The Constitution envisages decentralised planning and implementation. The administrative units in the country are Province, District and village. The authority of Provincial Governors increased in terms of planning, policy-making and implementation of the programmes within their jurisdiction. For the administration at the village level, Rural Islamic Council (RIC) has been established. The council is an elected body for four years period and has three members for a population up to 1500, and five members for a village having more than 1500 population. Besides, there are six other members of the Rural Islamic Council at village level, namely, members of the Islamic Consultative Assembly, Governors, District Administrator, Village Administrator and Director General and head of offices. However, other members have no voting rights. The Village Islamic Councils (number of Village Islamic Council - 23747) are responsible for implementing policies of the government and supervising the works being implemented in their areas as also collaborating with other agencies. The Village Islamic Council has judicial powers to settle disputes among individuals and places at the local level. The Rural Islamic Council at village level collaborate with the District Islamic Council and assist in implementation of various programmes. Above the Village Islamic Council, there is District Islamic Council at the district level and a district administrator is the head. The District Islamic Council has a Chairman, Vice-Chairman and one secretary selected for two years period.

The executive management of the country has two parts, namely, consultative management and sovereignty management. The Islamic councils at various levels have predominantly supervision and consultative role whereas sovereignty management is the main entity of the government at each level to perform and execute programmes.

Malaysia

The Malaysian administrative system has three layers – Federal Government, State Government and Local Government. Local Government (kerajaantemptan) is the third layer in the administrative hierarchy. After gaining independence from British in 1957, local government was restructured through Local Government Act, 1976 (Act 171) and Town and Country Planning Act, 1976 (Act 172). This Act outlines the form, organisational structure, functions and responsibilities of local government. The changes enforced by the Act 171 were – restricting the number of local governments in peninsula; most importantly, elections to these bodies were abolished. Therefore, under the provisions of the Act, the councillors were not elected rather they are appointed by the state government. This provision has prohibited democratic rights of people to exercise their franchise and these bodies are no longer democratically elected rather it is nominated, which subverts the basic tenets of democracy. Thus, the local government functions within the ambit of the State Government. The Local Government is divided into two types, namely, Municipality in urban areas and District Councils in rural areas. The local government structures are City Council (12 in number); Municipal Councils (39 in number); District Councils (98 in number) and modified Local authority (5 in number). At the district level, District Council in the rural areas is established and a district officer is head of the unit who is appointed by the state government. Below the district, there is a Village Development and Security Committee which is headed by a village Headman.

The powers and functions of the Local Government are enumerated in the Ninth Schedule List – II of the Federal Constitution, item number IV. The local government is responsible for planning, coordinating and regulating the use and development of land and buildings. Moreover, the local government also performs tasks entrusted by the state government. However, the State Governments have overriding powers on local government since it is established by the State Government. A National Council for Local Government has been constituted for formulating policies pertaining to the local government in consultation with State and Federal Government. This arrangement prohibits taking such decisions that is detrimental to the local bodies. The finance of the local government is allocated by the federal and state governments.

The Federal and State Government share responsibilities pertaining to rural development and poverty alleviation. Local Government Institutions are not involved in rural development work rather various ministries and agencies are directly or indirectly involved. Some of the agencies are Regional Development Boards, Development of Orang Asli Departments (JAKOA); Council of Trust for Indigenous People (MARA); etc. These bodies functions under the Ministry of Rural and Regional

Development (MRRD). Besides, other ministries like health, social welfare, agriculture, etc. also have programmes targeting development of rural areas.

In rapidly changing scenario, Local Government will have lot of challenges and these bodies have to devise new approaches, strategies as well as practical and effective answers and solutions. In view of these challenges, national efforts are required to reform the public service in meeting the current needs. Local governments together with other public agencies are undertaking a number of reform programmes based on a series of strategies. These reform efforts are intended to create excellence in the public service based on the core values of quality, productivity, innovation, integrity, accountability, discipline and professionalism. Local governments in Malaysia are now instruments of national development and changing fundamentally from a service provider to a facilitator of growth. Besides, local governments have assumed a more developmental role in creating an enabling environment for businesses to thrive and for prosperity of citizens.

Pakistan

The Pakistan has federal and parliamentary form of government and has three layers of administrative system - Federal Government, Provincial Government and Local Government. It has bicameral legislative body. The local government system does not figure-in the provisions of the Constitution rather it comes under the jurisdiction of the provincial government. In order to get support of community in governance, local government system was introduced through Basic Democracy Ordinance, 1959 and Municipal Administration Ordinance, 1960. The intention was to get direct participation of the people in managing their own affairs through representative bodies down to village level. It has four sets of hierarchical bodies namely, Union Council in rural area; Town Committee in urban area; Tehsil Council; District Council and Division Council. This scheme suffered due to built-in-structural contradictions and could not succeed as expected. Subsequently, each province has passed own set of local government law in 1970s. However, in order to strengthen the grassroots level democracy, the Local Government Ordinance, 2001 was promulgated, which provides for establishment of Local Government System. The local government is constituted at the district level, called Zilla Council; Tehsil level, called Tehsil Council; and lowest level at village is called Union Council. All these bodies are democratically elected. The council is elected for four years period. The striking feature of the system was that the age of voters have been lowered down from 21 to 18 and the women representation has been enhanced to 33 per cent. Moreover, representation of peasants, workers and minorities has been ensured. The chairman of the District Council is Nazim and vice-chairman is Naib Nazim. They are elected and their academic qualification has also been prescribed. According to a provision, the Nazim and Naib Nazim cannot hold the office for more than two terms. This prohibits a person not to continue in the office for a long time and allow others to get into the system. In order to maintain organic link the Nizam of Union Council is ex-officio member of the District Council and the Naib Nizam of Union Council is member of the Tehsil Council. The councils at the district and below levels are empowered to levy taxes. The elected council also has legislative powers. The departments and sectors allocated to local government are agriculture, education, health, law, revenue, community development, finance and planning, works and services and information technology. The Nazim as the head of the district level body is responsible for coordination between different departments. For participation of the people at the village level, a Citizen Community Board is constituted and thereby community is involved in the planning and implementation of projects.

Presently, the Democratic Government of 2008 has withheld the elections of the local councils and the Local Government Ordinance, 2001 is under review by the respective Provincial Governments for suitable modifications as a sequel to the 18th Amendment to the Constitution. So, these bodies are not in position. Moreover, under the provisions of the 18th Amendment in 2008 to the Constitution of 1973, the subjects of Local Government and Rural Development along with other subjects have been transferred from Federal Government to the Provincial Government. Hence, the Ministry of Local Government and Rural Development at the Federal level has been abolished.

Philippines

The administrative system of the Republic of the Philippines comprises a Central Government, Provincial Government and Local Government. The territorial and political division of Provinces and Local government are demarcated and they enjoy autonomy.

The democratic Constitution of Philippines, 1987 provides for Local Government Code, which was enacted in 1991 and became operational in 1992. Hence, Local Governments are Constitutional bodies.

In Philippines, the nature of local government is considered as frontline institution. The decentralised government units below the Centre are: Province, Municipality, City, Barangay, and the Regional Government in the national capital region at Manila and Regional Autonomous Governments in Regions IX (Western Mindanao) and XII (Southern Mindanao) (Guzman and Padilla, 1985). Presently, the number of administrative units below the central government is - 77 Provinces; 69 Cities; 1538 Municipalities; 41,359 Barangays.

The Section 17 of the Code has radical provision for devolution of powers, authorities, responsibilities and accountability to be transferred to the local bodies. As per the code, the basic services devolved to local government are health services with infrastructure provision, such as, school, clinic, local road building, agriculture, maintenance of public work and highways, environmental protection, etc. The Barangay is the lowest unit of local government system, which may be co-terminus with village. The Barangay has usually seven elected members and head is called Barangay Captain (Punong Barangay). The Barangays are responsible for agriculture support services which include distribution of planting materials, maintenance of health centres and day-care centres, general hygiene and sanitation, Barangay roads, bridges and water supply, infrastructure and Barangay justice. The local government is empowered to mobilise own revenue resources as also they can enter into international aid agreement.

The rural development activities between line agencies like Department of Agrarian Reform (DAR) and Local Government Units (LGUs) are governed by the provisions of the National Convergence Initiative (NCI) of 1999. It comprises the Department of Agriculture (DA), Department of Agrarian Reform (DAR), and the Department of Environment and Natural Resources (DENR). It aims to develop and operationalise a common framework for sustainable rural development that will facilitate the convergence of the resources of the three agencies for optimal use maximum development in rural areas. The LGUs is given a more pro-active role in identifying and implementing convergence initiatives at the local level. Specifically, the DAR works with the LGUs in the identification of projects and programmes, mobilising all types of resources (financial, expertise and manpower complement), coordination with other stakeholders to complement the initiatives. All the rural development projects and programmes are congruent with the local development plan of the LGU.

Sri Lanka

Sri Lanka has a long history of local self-government dating back to colonial period and changes were made after gaining independence. Sri Lanka is a Republic with democratically elected head of the country having multi-party system. The administrative units are divided into nine Provinces and 25 Districts. There are three types of local authorities, i.e., Municipal Council, Urban Council and Pradeshiya Sabha. All these units are elected bodies and the term of the office is five years. There are 14 Municipal Councils, 37 Urban Councils and 258 Pradeshiya Sabha. The municipal councils are established in cities and large towns and urban council for semi-urban areas and Pradehsiya Sabhas for rural areas. The powers and functions of the municipal councils are provided under Section-40 of the Municipal Council Ordinance. They are responsible for recruitment of officials, acquisition of assets, licensing, institute local actions, budgeting, etc. The Urban Councils have similar responsibilities like municipal councils. According to the Section 18 and 19 of the Pradehsiya Sabhas Act, they are responsible for providing services like public health, maintenance of public roads, regulating market places, etc. But, due to financial constraints and available human resources Pradehsiya Sabhas are not in a position to provide these services as mentioned in the Act. The Committee system operating in Local Authorities is very important element of management. The Committees are called Standing Committee in Municipal Councils whereas in other bodies namely, Urban Council and Pradehsiya Sabha it is called Committees. The Committees have legal status. In case of Pradehsiya Sabha, general public can be included whereas in Municipalities on elected members can be in the standing committee.

The Local Authorities will have more challenges in future like increased demand for good services, shortage of infrastructure, inadequacy of finance and dependency syndrome, lack of competent staff, etc. These bodies have to prepare for these challenges. There is need for capacity building of functionaries.

Emerging Issues

On the basis of the existing decentralised system of governance in the countries discussed above, some critical issues are emerging that needs to be addressed in the seminar to strengthen decentralise efforts and to make it more relevant and purposeful.

Notwithstanding the fact that whatever may be the political regime in the countries mentioned above, there is a broad-based movement towards greater decentralisation. Simultaneously, there is a dilemma whether decentalised governance can be an effective means to achieve the critical objectives of sustainable human development, particularly rural development and poverty alleviation; improved and more equitable public delivery system; increased popular participation; and enhanced government responsiveness. Thus, it is a complex issue that requires periodical review and examination. However, decentralisation has the potential to address important issues at all levels of government, accommodate multiple interests and provide a participatory policy- making the process and the system more accountable and responsive. Moreover, a well-established local democracy is a pre-requisite for building a stable productive society which can take care of their interest. Therefore, Seminar would like to devise a better framework of decentralisation woven with enhanced central and local capacity to govern, which protects the interest of the people and ensures accountability and openness.

Experiences from the countries reveal that decentralisation is good both for democracy and efficiency. Therefore, the process of decentralisation requires redefining structure, procedures and practices of governance, which is closer to citizenry, gives importance to a general sensitisation of the public and creates a heightened awareness.

Local government appears to be more suitable and conducive institutional apparatus for planning and implementing development policies, programmes, and service delivery. As observed, the task assigned to local government varies from country to country. However, emphasis is placed upon strengthening of local government institutions, which is steaming out of frustrating experiences of highly centralised system. Therefore, strengthening local government is inevitable. In view of this, the Seminar would like to discuss and suggest as to how local government institutions should further be strengthened with more devolution of powers, functions, functionaries and freedom.

Election to each level of local government varies from country to country. It is said that directly elected members are more accountable to their constituents than indirectly elected. Direct election also has cost concern. The Seminar may like to discuss the issue whether or not direct election to be held at all levels of local government. What should be the organic link between the upper and lower tier? Similarly, the election of Chairperson and Vice-Chairperson varies from country to country and many cases between different levels of local government. What could be more appropriate mode of election to Chairperson? Whether other categories of membership like ex-officio, nominated, etc. may be consider for the local government.

Political parties are among the main actors in governance, influencing the nature of democratic polity in a country, and the coherence of their programmes, their ideologies and leadership has a major impact on local democratic development. Political parties play an important role in enabling and limiting representation at the local level and have important implications for centre-local relations. Moreover, the growth in political parties over a period of time coincided with the increase in elections. Participation of political parties in local government election varies from country to country. This is a pertinent issue to consider whether political parties can take part in local government.

One of the fundamental democratic principles is to ensure fair and adequate representation for all social groups including women. The situation varies from country to country depending upon a range of circumstances. What would be the modalities to deal with issues of inclusiveness? A number of Asia-Pacific countries have special arrangements to deal with highly specific local issue for greater autonomy for indigenous people. What could be the criteria for such autonomy?

Conclusion

Efforts and experiences on decentralise governance drawn from these countries provides learning points and will have far reaching impact. However, it entails continuous strengthening of institutional capability and capacity building efforts of functionaries both elected and officials, reforms on the basis of experiences, innovations and willingness to learn from others and sharing best practices.

References

UNDP publication on Local Democracy in Asia-Pacific: Representation in Decentralise Governance. Regional centre in Bangkok, 2006.

CIRDAP Country Status Report on Bangladesh, Fiji, Iran, Malaysia, Pakistan, Philippines, Sri Lanka, 2011.

Asia-Pacific Journal of Rural Development, Vol. XXII, No. 1, July 2012; Special Issue on Decentralised Approach to Rural Development, Theme Editor, S.K. Singh.

Singh, S K. Capacity Building for Local Governance: A Suggestive Framework for Select Member Countries of CIRDAP; APJORD, Vol. XXII, July 2012, pp. 25-46.

Country Report on Local Government System: Indonesia, UNDP and SMERU, 2002 Regional Autonomy in Indonesia: Field Experiences and emerging Challenges.

2

Urban Local Governance in India-An Analysis

—*Shankari Murli*

Introduction

The paper is devoted to the theme of capacity and capabilities building in Urban Local Bodies (ULBs). The need for such a study is significant in the context of the rapid urbanisation in India. Nearly a third of the population is now residing in urban centres (31.16 per cent as per 2011 Census figures), and this population is growing fast at 31.8 per cent compared to rural population growing at 12.2 per cent). The theme of this paper is the study of local democratic governance mechanisms in cities as compared to rural areas. In this scenario of rapid transition from rural to urban settlements, there is both a process of addition of new statutory towns as well as a reframing of the boundaries of existing urban centres to include former rural areas. This process needs to be studied with emphasis on decentralisation at local government levels. This transition and integration of the former rural settlements and the level and quality of services provided after incorporation by the urban local body and the resultant urban accountability structures offer insights on the path of urbanisation. The paper is divided into six sections. The second section is an overview of decentralisation in India. A brief history of ULBs in India is the third section followed by the section on the recent urban trends. The fifth section emphasises the need for ULBs to be developed as institutions of democratic decentralisation, especially in comparison to the more formally structured Panchayati Raj Institutions (PRIs). The concluding section sums up these issues.

Decentralisation in India

The entire decentralisation discourse and practice in India has had strong rural roots and a rural bias. Decentralisation in India had two distinct pushes leading to the 73rd and 74th Constitutional Amendments – the indigenous Gandhian concept of the village being a self-reliant unit[1] as well as the impetus given by the Structural Adjustment Package of the IMF in 1991. While the former is covered in detail in most Indian writings on decentralisation and Panchayati raj in India, the second aspect is significant, especially in the post-1991 reform period in the country.

The international agencies (World Bank and International Monetary Fund) adopted this agenda from the decentralisation theory from public economics. The theory originated from the Decentralisation theorem (Oates, 1972). Oates had followed the public economics discourse and the Arrow-Musgrave-Samuelson paradigm of an idealised government which maximises social welfare and provided public goods while promoting redistributive justice and anchoring the macroeconomic policy (Oates, 2005). The theorem established that a good/ service could be most *efficiently* provided locally. This found favour among those who saw a need for less government and more self-determination and private enterprise. Therefore, it was felt that decentralisation was a panacea for the ills of developing/ lesser developed countries. This theory and its advocates propagated the advantages of decentralisation without differentiating between rural and urban communities. The era of the 1980s and early 1990s witnessed the collapse of many national economies. The IMF and the World Bank took an evangelical position on decentralisation as part of the reform agendas among all the developing, transitional and former Soviet Union countries. Decentralisation became an integral part of the standard package of good governance reforms. It offered public economics benefits of tax-assignment and economic efficiency and stability while it also appealed to the policy-makers, offering political mileage from extending political largesse and sharing of revenues and expenses from within the earlier centralised stronghold of planners and bureaucrats. This also fanned a demand for such decentralisation from the local leaders and non-governmental agencies functioning at the local levels who wished to participate in the policy, decision and allocation making processes.

The implementation of political, financial and administrative decentralisation, through the multiple agencies of governmental, non-governmental and private agencies was not always smooth. The critics felt that none of the touted benefits could be seen in countries/ areas where budgets were not citizen-focused and the institutional capacities of lower level of governments were non-existent. In such cases introduction of decentralisation would only lead to higher costs, lower efficiency in service delivery, and even heightened inequity and macroeconomic instability (Prud'homme, 1995). In India too, the need for reforms was acknowledged but there was little follow-through. The economic crisis of 1991 and the Structural Adjustment Package led to the two amendments bestowing constitutional status to the Local Self Governments in the country, as much as the traditional Gandhian focuses on self-governing, self-sufficient rural communities. The 73rd Constitutional Amendment granted constitutional sanction to the traditional system of panchayats, but did so with specific codal provisions of elections, representation and functions. The 74th Amendment did the same for urban areas, though in a different manner.

Financial and administrative decentralisation did not follow the political signals of decentralisation, nor were all the State governments equally motivated to decentralise funds, functions or functionaries. The government machinery had not kept up with the pace of economic reforms. The earlier rules, regulations, codes and manuals, many of them codified in the nineteenth century, are still prevalent though often they have little relevance to the day-to-day business of governance.[2] The administrative pyramid of India focused primarily only on the top two tiers of the Centre and the States without realising the magnitude of the third tier of local governance which has in turn been divided into three layers of district, sub-district and village levels in terms of the 73rd Constitutional amendment. Even a cursory look at the numbers at each level reveals how there has been too much concentration of political, fiscal and administrative power at the centre leaving a vast slice of the country out of the planning and decision-making processes. While the Seventh Schedule of the Indian constitution allocated the powers and responsibilities among the Centre and the States, the 73rd and the 74th Amendment required the introduction of the Eleventh and the Twelfth Schedules specifying the powers, authority and responsibilities of the Panchayats and the Municipalities respectively. The traditional accountability mechanisms of Financial control (Avasthi, 1980) in the form of Pre-budget and Post-budget controls, system of Parliamentary Committees like the Public Accounts Committee and the departmental sub-committees captured the account of funds till the stage that they were within the purview of Consolidated Fund of India or the States. This creation of the third tier impacted the effectiveness of schemes and aided decentralisation of administration to cover a comprehensive devolution of powers and autonomy and not mere de-concentration of administrative and political power without the attendant autonomy. Further, a detailed examination is required of the extent to which these constitutionally enshrined political local bodies have achieved their goals of improved accountability to the people, participatory decision-making, reduction in delays and corruption exemplified by the centralised bureaucracy, better targeting of scheme beneficiaries and an overall efficient, effective and equitable development at the local level.

In India, as in most countries, the first wave of decentralisation occurred in the political realm in 1992 with the creation of Local Bodies of the three levels of PRI with their election procedure clearly laid down. Their responsibilities and functions have been spelt out in the 11th and 12th Schedules. There are two broad features of the decentralisation discussion in India. Firstly, it tends to focus largely on the political decentralisation, which is most visible feature, at the cost of the less clearly mapped fiscal and administrative decentralisation. Secondly, it tends to stop short at the state level itself to determine State-wise patterns. The sub-state level decentralisation at the third-tier has not yet been studied in enough detail or perspective in academic literature or reviewed systematically in administrative circles. In fact, the 73rd and the 74th Constitutional Amendments in 1993 are quite recent as is the theme of this conference. There are many advocates who believe that this set of legislation, if given sufficient time, is enough to rectify a number of problems plaguing the country and hampering its development. The responsibility for ensuring the conformity with the constitutional provisions lies with the Central Government but the actual modalities for the devolution to lower levels of government lies with the States as per the Seventh Schedule. This leads to a wide range of variations and unevenness in the ground-level decentralisation across the country. The then Prime Minister, Rajiv Gandhi had said during an earlier Parliamentary debate in 1989, which was the precursor to the 73rd amendment:

"It would be for State legislatures to lay down the legislative parameters of devolution and for State governments to give practical effect to those parameters. We recognise that the precise pattern of devolution might vary from State to State."[3]

The freedom vested with the State governments has led to a veritable patchwork of various provisions tacked on to the Conformity legislations passed by the States in the wake of the 73rd and 74th Amendments. However, in terms of theory, the guiding principles for the downward devolution of powers and responsibilities in the form of Functions, Funds and Functionaries are:

- **The Principle of Subsidiarity:** which lays down that functions, funds and functionaries should be devolved to the level at which it is most efficient for providing that service.
- **Economies of Scale:** to ensure that all material purchase, service outsourcing or construction/production decisions are taken at the level where maximum economies of scale are afforded.
- **The Principle of Equity:** to ensure that all regions and all categories of people are covered in an equitable fashion – with compensation and positive discriminations, wherever required to help the disadvantageous groups.
- **Heterogeneity:** According to the principle of heterogeneity, there is a need to understand and appreciate the genuine differences in the tastes and preferences of different sets of people, so that there is no single prescribed product or service being provided to diverse groups of population.
- **Public accountability:** The devolution of funds, functions and functionaries in the public domain necessitates that all aspects of the devolution should conform to the highest standards of public accountability and have well-defined responsibility matrices and clear Audit Trails.

History of Urban Local Governments in India

Long before the 74th Constitutional Amendment in 1993, India has had a rich history of urban local governments and bodies vested with the basics of urban governance. However, these predated the Constitution and to that extent, they enjoyed only executive sanction by the state governments and were *ultra vires* with no constitutional backing. A brief history of decentralisation in India reveals municipal governments as early as in the seventeenth century from the East India Company, starting in 1688 with Madras, followed by Calcutta and Bombay. This laid the foundation of the subsequent path of urban governance in India. In 1882, the Ripon resolution declared the setting up of local boards for self governance composed of two-thirds elected members, presided by a non-official Chairman.

The need for such local government bodies, as well as their viability, was clearly recognised by the British colonial administration. On the other hand, their transformation into political nurseries to the fledgling freedom fighters was unwelcome. Therefore, efforts were made to clip their responsibilities and powers and assimilate them into the federal polity with two tiers of government – Centre and State. They were not granted formal political autonomy, even though the Royal Commission on decentralisation in 1909 deplored the lack of autonomy to urban local bodies. The Montague-Chelmsford reforms of 1919 made local bodies a subject transferred to the provinces. The issue of empowerment of Local Self Government institutions became one of the many issues in the struggle for greater autonomy and eventual independence of the country and was mentioned in the Article 40 of the Constitution in the non-mandatory Directive Principles of State Policy chapter. However, both the rural and urban bodies have historically remained outside the scope of the formal vertical hierarchy of government.[4] The constitution of independent India made no specific concession to them. It was only after the 73rd Amendment was passed that granted status to the rural local bodies that as a corollary to it, the 74th Amendment was passed which gave India its first constitutionally mandated urban local administrative units. Thus, ULBs had to traverse a long distance to develop as institutions of democratic decentralisation.

Recent Trends in Urban India

Urban growth is the most visible sign of economic development in India. Urban growth has overtaken growth in rural India as per 2011 Census, both in terms of the increase in number of urban centres as well as the growth of population in them, with rural-urban and urban-urban migration. For the first time in India, urban population growth overtook rural growth with the decadal population urban growth rate for India at 31.8 per cent, against 12.2 per cent for rural India. The increase in the number of statutory and census town and the share of urban population in India can be seen in the table below. Nearly a third of the country is living in urban settlements and this number is poised to grow further, both due to natural population growth in the urban centres as well as migration. Another major factor of urban growth is the fact that as population of a settlement increases to a threshold, it fulfils one of the criteria for that settlement to be classified as an urban centre.[5] The satisfactory governance of this burgeoning population is a challenge for administrators, policy-makers, academics and even of the common citizens.

Census Year	*Statutory towns*	*Census towns*	*Total number*	*Share of urban population (Per cent)*
2001	3799	1362	5161	27.81
2011	4041	3894	7935	31.16

Census 2011.

Furthermore, with the increase in urbanisation and the rapid growth of urban centres in the country, there is a trend towards a breakdown of the rural-urban dichotomy. The density, diversity, dynamics and resultant complexity of urban centres is spreading outwards into the surrounding areas. There is a gradation of urban-ness and rural-ness around cities (Ramachandran, 1991) without necessarily having a discernible "tipping-point" in between reducing the perceived rural-urban disparity (Rajasekhar and Sahu, 2004). This requires a holistic spatial analysis of the complex network without too much reliance on a strict urban and non-urban classification. In addition, unlike the administrative units of Union and State or Union Territory governments, there is a clear break at the level of local governments between urban and rural settlements. The decades which have followed have seen the maximum growth of cities due to natural growth, migration, better economic opportunities and infrastructure, including education and health. For all these reasons, it is significant to study the accountability, responsiveness and transparency of these Local Self-Government bodies. This places the urban governance institutions in the context of the larger decentralisation process in India and compares the constitutional provisions of the 73rd and the 74th Amendments.

Need for Strengthening ULBs

Having established the trends of urbanisation in the country and the historical background of the ULBs, this section highlights the significance and need for an effective elected urban local body especially in the rapidly urbanised country.

As indicated in an earlier section, there has been great variation and unevenness in the acceptance of democratic and functional local bodies by different states and this can be seen by studying their conformity legislations. This variation is even more marked in the case of urban local bodies and the conformity legislations consequent to the 74th Amendment. The intense focus and monitoring of the panchayati raj bodies, both due to their large numbers and the political significance, has meant that despite the variations, the position of rural local governments is far more regulated and compliant to standards than in the case of urban governments.

There is undoubtedly much resistance to the emergence of local leaders at the third tier in rural areas, but this is even more so in the case of urban local politicians. The most significant reason for this that while rural local elections are not contested on party lines, urban politics is completely conducted along party lines. The local candidates are selected, supported and elected by their party affiliations with some stray independent candidates, if any. The jury is still out on how desirable this difference is and whether or not local bodies should be aligned along state and national party lines. Many notable votaries of democratic representation have supported this. Abdul Nazir Saab, a former and indeed notable, Karnataka Minister for Panchayati Raj, who worked tirelessly in ushering in a new era of PRIs in the state, once said: "anyway in the villages there is Ramanna-Bhimanna politics. It is a reality. Isn't it healthier that they align on Democratic Party lines rather than on caste, religion, etc?" Regardless of this debate, the fact exists that due to party affiliation, the elected leaders of the urban local bodies tend to be compromised being relative juniors in the party hierarchy. Furthermore, their priorities and policies are guided by their party compulsions rather than local needs.

The size of urban electorates, even with the outdated and limited voter-lists, far exceeds the voter base of most gram panchayats. Thus, each urban ward has a single elected representative for far more people than the typical gram panchayat member who is elected from among and represents about 5000 persons.

The gram sabhas, perhaps due to better awareness in some states and relentless monitoring in other states, tend to meet at least twice a year with the provision of meeting for a special Gram Sabha for specific issues. These Gram Sabha meetings are the basic core of democratic representation with planning, monitoring, beneficiary identification and social audit provisions built in. While there are many studies which highlight to sorry state of Gram Sabhas, in the case of ULBs, the corresponding feature of Ward Sabhas and ward committees is practically non-existent.

Nature of decentralisation in India is different from the type of federal systems in Brazil and is more in the nature of nested governments in a hierarchy rather than autonomous local governments (Vyasulu, 2012). In such a context, the administrative demarcation of urban and rural local governments adds to the weakening of the decentralised governance by introducing the dual and mutually exclusive systems. Furthermore, this asymmetric nature of federalism influences public service delivery. The ULBs are largely under the control of the state governments in planning, monitoring, beneficiary identification and they do not enjoy sufficient accountability and transparency in their working. The state election commissions, state finance commissions and even the District Planning Committees are more focused on rural areas than the urban centres. Most large cities do not even have the mandated Metropolitan Planning Committee.

Citizenship concepts in urban India are rather underdeveloped with most urban dwellers also retaining their native rural identities. This undermines the role of citizens in local self-government and leads to poor citizen participation in local and civic affairs. Most cities and towns in India are not settled well-enough to instill civic identities and pride among the residents. Many residents are also first- or second-generation migrants from other urban or rural areas. There is neither a supply of democratic institutions nor a concerted demand for them in most ULBs.

The traditional concept of accountability in India as a colonial British construct is of post facto accountability which is not need driven, based on what the citizenry wants or demands. In fact, the degree of accountability and transparency which is seen in the PRIs is also not built-in to the ULBs. The hierarchical structure is also not conducive to effective functioning since the head of the Ward Committee has little or no control over the functional bureaucracy such as the Executive Engineer. The dysfunctional state of the ward committees and ward sabhas led the Union government in the ministry of urban affairs to link their releases under the JNNURM and other schemes to the passage of affective Community Participation Bills, along the lines of their Model Nagar Raj Bill. Since the states were keen to receive funds for urban settlements, they have put in place some form of the Nagar Raj Bill as conformity legislation. However, with the great degree of variation across states, this Community Participation Bill does not achieve its purpose of empowering and involving citizens in the urban affairs, especially not in planning, monitoring, beneficiary identification and social audit.

Ward Committees are largely nominal and even have nominated members supplanting the elected representatives. Ward sabhas, where they exit are large and comprise mixed populations, do not function as effectively as their rural counterparts, the gram sabhas. These areas need some serious attention for the ULBs to effectively perform and function as institutions of democratic decentralisation.

In addition to the above mentioned problems, there are deficits of resources, technology and manpower; inefficiencies in utilisation of resources; absence of clear hard budget constraints; lack of financial and political transparency and accountability; an excess of mixed electorates with, highly polarised voters by political, economic and social lines; populous neighbourhoods; and multiplicity of agencies.

This pessimistic scenario can however, be redressed with some coordinated efforts given the higher rates of literacy among urban citizens. This process needs to be initiated at multiple levels in a coordinated fashion for it to work. The deficit of institutional framework to ensure democratic ULBs even in comparison to the PRIs is more surprising given the expectation that urban areas are more literate and politically aware. However, there seems to be a neglect compared to the constant emphasis on PRIs. Moreover, there is little political interest in grooming leadership in the ULBs. Similarly, the administrative and functional structures are also well-entrenched and likely to resist giving up any position to new agencies, administrative or political.

With suitable initiatives the situation can be turned around to strengthen urban local bodies. Some of the initiatives required are - amendments to the various conformity legislations, community mobilisation, extensive voter registration, organisation of wards on the basis of comparable size and population, enforcement of legal provisions, mandatory proceedings and their recording, introduction of tiers of urban municipal government, clarity of roles of political and executive personnel, evaluation of the mayoral system and a structured system of Administrative and Financial Accountability.

Conclusion

In conclusion, it would be pertinent to repeat that ULBs have had a long historical role in India – this role has been blessed with constitutional sanction only by the 74th Amendment. As compared to the PRIs initiated after the 73rd Amendment, there are multiple areas of political, functional and administrative empowerment deficits. These can be tackled and overcome only by coordinated action by citizens, governments as well as other agencies in a multi-pronged action. These initiatives need to be specific and two-way with dual ownership by public agencies and the citizenry. This is the need of the hour.

References

Avasthi, A (1980): Centralised Administration, Tata-McGraw Hill, New Delhi.

Census of India reports and data from the website http://censusindia. gov. in/

Oates, Wallace E., (1972): Fiscal Federalism, Harcourt Brace Jovanovich, New York.

________(2005): Toward A Second-Generation Theory of Fiscal Federalism, Published in International Tax and Public Finance Volume 12, Number 4 / August, 2005 Accessed:http://www. econ. umd. edu/~oates/research/ 2ndGenerationFiscalFederalism. pdf

Prud'homme, Remy, (1995): 'On the Dangers of Decentralisation', World Bank Research Observer, Vol.10, No. 2.

Rajasekhar, D and G B Sahu (2004): The growing rural-urban disparity: Some issues, ISEC Working Paper no.156.

Ramachandran, R. (1989): Urbanisation and Urban systems in India, OUP, Delhi.

Vyasulu, Vinod (2012): Reflections on Budgets and Governance in India, Centre for Budget and Governance Accountability, New Delhi accessed online from:http://www. cbps. in/wpcontent/themes/cbps/pdf/Reflections_on_ Budgets_Governance

Notes

1. The famous quote of Gandhi about India living in her villages.
2. Refer Administrative Reforms Commission India reports at the website: http://arc.gov.in/
3. Rajya Sabha Debate 13 October 1989.
4. This paper focuses on urban local government and touches upon rural local bodies in India only to the limited extent that they impact the system of urban local government.
5. The 3 criteria for defining a settlement as an urban centre in India are: 1. Population over 5000; 2. over 75 per cent male working population engaged in non-agricultural activities; and 3. a population density of >400 per sq km.

3

Ward Committees, Citizen Participation in Urban Governance: Experiences of Kerala and Maharashtra

—Yacoub Zachariah Kuruvilla
and Smita Waingankar

Introduction

This paper documents the experiences of citizen participation in urban governance through ward committees in two states, Kerala and Maharashtra. Ward committees was an important institution which was created by 74th Constitutional Amendment Act (74th CAA) to promote citizen participation in urban governance. However, the experiences with ward committees in different states have not been encouraging (Sivaramakrishnan, 2006; Baud, 2009).

Both scholars and policy-makers have pointed out Kerala as a potential model state in terms of legal framework for enhancing participation of citizens in decision-making of local self-government institutions (LSGIs). However, a detailed academic study of the experiences of functioning of wards committees in urban LSGIs of Kerala not yet been undertaken. This paper documents the experiences of ward committees in the city of Kochi in state of Kerala and highlights the key findings from there.

Maharashtra is one of the more urbanised states in India with more than 40 per cent of its population living in urban areas. This paper analyses the existing legal framework for ward committees in its municipal Acts and reviews the process and explains the implications of the Amendments bought to these Acts in the year 2009 to strengthen citizen participation in urban governance.

These amendments were bought in the context of Community Participation Law (CPL), a reform conditionality outlined under Jawaharlal National Urban Renewal Mission (JNNURM). JNNURM is the most massive centrally aided urban development programme in post-independent India. The Community Participation Law sought to establish ward committees in each electoral ward and area sabhas at polling booth level with each municipal electoral ward. This paper reviews the status of CPL in both states.

The broad findings of the paper are that while Kerala has been considered as a potential model for citizen participation in urban governance through ward committees, there are serious deficits in devolution of power to urban local-self-governments that reduces the effectiveness of ward committees as an institution of participatory governance. In case of Maharashtra, the legal framework for ward committees is not in the spirit of 74th CAA and denied the principles of proximity and broad representation to citizens. The paper also finds that centralised approach to decentralisation as seen in JNNURM has failed in ensuring that states and urban local governments create spaces for citizen participation in civic affairs. The paper concludes with the need to recognise the variety of political institutions and culture as well as variety of urban local governments in terms of population and area in developing a framework for citizen participation in governance. This would require collaborative efforts from political leadership, governments at all tiers, academia and civil society to deepen decentralisation and participatory governance in urban areas.

Background

In India, as in many other countries of the world, research on the subject of public participation in urban governance has seen growing interest, especially due to economic factors such as globalisation and trade liberalisation, and political factors such as decentralisation and devolution of development functions to local governments. In India, the discussions on citizen participation in urban governance gathered momentum after the enactment of the 74th Constitutional Amendment Act, 1992 (74th CAA), which is considered the landmark legislation for urban local governments in India providing them statutory status.

A closer scrutiny reveals that municipal governance has a long history in this country. Urban local governments in terms of a representative organisation that is responsible to voters enjoying a wide ranging set of powers and functions of administration and taxation is a creation of the British colonial rule. Lord Ripon who is considered as the father of local self-government in India for his promulgation of resolutions of 1881 and 1882 endeavoured to make local bodies strong, autonomous and broad based. According to him, the main objective of local self-governments was to serve as a school for training representatives in civic matters (Pinto, 2000). He was the first to call for elected municipal boards in India as against nominated municipal boards that was in practice during his time. However, his resolutions were not implemented in their full spirit by the British officials who continued to maintain centralised control over the municipalities and all citizens were not eligible to either contest or vote for municipal elections.

Post-independence, municipalities in India were neglected. In the Indian constitution there was no provision for municipalities, unlike village panchayats, establishment of which became a part of Directive Principles of State Policy within the Indian constitution. According to the Indian constitution, local self-government is a subject under the State List, thereby handing the control of local bodies to state governments. The period between 1950 and 1992 was marked by increased control by state governments over municipal bodies. Municipal corporations saw a steady erosion of their powers, functions and resource base over time. State governments regularly superseded municipal bodies and kept them in suspended animation. The participation of ordinary citizens in urban local government during this period was restricted to voting in elections, which were often held irregularly or not held for long periods of time (Bhattacharya, 1976; Pinto, 2000; Sivaramakrishnan, 2006).

The 74th Constitutional Amendment Act, 1992 provided for a third tier of government namely, municipalities in urban areas as institutions of local self-governance endowed with powers and functions. The provisions for wards committees as outlined in the Article 243 S of the 74th CAA was significant for providing space for citizen participation in urban local governance. The Joint Parliamentary Committee (JPC) recommendations on the amendment bill show the rationale for including citizens in ward committees.[6] In order to maintain the sanctity of division of powers in the Indian Constitution, 74th CAA provided State legislatures with discretionary powers to decide on the composition, powers and functions of ward committees. This step was taken to ensure that central government did not transgress into state governments functional domain as local government is a state subject in the Indian constitution. In the next section, the paper briefly reviews academic literature on participatory governance.

Participatory Governance: Citizen Participation for Effective Governance

Ward committees were envisaged as participatory forums for urban governance that would bring urban local bodies closer to citizens and provide a platform for citizen engagement in process of city planning and development. According to different scholars, citizen involvement in governance through participatory forums is expected to improve representation of citizens especially of the poor and marginalised. It is also expected to increase effectiveness of public policy by providing feedback to policy-makers or by allowing citizens to shape policies according to their needs. Such forums can play a role in developing mechanisms to extract accountability of elected representatives and local officials by providing a space for citizens to critically evaluate their performance. All of these outcomes are believed will contribute to larger goals of improving democratic legitimacy and develop an engaged citizenry (Chottray and Stoker, 2009).

Governance seeks to understand the way we construct collective decision-making. It looks at how mode of decision-making can be done with effectiveness and legitimacy in view of challenge to traditional ways of decision-making by complexity of social problems, strength of organised interests and interdependencies brought by new era of globalisation (Chottray and Stoker, 2009).

Participatory governance as a subset of governance theory emphasises democratic practices. It offers a set of theory and practices of public engagement through deliberative processes. It extends citizen role beyond that as a voter to include a more direct deliberative involvement in pressing policy issues. It seeks to develop practices that are found in a more equal distribution of power, a fairer distribution of resources, the decentralisation of decision-making processes, development of a wide and transparent exchange of information, the establishment of collaborative partnerships, an emphasis on inter-institutional dialogue and greater accountability (Fischer, 2010). Contemporary forms of participatory governance reflect thinking beyond representative democracies and establishment of new voice mechanism for direct connection between people and bureaucracies that affect them. Participatory governance has thus been linked to community or neighbourhood level governance as also with more active forms of citizenship.

One form or type of governance that combines participation, deliberative democracy and participatory governance is known as empowered deliberative democracy (EDD) developed by Fung and Wright (2001). EDD takes many of its normative commitments from analyses of practices and values of communication, public justification and deliberation. It extends application of deliberation to practical problems. It locates deliberation in specific organisations and practices in order to marshal social experience and understandings of practical deliberation and directions for its improvement. Three general principles of EDD include a focus on specific, tangible problems, involvement of ordinary people affected by these problems and officials close to them and the deliberative development of solutions to these problems. The authors have also highlighted the broad criticisms of EDD such as constraints on the scope of deliberative decision and action due to limitations imposed by external actors, 'balkanisation' of the polity and political decision making.

The question of why citizens should be allowed to participate in city governance process has been answered by Sorensen and Sagaris (2010). According to them, there are five answers to this question. Citizens provide local knowledge and experience is essential wherever governments seek to make cities more liveable. Local participation may build active support among residents that is crucial to success of local programmes. Local people have strong incentives to improve their own environments and when given an opportunity to make a difference, often work very hard to ensure that policies succeed. Citizen engagement in planning may help to strengthen social cohesion and capacity for environmental management. Fifth, the process of public engagement may generate or strengthen a sense of shared interests and place identity.

Melo and Baiocchi (2006) have identified the need for a research agenda that combines debates in urban governance and deliberative democracy to enquire into the role of deliberation in city governance. They also raise some research questions that are of crucial importance for debates on deliberation and governance include whether pro-poor institutional biases could be built into participatory structures, what are the conditions under which participatory arrangements can be both democratic and governance-enhancing? What are the factors that facilitate or hinder emergence of local horizontal governance arrangements? Which factors account for the relative success or failure of this coordinating devices in certain places? And whether minimum levels of associational density is necessary for such arrangements to work?

Ward committees can be considered as participatory forums initiated by state in which citizens can participate through fair deliberation in distribution of resources and planning processes locally thereby setting framework for allocation of resources. In the next section, the paper provides an overview of the experience of ward committees in India as forums of participatory governance documented in academic literature.

Ward Committees in India: Falling Short of expectations

Ward committees were expected to act as "bridge between municipal government and citizens" (Sivaramakrishnan 2006). In other words, they were to act as institutions of neighbourhood governance and increase proximity between elected representatives and citizens and also provide a space for citizen participation in local level planning. The academic literature on ward committees in India is limited to a few collected volumes and journal articles. The prominent academic literature on ward committees are volumes edited by Sivaramakrishnan (2006), Baud and De Wit (2009).

The first major study on ward committees by Institute of Social Sciences, New Delhi which is documented in Sivaramakrishnan (2006) found that only 19 states out of 29 states had enacted an enabling state legislation for the purpose of ward committees. Further, only eight states had constituted wards committees. While, only the states of Kerala and West Bengal have a ward committee for each ward, Kerala has moved beyond the 74th CAA in providing for ward committees in all municipal bodies with more than one lakh population.

The findings of the study showed that in Bangalore, three electoral wards are combined to form a wards committee. In metropolitan cities of Delhi, Chennai and Mumbai, more than 10 electoral wards are combined to form a wards committee thus negating the very purpose of wards committee which was to be more proximate to the local citizens of the respective wards. In Delhi and Tamil Nadu, there is no provision for inclusion of members from the civil society. Maharashtra has restricted civil society representation to three members who are registered as voters in the wards within the jurisdictions of the wards committee. However, these representatives are nominated by the elected councillors making it difficult for them to act as truly independent voices. Thus, the representative character of wards committees in many states can be questioned.

The study pointed out that ward committees have been constituted only in a small number of cities and there are issues with their design and functioning. Ward committees in most cities do not satisfy the primary criteria of proximity to citizens which was the rationale for creating ward committees in the first place. In most ward committees, composition is restricted to the councillors or sprinkling of representatives of voluntary associations. Hence, even in institutional design these ward committees failed to ensure fair deliberations and did not enhance legitimacy and accountability of elected municipal representatives and officials (Sivaramakrishnan, 2006).

Baud (2009) confirms that Ward Committees hardly perform satisfactorily anywhere. They have limited powers and resources with limited impact on participation improved governance or service delivery. While problems can be partly attributed to design issues in terms of delegated tasks and finances, civil society representation is also poorly organised and links to citizen organisations are weak.

Thus, both Sivaramakrishnan (2006) and Baud *et. al* (2009) have pointed out that most states of India have not implemented an enabling institutional design for ward committees in terms of its proximity to citizens, representation of civil society in the committees and devolution of powers and functions to ward committees for effective ward level governance.

There has been a considerable lack of interest in and research into the impact and implications of 74th CAA and ward committees in enhancing citizen participation in urban governance. Two decades have passed since enactment of 74th CAA and academic literature seems to find only a potential model state for participatory urban governance, Kerala. In the following section, the paper reviews academic literature on ward committees in Kerala and points out that the assumption of this model state in academic literature is based on review of legal framework for urban governance rather than an empirical examination of the functioning of ward committees in cities and towns of Kerala.

Ward Committees in Kerala: A model for citizen participation in urban governance through ward committees

Sivaramakrishnan (2006) finds ward committees in Kerala is designed to be highly participatory, providing proximity of people to elected representatives as every electoral ward has a ward commiittee or ward sabha. Their smaller size and representative character enables to them to serve as a platform for seeking and obtaining accountability from the councillor as population sizes of wards are smaller.

According to De Wit *et. al* (2009) Kerala has been the most ambitious in establishing and empowering ward committees. Ward committees in Kerala have tasks that include preparing and supervising ward-level development schemes, identifying beneficiaries of welfare schemes among others. They state that there is a need for distinction between institutional design of ward committees in statutory legislations like municipal acts and composition of members, powers and functions of ward committees in actual practice. Further, they point to reported shortcomings such as large size of each ward committee and reluctance of authorities to delegate powers have reduced them to a mere consultative body unable to implement ward development plans as per legislation. Despite such cautions, De Wit *et. al* (2009) states that experience of ward committees in Kerala can provide lessons to strengthen legislation on ward committees both at national and state level because of its potentially participatory and representative institutional design.

A review of literature on functioning of ward committees in Kerala shows that based on studies of legal provisions of ward committees, Kerala has enhanced principles of proximity, representation and devolution of powers for ward committees. These studies have highlighted ward committees in Kerala as pioneers in implementing these principles through legal provisions. These studies highlight the fact that ward committees in Kerala in terms of legal provisions enable proximity of citizens to municipal governance, representation of different civil society groups and have been devolved a set of powers and functions for ward level municipal governance. In the next section, the paper reviews the context and processes that enabled such an institutional design in Kerala as a part of the People's Planning Campaign (PPC) and provides an overview of the salient features of this legal framework.

People's Planning Campaign and Ward Committees in Kerala: Institutional Design to enhance citizen participation in urban governance

In 1994, The Kerala Municipality Act was enacted to conform to 74th CAA. In this Act, the ward committee was to be chaired by the elected councillor who would also nominate the ten members on the committee. In 1996, the Left Democratic Front (LDF) government initiated the 'People's Planning Campaign' in Kerala for democratic decentralisation to empower both rural and urban local governments through devolution of powers and financial resources. Further, to carry the process forward, it appointed a 'Committee on Decentralisation of Powers' led by S. B. Sen seeking legislative changes for democratic decentralisation.

According to scholars, the biggest achievement of Peoples Planning Campaign (PPC) was institutionalisation of decentralised planning by local self-government institutions. The decentralised system of planning has been institutionalised and is the core of local government system in the state. The new system is well backed by constitutional amendments, established conventions, approved rules and procedures, a wide variety of organisations and support of people. PPC in Kerala is considered by scholars as an example of empowered deliberative democracy and participatory governance (Fung and Wright, 2001).

The recommendations of Sen Committee were enacted as amendments to Kerala Municipality Act in 1999.[7] These recommendations enhanced proximity of citizens to ward committees, broadened the representation in ward committees by including a wide variety of political and social organisations and provided ward committees with a definite set of functions and rights.

Section 42 of the Kerala Municipality Act, every electoral ward of a municipality with more than a lakh population needs to have a ward committee. Based on provisions under Section 6 of the Kerala Municipality Act, the average number of voters in an electoral ward are about 8,000 to 10,000. Thus, these legal provisions enhanced proximity of ward committees to citizens.

Section 43 of Kerala Municipality Act provides membership of ward committees to members of neighbourhood groups (NHGs) and resident welfare associations among others.[8] The representation of civil society members is open to all residents of the ward, irrespective of their economic or social backgrounds. Therefore, one finds middle income and lower income representation in ward committees through resident welfare associations and neighbourhood groups. Together, they form the majority of the ward committee members.[9] Thus, significant memberships of ward committees were to be ordinary citizens of the ward.

Another set of recommendations of Sen Committee were enacted as Section 45 of Kerala Municipality Act. These provisions are related to powers and functions of the ward committee which includes setting priorities for the development of the ward, identification of beneficiaries of development schemes in the ward and review of the implementation of development schemes and municipal services at ward level.

The powers of the ward committees also include the right to receive information about all schemes being implemented in the ward as well as proposed schemes for the ward. It also has the right to discuss annual plan and budget of the municipal corporation and placing its suggestions and recommendations for discussions in the municipality.

To summarise, the population that a ward committee has to serve in Kerala is relatively smaller, enabling easier access for citizens to raise issues with ward committee members. Also, ward committee members being residents of this ward are likely to be familiar with civic issues of their ward which may have a bearing on deliberations in the ward committees. Citizens can now access, recommend and bring forth issues to a ward committee. Through inclusion of members from neighbourhood groups in ward committees, two vulnerable sections of the society namely, women and urban poor have been given representation in the ward committees. Ward committees in Kerala have provided membership to a wide range of civil society organisations in the wards. The possibility for more democratic discussions and deliberative decision-making in ward committees is potentially enhanced by the representative structure of ward committees. Similarly, the extent of transparency and accountability of municipal councillors and elected officials may also be potentially more in representative ward committees.

However, the impact of PPC on participation of citizens in municipalities of Kerala has not been investigated and documented. Perhaps a reason for absence of studies on participation in urban governance during and after PPC is because the amendments of 1999 came towards end of PPC and it was perhaps too early to evaluate its impact at that point. Ward committees in Kerala have been functioning for more than a decade now. However, a detailed documentation of the experience of functioning of ward committees in municipal corporations of the state was not available. In the following sections, paper reviews the experiences of ward committees in Cochin Corporation based on a research study conducted in 2011 about participation of women members and functioning of ward committees (Kuruvilla, 2011).

Ward Committees in Cochin Corporation

Cochin Municipal Corporation was formed in 1967. Kochi is Kerala's commercial capital and is the centre of its biggest urban agglomeration. The dynamic economy of the city has attracted many migrants at various points of time and continues to do so. At present Kochi Corporation is divided into 74 electoral wards. All electoral wards have functioning ward committees. The study focused on four ward committees of Cochin City Corporation.[10] The wards were selected purposively based on criteria of having experienced ward councillors who have seen the transformation of local governments in Kerala after 74th CAA, have been a part of People's Planning Campaign and have a long experience with ward committees. Interviews were conducted with elected ward councillors and ward committee members from resident welfare associations and neighbourhood groups which are two of major groups of members in ward committees. While, the main aspect that was studied was participation of women in ward committees, broader issues with functioning of ward committees were also part of the study. The findings on functioning of ward committees in Cochin have been highlighted in the next section.

Functioning of Ward Committees in Cochin: Open agendas, fair deliberations and mixed outcomes

The first part of findings is related to agendas of discussion, manner of deliberations and outcomes of ward committees in Cochin. Based on evidence from fieldwork, the agendas forward committee meetings are found to be mostly open ended, with members being free to raise different issues related to municipal governance at ward level. With regard to deliberations in ward committees, it is found that vocalisation is the predominant form of participation in ward committees. In this form of participation, silence of ward committee members is also a form of participation used to signal as an assent to a particular issue being raised by other members.

With regard to outcomes of ward committees, the evidence from the study shows that there are both positives and negatives to the functioning of the present institutional design of the ward committees in Cochin Municipal Corporation. The positives noted by ward committee members included some opening up of municipal decision-making process, ability to use knowledge of the members to enhance effectiveness and responsiveness of elected members and municipal officials and providing members with further learning of civic issues of Cochin and being able to see these issues beyond locality or ward level. The negatives included ignorance of their recommendations by Municipal Corporation, red tapism and apathy of municipal bureaucracy slowing down the implementation of ward committee recommendations, lack of interaction of members outside ward committees and failure to connect with ordinary citizens.

Based on these findings, it can be concluded that ward committee processes may be happening in a reasonably satisfactory manner with active participation of members, translating the demands and suggestions of the ward committee has been more difficult because of the many external factors that constrain CMC from responding to the demands of ward committees. In response to questions on agenda setting in the ward committees, the responses by different members of the ward committees pointed to agenda setting as not being a critical aspect of ward committee meetings. While, some of the most important items on the agenda of a ward committee are discussion of annual plan of the CMC and selection of beneficiaries for different welfare schemes, members have the freedom to raise any issue that is related to the municipal ward or CMC. The elected councillors felt that ward committee agenda has been reduced to discussion of fund utilisation only rather than about development issues of the ward.

The very idea of a formal agenda is absent in ward committees of Cochin Municipal Corporation. It was found that ward committee members in fact preferred the idea of having an open agenda for the meetings. This allowed them to raise issues and questions regarding a whole range of development schemes and activities implemented by CMC. However, the observations of councillors showed that they preferred a more formal agenda. While, they believed that broader issues of development of the city need to be discussed in ward committees.

While an open agenda may allow for diverse interests to be represented in the suggestions of the ward committees, it also increases the demands on the councillor because he or she is the link for ward committees with Cochin municipal corporation. Such demands also raise the question about adequate resources (financial, technical and administrative) to meet these demands. An open agenda also has implications for responsiveness of the councillor and the municipal corporation. As shown in the next set of findings regarding limitations of Municipal Corporation in terms of powers and resources, the open agenda has potential of setting high expectations which elected councillors may not be able to deliver due to administrative, financial and legal constraints.

Deliberations in the Ward Committees

In response to questions on how members participated in the ward committees, most of the members responded that vocal participation was the most preferred manner of participation in ward committees. In most cases, members who had a question or wanted to raise a issue were allowed to do the same without any hindrance from other members or the councillor who is the chairperson of the ward committee.

It was found that major issues in the wards like problems with water supply or road was found to receive support in deliberations of all members. But issues related to a particular group like welfare pensions or some infrastructure need of a particular locality was usually raised by only the concerned members. Also, all members pointed to the fact that while ward committee members may not actively or vocally support needs of other members, there was no opposition or contestation regarding issues raised in the ward committees.

The explanation for this finding is that for members, the stakes at hand in the ward committees are not that high. While, for NHG members, ward committees are useful to raise micro-level issues in implementation of schemes for poor or formulating new demands on CMC, a larger level question on changing the benefits or eligibility norms in welfare schemes may not be possible within this forum and can be taken up through the CDS for CMC and at a state level through Kudumbashree at the state level.

The fragmentation of responsibilities for service delivery of urban services means that it is far more difficult especially at ward level to fix accountability on any of the institutions. The major arterial roads in West and East Kochi are national highways under National Highways Authority. Similar is the case with water supply which is entirely controlled by a state level parastatal known as Kerala Water Authority whose accountability flows upwards to central and state governments rather than Municipal Corporation and its citizens. This means that ward committees have many constraints even in raising issues with service delivery of critical urban services like water supply, sewerage and highways. This reduces the effectiveness of the outcomes that can be achieved by the ward committees.

Outcomes of Ward Committees

Most members evaluated the outcomes of the ward committee as having positives and negatives. The positives were that new councillors and officials had to provide information on development schemes in the ward. In other words, there has been some opening up of municipal decision-making. As members have gained knowledge about municipal affairs through their participation in ward committees, slowly larger and broader questions about city planning, issues affecting women in the city, environmental concerns are all being raised in ward committees. Thirdly, the linkage of members in the ward committees to different social organisations means that the knowledge acquired by different members through personal and professional activities can be used to enrich the discussions of the ward committees.

For many members, the major problem was that suggestions of ward committees were either not taken up at all by the municipal corporation or stuck in the red tape of municipal bureaucracy. While members are now aware of municipal decision-making processes, many residents of the ward are not concerned about functioning of ward committees and exercise of its functions and powers. The lack of connection with residents of the ward was also sighted as a problem.

A major issue highlighted by members was that quarterly meetings of ward committees were ineffective to tackle ward level issues, often forcing members to meet councillors and officials directly. The lack of executive powers for the ward committees in implementation and monitoring of ward level programmes was pointed to members as a major limitation. However, despite observation of the members on these negative aspects of the ward committees, there have been no discussions on strengthening the ward committees or improving the awareness of ward committees among residents of the ward.

In summary, the findings from the study show that ward committees follow an open agenda which while promoting representation of diverse interests in ward committees also has implications for the responsiveness of councillor and municipal officials. The deliberations of ward committees are found to be non-confrontational because issues discussed at micro-scale with low stakes. The ward committee member's evaluation of the outcomes of the ward committees reveals a mixed picture with both positives and negatives. However, the overall evaluation has been that agendas and deliberations of ward committees are not quite translating into real and tangible outcomes due to limitations of the Cochin Municipal Corporation in responding to demands of ward committees.

In the next section, the paper elaborates on the limitations of Cochin Municipal Corporation to respond to demands of ward committees is a result of the slow pace of urban decentralisation in Kerala and lack of integration of functioning of Cochin Municipal Corporation with activities and programmes of ward committees.

Limits of Urban Decentralisation in Cochin Municipal Corporation and its Ward Committees

Ward committees in municipal corporations have been assigned certain functions and powers to act as institutions of municipal governance at the ward level. However, conversations with councillors and other ward committee members revealed a perception of weakening or 'fracture' of the link between activities of CMC with those of the ward committees. This perception is linked to slow pace of the process of devolution of powers to urban local bodies like CMC in Kerala. CMC has limited functional and financial autonomy which affects its capacity to respond to demands of ward committees. Further, there are very little inter-linkages between day-to-day functioning of CMC and ward committees. In the following section, the paper examines the views of the ward committees on the extent of decentralisation in Cochin Municipal Corporation.

Urban Decentralisation in CMC: View of Ward Committee Members

Ward committees have been provided a whole range of functions and powers under the Kerala Municipal Act, 1994 from prioritising local needs to monitoring the implementation of different municipal schemes and programmes. In course of my conversations with ward committee members, I received different view-points on the issue of decentralisation with regard to Cochin Municipal Corporation (CMC) and role of ward committees in the governance activities of CMC from ward committee members and the councillors. Both RWA and NHG ward committee members felt that the responsibility of effective functioning of ward committees rested on the shoulders of ward councillors as chairperson and municipal officials as coordinators.

From the point of view of councillors, they feel that decentralisation of powers is a myth as far as urban local bodies like CMC is concerned. They felt that power was still concentrated with state legislative assembly and the executive. The important decisions are still taken by committees of officials based in the state capital to which the mayor is only an invitee. Councillors questioned decentralisation model in Kerala especially in urban local bodies because all their actions require some kind of approval at the state level.

Hence, there are divergent views on why the exercise of ward committee powers does not achieve desired results. The view of the ward committees is that councillors and municipal officials need to have a faster response to demands from the ward committees. The views of the councillors have been shaped by their long experience in Cochin Municipal Corporation (CMC) as elected members is that in many matters the CMC does not hold power to make decisions. In important matters like finances and staffing, the state government holds the most powers and CMC has to wait till decisions are taken at that level. In the following section, the paper reviews some examples of how crucial decisions related to municipal governance are not within the control or domain of CMC and its implications for functioning of ward committees.

Limited Functional and Financial Autonomy for Cochin Municipal Corporation

The annual budget of Cochin Municipal Corporation can be finalised only after presentation of the state budget as the amount of the grants for CMC from state government will be known only after this process. Further, all its projects needs to be approved by a State Level Technical Group (SLTG) which has an advisory and monitoring role in finalising projects of the civic bodies. These processes take time which mean significant delays in formulation and approval of projects of Cochin Municipal Corporation. The impact of delays will be felt even for ward level projects and can be considered as one of the reason why ward committee members have pointed to significant delays in implementation of some of the ward level schemes.

Another example of where ward committees do not have any major role to play is in the case of urban development schemes of central government and those funded through loans of multilateral financial institutions. In such schemes, often guidelines are set in advance and Municipal Corporation only formulates schemes according to these guidelines. The monitoring of such schemes is done by agencies appointed by central and state governments. While, departments of Municipal Corporation may support the monitoring of such schemes, there may be limitations to involvement of ward committees in monitoring the implementation of such schemes.

For example, while JNNURM and BSUP which has an elaborate set of guidelines regarding implementation and monitoring and actually have called for ensuring participation of citizens through institutions like ward committees, there is no mention of involving citizens in the monitoring or social auditing of these schemes through institutions like ward committees. Neither has a decision being taken at state level or CMC level to involve these institutions.

There are two major issues arising out of this manner of implementation of schemes and projects at municipal corporation level. First, I characterise guidelines under such schemes as moves towards centralisation of powers, which is contradictory to aims of decentralisation envisaged under 74th Constitutional Amendment Act. Second, this manner of implementation of schemes raises questions of accountability for municipal corporations and its citizens. Such schemes have a reduced role for urban local governments and their citizens in the implementation and monitoring of such projects.

The moves towards centralisation do not augur well as far as urban decentralisation is concerned for municipal corporations like CMC or institutions of governance at sub-municipal levels like ward committees because their roles in governance is reduced. Municipal corporations and ward committees have been created as institutions of municipal governance that can be made accountable to citizens at different levels and act as a system of checks and balances in local governance. But, if major projects are removed from the purview of urban local bodies, their role in ensuring accountability in implementation of these projects is considerably weakened. State government and central government play a major role in financial and administrative matters of municipal bodies. This means that role of Municipal Corporation and ward committees in role of governance and enhancing accountability in implementation of schemes and projects is reduced.

In the next section, the paper throws to light some of institutional and political factors for lack of integration of ward committees with functioning of Cochin Municipal Corporation.

Lack of Political and Administrative Integration of CMC with Ward Committees

The role of ward committees in the day-to-day functioning of Cochin Municipal Corporation (CMC) is limited or even negligible. The role of ward committee members is limited to giving suggestions, pointing out problems in implementation of schemes and supporting the ward level programmes planned by the councillor or CMC. A major limitation in terms of institutional design noted by ward committee members is the fact that ward committees are held only quarterly. This means that issues lose their relevance over time as newer issues gain priority. The councillors have pointed out that they do not have any separate resources (office, staff) for organising ward committee meetings. Councillors have also pointed out that local political leadership is reluctant to engage with civil society organisations like neighbourhood groups and resident welfare associations in ward committees. Hence, ward committees and greater decentralisation is not an important priority for political parties.

To summarise, the above sections have shown that there is a near consensus view of ward committee members that powers for ward committees are limited. The councillors have described the pace and extent of urban decentralisation in Kerala as slow and limited. These factors have reduced the effectiveness of ward committees as institutions of local governance. Further, I have described that there is limited financial and functional autonomy for Cochin Municipal Corporation reducing its capacity to govern and respond to demands of ward committees. Finally, I point to the fact that Cochin Municipal Corporation itself has not integrated its day-to-day functioning with ward committees. I have shown the institutional and political factors that have played a role in this lack of integration.

Institutional Design not the only Condition for Effective Participatory Governance

The study of ward committees of Cochin city in Kerala shows that creation and providing a 'model' legal framework for ward committees to institutionalise citizen participation will not directly translate into effective outcomes. The ward committees need to be part of a larger municipal system that can respond to demands and needs thrown up by opening municipal decision-making processes to citizens through devolution of administrative and financial powers and autonomy based on the principle of subsidiarity.

Despite the People's Planning Campaign and institutionalisation of participatory local governance process, the situation regarding citizen participation in urban governance is still far from ideal in Kerala. While scholars have made claims regarding the participatory potential of institutional design of ward committees in Kerala, it is clear that the legal design has not been supplemented with devolution of powers and support mechanisms such as functionaries and financial resources. The fragmentation of delivery of urban services and accountability lines that move upward to state and central levels raise questions about artificial divisions that lead to ineffective governance and create constraints in ensuring accountability from elected representatives and officials of LSGIs as well as other service agencies.

However, Kerala refused to implement Community Participation Law as mandated by the Central government for access to funds under JNNURM justifying the present 'model' system of urban governance and citizen participation in ward committees.[11] This argument has been accepted by Central government as Kerala has received funds from the mission.

The findings from study of ward committees point to the need for shifting the debates in academic discourse on urban decentralisation to the issue of devolution of powers that will enable ULSGI's to function as autonomous institutions that can deliver effective services through citizen participation in urban governance. In the next section, the paper reviews the experiences of functioning of ward committees in the state of Maharashtra.

Ward Committees in Maharashtra- Jurisdiction, Membership and Functions

The experiences of functioning of ward committees in Maharashtra is based on analysis of the legal framework for ward committees in each of its municipal acts, discussions in two meetings held in Mumbai and Pune on Community Participation Law in which authors were involved actively and informal meetings and discussions with civil society organisations and elected representatives on participation of citizens in urban governance in Maharashtra.

Maharashtra urban local self-governments are governed by four municipal acts.[12] In Maharashtra, all the four municipal acts provide Ward Committees for a group of electoral wards in municipalities with more than 3,00,000 population which follows the recommendation of the 74th CAA. However, not all municipal corporations have constituted ward committees. As on December 2010, ward committees were constituted in 19 municipal corporations out of the 23 in the state. Further, ward committees in Maharashtra have been constituted for a group of electoral wards or for an administrative ward that consists of many electoral wards unlike in Kerala where ward committees are constituted for each electoral ward.

In Maharashtra, membership of ward committees is restricted to elected councillors from the electoral wards of the administrative ward, the ward officer or divisional officer of that ward and not more than three members of non-governmental organisations/community based organisation (NGOs/CBOs) who are nominated by the councillors and are residents of the administrative ward. However, it required a Public Interest Litigation (PIL) filed by YUVA, an NGO based in Mumbai for the Bombay High Court to direct the Mumbai Municipal Corporation to ensure nomination of three NGO/CBO members in ward committees. Even in 2010, NGO/CBO members were nominated in ward committees of only seven municipal corporations of the state.

These experiences have led to many active civil society organisation being sceptical about the process of nomination in the ward committees of the municipal corporations of the state. Further, unlike Kerala there are no residential welfare associations or neighbourhood groups which can be directly considered for membership in ward committees.

The main functions of ward committees in Maharashtra is to ensure speedy redressal of common grievances of citizens regarding urban services, make recommendations on estimates of expenditure pertaining to ward under different heads before being forwarded to the municipal commissioner and provide administrative and financial sanction for municipal works of upto Rs 10 lakhs which has been provided for in the municipal budget. Hence, we can see that legal framework for ward committees in Maharashtra faced many shortcomings in terms of proximity to citizens, representativeness and rights and powers for local level planning. This can be more clearly illustrated with the example of ward committees in Municipal Corporation of Greater Mumbai.

Ward Committees in Municipal Corporation of Greater Mumbai: Proximity and Representation Questioned

The Municipal Corporation of Greater Mumbai (MCGM) is divided into 227 electoral wards and 24 administrative wards. The wards committees in MCGM started functioning in January 2000. The Bombay Municipal Act has limited the number of wards committees to twenty five. However at present, only 16 wards committees have been constituted in MCGM. The average number of electoral wards in each ward committee in MCGM is fourteen. Each ward committee has been constituted for seven to eight lakhs population. Size of wards committees will be one of the major issues which hamper the proximity between voters and elected coucillors. The size of ward committees is crucial as it is impacted on facilitating community participation, enhancing accountability, operationalising transparency and also decides the volume of cost and functionaries. While, MCGM has managed to decentralise its administration system to administrative wards, the municipal bureaucracy is more powerful at the ward level and is accountable to Municipal Commissioner rather than the ward committee of the administrative ward.

Community Participation Law in Maharashtra: Flawed idea of community participation

The Maharashtra Government signed an MoA (Memorandum of Agreement) with the Union Government for JNNURM, which specified the timelines for implementation of conditionalities such as Community Participation Law (CPL). In the MoA, Government of Maharashtra (GoM) agreed that it would pass the Community Participation Law (CPL) in the year 2008 and prepare and notify the rules for operationalisation of the CPL in the year 2009. A brief overview of the actual process is provided below.

In the budget session of the year 2008, Maharashtra Legislative Assembly (Vidhan Sabha) passed the bill titled 'Maharashtra Municipal Corporations and Municipal Councils (Second Amendment) Bill, 2008.' without any discussion. No single member of house was aware of the objectives and substance of the law. Thus, it was passed in Vidhan Sabha without any serious discussion. The media and few civil society organisations raised serious objections on passing this crucial bill in the Vidhan Sabha (Legislative Assembly) without knowing the implications of this bill on local government politics. In the same year this bill was discussed in Vidhan Parishad (Legislative Council). The members of the house raised serious questions and objections on the draft provisions of the said bill. The major concern of the members was that formation of Area Sabha with independent Area Sabha representatives would be a threat to councillors due to creation of a new set of power centres sub-ward level who may eventually become potential competitors. This bill was sent to the Joint Parliamentary Committee for revision.

The revised version of the bill was passed by both the houses in July 2009. However, the elected councillor became the chairperson of the Area Sabha in the Amendment Act of 2009 thereby ensuring their dominance at the electoral ward level. Further, Area Sabha was reduced to public meetings to be held twice in a year. The Amendment Act did not restructure the ward committees to the electoral ward level as suggest by the Model Bill. Therefore, The Act completely violated the spirit of the Model Nagar Raj Bill and was based on a flawed idea of community participation. Further the Amendment Act could not provide for a synergetic division of functions, roles, powers and rights between ward committees and area sabhas based on principle of subsidiarity.

After civil society intervention, the Maharashtra government appointed a seven member of the study group[13] to review the Amendment Act and provide recommendations on the same. The study group submitted the report in February 2011. However, no further action has been taken on the report and neither has the rules for the formation of Area Sabhas been notified essentially making Community Participation Law in Maharashtra, a non-starter.

Legal Framework and Devolution of Powers Necessary for Effective Citizen Participation in Urban Governance

In the following sections, we analyse the experiences and findings from both the states and highlight the key emerging points regarding citizen participation in urban governance through ward committees. Despite, Peoples Planning Campaign in Kerala and strong legal framework for enhancing participation in urban governance through ward committees, the experience of functioning of ward committees showed the shortcoming and deficits in actual devolution of powers and functions to urban local governments in the state.

Despite an enabling framework in Kerala, decentralisation of key powers, financial resources and functionaries in terms of staffing yet to happen, hence dynamism of the participation process is lost, issues of higher stake often has to be decided at higher tiers even when they are within domain of municipalities. While devolution of powers may not be a sufficient condition, they are a necessary condition to ensure effective participation. There is a need to do proper activity mapping for urban local bodies to ensure effective participation in forums like ward committees. Further urban local bodies need to be put at centre of service delivery within their jurisdiction even when it may be delivered by parastatals or other agencies. Only such measures can ensure accountability.

In Maharashtra, the legal framework for ward committees was extremely weak even after 74th CAA as principles of proximity to citizens, representativeness and functions and powers for intervening local level planning. The process of enactment of Community Participation Law has explicitly shown serious flaws in the approach of the government in Maharashtra which saw the law only as an instrument to ensure continued funding under JNNURM.

The JNNURM call for enactment of Community Participation Law has been ignored by both Kerala and Maharashtra. While Kerala has justified its decision to not implement CPL model suggested by the mission on the basis of participatory process in place at present, Maharashtra had changed the Model to suit the political sensitivities in the state and once JNNURM funds has been assured, it has opted to neglect implementation even of Act legislated by its own assembly. However, funds have been received by both states and work under JNNURM is continuing. Hence, we have seen a complete failure of carrot and stick approach to achieve community participation in urban governance. One has to wait and see what form the next phase of JNNURM will propose measures to enhance citizen participation in urban governance.

Finally, the paper concludes with the need to recognise the political culture of each state in designing measures to enhance citizen participation in urban governance has become clear from review of the experiences of both the states. While, Kerala has stable political coalition culture which is responsible both for the successes and failures of urban decentralisation in Kerala, Maharashtra despite having the same coalition ruling for more than 15 years has not seen many measures to enhance citizen participation in urban governance. The culture of public action in Kerala and density of active social and political organisations still provides an opportunity for furthering urban decentralisation and promoting an even greater participation of citizens in urban governance. In Maharashtra, there is a need for a debate between political system, academia, elected representatives of urban local bodies and organisations that work among urban citizens to evolve a system for urban governance that will provide a greater say for citizens in affairs of their own urban local governments.

References

Baud, I. S. A, J De Wit (ed.) (2009) : New Forms of Urban Governance in India: Shifts, Models, Networks and Contestations (New Delhi: Sage Publications).

Bhattacharya, M (1976) : Management of urban government in India (New Delhi: Uppal Book Store).

Chhotray, V and G Stoker (2009) : "Participatory Governance" in *Governance Theory and Practice: A Cross-Disciplinary Approach* (Basingstoke:Palgrave Macmillan) 165-190.

De Wit, J, N Nainan and S. Palnitkar (2009) : "Urban Decentralisation in Indian Cities : Assessing Performance of Neighbourhood Level Wards Committees" in Baud et al. (ed.) *New Forms of Urban Governance in India: Shifts, Models, Networks and Contestations* (New Delhi:Sage Publications) 65-82.

Fung, A and Wright Erik Olin (2001): "Deepening Democracy: Innovations in Empowered Participatory Governance", *Politics and Society*, 29 (1) : 5-41.

Kuruvilla, Y (2011) 'Participation of Women in Urban Governance: Role of Neighbourhood Groups in Ward Committes of Cochin, Unpublished M. Phil Thesis, Centre for Regional Studies, University of Hyderabad, Hyderabad.

Melo, M. A. and G. Baiocchi (2006): "Deliberative Democracy and Local Governance: Towards a New Agenda", *International Journal of Urban and Regional Research* 30.3, 587-600.

Pinto, R. M. (2000): Metropolitan City Governance in India, (New Delhi:Sage Publications).

Sivaramakrishnan, K. C. (ed.) (2006) : People's Participation in Urban Governance: A Comparative Study of Working of Wards Committees in Karnataka, Kerala, Maharashtra and West Bengal, (New Delhi: Concept Publishing Company).

Sorenson and Sagaris (2010): "From Participation to the Right to the City: Democratic Place Management at the Neighbourhood Scale in Comparative Perspective", *Planning Practice and Research,* Vol. 25, Issue 3, 297-316.

Notes

1. The Joint Parliamentary Committee to which the amendment bill was referred felt that " in the larger municipal bodies, citizens do not have easy access to elected representatives since the ward sizes become very large. The Committee therefore is of the view that in municipalities having a population of three lakhs or more ward committees should be constituted". (Sivaramakrishnan, 2006, p. 6).
2. The Preliminary report of Sen Committee can be accessed at http://www.scribd.com/doc/45038501/Preliminary-Report-of-the-Sen-Committee-on-Decentralisation-in-Kerala.
3. However, the provisions for representation of civil society were not initially a part of the conformity legislation passed by the state assembly in the aftermath of the 74th CAA. The provisions came as a result of amendments to Kerala Municipal Act in view of recommendations of the Sen Committee on legislative changes to be adopted for strengthening local-self government institutions as a part of the People's Planning Campaign (PPC). The provisions provide for representation of trade unions, political parties, trade and industrial associations, cultural associations and educational institutions.
4. There are 15 members from resident welfare associations and 20 members from neighbourhood groups in the ward committees. Generally, the total membership of ward committee is around 60.
5. The wards selected for the study were Fort Kochi Veli and Cheralayi in West Kochi and Puthukalavattom and Karanakodam in the East.
6. Refer Memorandum of Association (MoA) signed by Kochi Municipal Corporation for JNNURM available at www.jnnurm.nic.in
7. The Acts and relevant sections are as follows:
   1. The Mumbai Municipal Corporation Act 1888; Section 50TT,
   2. The Bombay Provincial Municipal Corporations Act, 1949, Section 29A
   3. The City of Nagpur Corporation Act, 1948; Section 38A
   4. The Maharashtra Municipal Councils, Nagar Panchayats and Industrial Township Act 1965; Section 66A
8. Government Resolution, Government of Maharashtra - MMC 2009/317/C.N.128/UD-32 dated 5th August 2009.

4

Structural and Functional Aspects of Panchayats and Autonomous Councils in Assam

—*Harsha, S.*

An attempt has been made in this paper to outline the Structural and Functional aspects of Panchayts and Autonomous Councils. A study of structural and functional aspects of an institution points out the autonomy enjoyed by the institution and the provisions for people's participation, accountability and transparency.

Panchayati Raj Institution in Assam

Panchayati Raj Institutions (PRI) in different forms and at different times has been in existence in Assam since ancient times. Apart from various welfare activities, these organisations also played an important role in settlement of local disputes. During the Ahom rule itself the existence of Raijmel, Dekamel and Gavorumel etc. functions as local self-government in Assam.

It is a well known fact that the system of Panchayats in the independent India was introduced in the light of specific mention made in the Directive Principles of State Policy under Article-40 of the Constitution. The Assam Panchayati Raj Act was passed in 1948 providing for the two tier structure right after the independence and before the new constitution became operative. A new Panchayat Act in Assam was passed in 1959 which was in conformity with the Balwantrai Mehta Committee Report which provided the three tier PRI structure. Again this Act was replaced by

Panchayati Raj Act 1972 which again substituted by an Act of 1986. Thereafter with the enactment of the 73rd Amendment Act 1992, the Assam Panchayati Raj (APR) Act 1994 was passed by Assam Government that provides a three tier panchayat system comprising Gaon Panchayat, Anchalik Panchayat and Zilla Parishad. The Act of 1994 was enacted in conformity with the provisions of 73rd Amendment Act. As per the APR Act of 1994 the first Panchayat election was held in Assam in 2001 and constitution of all the three tiers were completed in June 2002 (assamgov.in).

Except the sixth schedule areas, the Panchayati Raj Institutions have been successfully established in all districts of Assam and to a large extent the Panchayati Raj Institutions have been functioning in accordance with the Assam Panchayati Raj Act 1994. Salient features of the Assam Panchayati Raj Act 1994 can be discussed under the following heads.

Salient Features of the Assam Panchayati Raj Act 1994

As mentioned above, the Assam Panchayati Raj Act 1994 extends to the entire state of Assam, except the autonomous councils constituted under the Sixth Schedule of the Constitution of India. In pursuance of the new provisions inserted in the Constitution, the Act has created a three-tier Panchayat System in the State consisting of Gaon Panchayat, Anchalik Panchayat and Zilla Parishad. It has also provided for Gaon Sabha for direct democracy at the Village-Panchayat area level and District Planning Committee for drafting development plans at the district level. It has also been mentioned in the Act that there will be two Commissions, namely the Finance Commission and the State Election Commission and it has assured necessary reservation policy for the SC, ST and women as per dictate of the 73rd Constitutional Amendment Act, 1992. Provisions of the Act can be discussed as follows.

District Planning Committee

The Act has envisaged District Planning Committee as a coordinating agency for the local self-government institutions existing in both rural and urban areas. Its function is to consolidate the plans prepared by Zilla Parishad, Anchalik Panchayats, Town Committees, Municipalities and Municipal Corporations and prepare a draft development plans for the district as a whole. District Planning Committee shall consist of both ex-officio members and indirectly elected members. Local Member of Parliament, local Member of Legislative Assembly, President of the Zilla Parishad and Chairpersons of urban local self-government bodies in the district are the ex-officio members. Not less than four-fifth of the total members of the body shall be elected from the members of Zilla Parishad and urban self-government bodies on rotation annually and in proportion to the ratio between rural and urban population in the district.

The Deputy Commissioner shall be a permanent invitee, the President of the Zilla Parishad shall be the ex-officio Chairperson and the Chief Executive Officer of the Zilla Parishad shall be the ex-officio Secretary of the District Planning Committee.

Gaon Sabha

The Act provides for a Gaon Sabha (constitutional equivalent of Gram Sabha) for every Gaon Panchayat area consisting of persons registered in the electoral rolls of the area. The Gaon Sabha shall meet at least once in three months to discharge the following responsibilities:

(i) To consider the report in respect of the development programme of the previous year and the development programme proposed to be undertaken during the current year;

(ii) To mobilise voluntary labour and contribution in kind and cash for the community welfare programmes;

(iii) To identify beneficiaries for the implementation of development schemes pertaining to the villages; and

(iv) To promote unity and harmony among all sections of the society in the villages.

These are all very important functions and if discharged seriously will endow the people of the villages with authority in their own affairs.

Gaon Panchayat

The State Government may declare a village or a cluster of villages or an inhabited area having population between 6000 and 10,000 as a Gaon Panchayat. A Gaon Panchayat is a body of corporate.

The Panchayat body shall consist of 10 members directly elected by the voters of the territorial constituencies and the President of the Gaon Panchayat who shall also be directly elected. A Vice-President shall be elected from and by the members in the first meeting to be called by the Deputy Commissioner or an Officer authorised by him.

The Gaon Panchayat is required to meet at least once in two months. In addition, it is to work through three standing committees namely,

Development Committee, Social Justice Committee and Social Welfare Committee. Important general functions of the Gaon Panchayat are:

- (i) Preparation of Annual Plan for development of the Gaon Panchayat area;
- (ii) Preparation of Annual Budget;
- (iii) Mobilisation of relief in calamities;
- (iv) Organising voluntary labour and contribution for community work; and
- (v) Maintenance of essential statistics of the villages.

The Gaon Panchayat is to identify and implement various agricultural schemes of amounts not exceeding Rs 50,000 with technical assistance from the concerned State Government Departments. The scope of activities of the Gaon Panchayat extends to a long list of items.

Among these special mention may be made of the following:

1. Development of wasteland and grazing land;
2. Development of fisheries in the villages;
3. Plantation of firewood trees and fodder development;
4. Distribution of house sites;
5. Construction and maintenance of village roads;
6. Identification of locality for distribution of electricity;
7. Selection of beneficiaries under poverty alleviation programmes;
8. Ensuring full enrollment and attendance of students and teachers in Primary Schools;
9. Implementation of family welfare programmes;
10. Participation in women and child welfare programmes;
11. Monitoring public distribution system; and
12. Maintenance of community assets.

The fund of the Gaon Panchayat consists largely of contributions and grants from the Central and State Governments and higher Panchayat bodies. But it has also power to levy taxes, tolls, rates and fees. For example, it may impose tax on sale of goods like firewood and thatch, private hat, private fisheries, fallow cultivable land etc. It can also realise cess or fees on registration of cattle sold, license for tea stall, hotel, cart, bicycle and boat. The Gaon Panchayat is entitled to get share of land revenue and local rates etc from the State Government.

Anchalik Panchayat

According to the Act, for each Development Block there will be an Anchalik Panchayat which will be a body of corporate. The Anchalik Panchayat will consist of:

(a) One member from each Gaon Panchayat to be directly elected from the territorial constituency of the Gaon Panchayat under the Anchalik Panchayat;

(b) The President of the Gaon Panchayats under the Anchalik Panchayat; and

(c) Local Member of Parliament and Member of Legislative Assembly.

The directly elected members shall elect from amongst the members, President and Vice-President of the Anchalik Panchayat. Anchalik Panchayat shall hold meeting at least once in two months. For discharging its functions each Anchalik Panchayat shall have three Standing Committees namely, General Standing Committee, Finance, Audit and Planning Committee and Social Justice Committee. The general functions of Anchalik Panchayat are as follows:

(a) Preparation of Annual Plan in respect of schemes entrusted to it by virtue of Act or assigned to it by the State Government or the Zilla Parishad and submission thereof to the Zilla Parishad for integration with the District Plan;

(b) Consideration and consolidation of the Annual Plans of all Gaon Panchayats under it and submission of consolidated Plan to the Zilla Parishad;

(c) Preparation of Annual Budget of the Anchalik Panchayat and submission to Zilla Parishad for approval;

(d) Performing functions as may be entrusted to it by the Government; and

(e) Assisting the Government in relief operations in natural calamities.

The Anchalik Panchayat shall identify and implement agricultural schemes of amounts not exceeding Rs 2,00,000 (four times that allowed to a Gaon Panchayat) and not below Rs 50,000 for agricultural development of the Anchalik Panchayat area with technical assistance from the concerned State Government Department. It has wider scope of functioning and greater authority in rural development works than the

Gaon Panchayat as it is the superior body. Some of the important areas of functions of the Anchalik Panchayat are as follows:

1. Maintenance of agricultural seed farms and horticultural nurseries;
2. Storing and distribution of insecticides and pesticides;
3. Training of farmers and extension activities;
4. Implementation of individual irrigation works;
5. Planning and supervision of implementation of poverty alleviation programmes;
6. Maintenance of veterinary and animal husbandry services;
7. Organisation of training programmes in khadi, village and cottage industries;
8. Implementation of housing schemes;
9. Planning and preservation of trees on public land;
10. Construction and maintenance of public roads and maintenance of public ferries and waterways;
11. Construction, repairs and maintenance of primary school buildings;
12. Implementation of adult literacy programmes;
13. Promotion of immunisation and vaccination programmes;
14. Promotion of programmes relating to the development of women and children; and
15. Monitoring the old age and pensions of widow and handicapped.

The fund of the Anchalik Panchayat mainly consists of grants made by the Central and State Governments and share of land revenue. It may also receive contribution and grant made by the Zilla Parishad and raise loans. An Anchalik Parishad has also tax-raising power. It can levy surcharge on land revenue at the rate of two paisa per rupee, tax on profession, trade, manufacture and production; levy fee for cinema hall, brick kiln, saw mill, rice mill, confectionary and bakery, private fisheries etc.

In addition it can levy toll at any toll bar established by it on road or in respect of ferry under its management. It may levy a cess or water rate for recovery of cost of minor irrigation works. An Anchalik Panchayat may borrow money from the government or from banks and other financial institutions with previous permission of the State Government.

The State Government shall appoint the Executive Officer of Anchalik Panchayat who shall be the ex-officio Secretary. Other staff will be either appointed or deputed by the State Government.

Zilla Parishad

For every district there shall be a Zilla Parishad having jurisdiction over the rural areas of the district. The Zilla Parishad shall consist of:

(i) The members directly elected from the territorial constituencies of the district (one member for a population of not less than 40,000);

(ii) The Presidents of Anchalik Panchayats of the concerned district; and

(iii) Local Member of Parliament and Member of Legislative Assembly.

The term of the Zilla Parishad is five years. President and Vice-President shall be elected from amongst the directly elected members in the first meeting of the Zilla Parishad to be called by the Deputy Commissioner. Every Zilla Parishad shall hold meetings at least once in every three months. The Zilla Parishad shall have four standing committees namely, General Standing Committee, Finance and Audit Committee, Social Justice Committee and Planning and Development Committee. The government shall appoint an Officer not below the rank of Additional Deputy Commissioner of a district as Chief Executive Officer (Ex-officio Secretary). Chief Accounts Officer and Chief Planning Officer are also to be appointed by the government.

The Zilla Parishad is to prepare plans for economic development and social justice of the rural areas of the district under its jurisdiction. It has also to ensure the coordinated implementation of such plan. Being the nodal agency of rural development in a district the Zilla Parishad is concerned with all the aspects such as planning, coordination, implementation, supervision and resource allocation. Some of the important functions of the Zilla Parishad are as follows:

(i) Opening and maintenance of agricultural farms and marketing agencies and infrastructure;

(ii) Establishments and maintenance of godowns and cold storages;

(iii) Arrangement of agricultural and horticultural extension and training centres;

(iv) Construction, renovation and maintenance of minor irrigation works;

(v) Publication of statistical and other information relating to activities of Panchayat institutions;

(vi) Land reclamation and land development works;

(vii) Development of regulated markets and grading and quality control of agricultural products;

(viii) Establishment of veterinary hospitals, dispensaries, breeding farms for cows and pigs, firms for poultry, duck and goat;

(ix) Promotion of social and farm forestry;

(x) Fish seed production and distribution and development of inland fisheries;

(xi) Identification of traditional skills in household industries, assistance of their raw material requirement, development of new designs, organisation of training programmes, credit-link establishment and marketing of finished products;

(xii) Construction and maintenance of roads other than National and State Highways;

(xiii) Establishment and maintenance of hospitals, primary health centres and dispensaries;

(xiv) Establishment and maintenance of primary secondary schools;

(xv) Management of hostels for the benefit of SC and ST students;

(xvi) Planning, supervision, monitoring and implementation of poverty alleviation programmes;

(xvii) Maintenance of social welfare institutions such as Poor Home, Orphanages, Rescue Shelters etc; and

(xviii) Sanctioning and distribution of pension for widows, old, physically disabled, destitute etc.

The Zilla Parishad fund mainly consists of the amount transferred from the consolidated fund of the State Government and contribution and grants from the government. The power of taxation is very limited. It can levy tolls on ferries, collect registration fees of boats and vehicles, realise lighting rate, water rate etc where the services are provided by it. It can raise loan with government approval for executing any development work.

The Zilla Parishad shall always be under the tight grip of the State Government as per provisions of the Act. The annual budget of the Zilla Parishad would become effective only if approved by the State Government. At every step the activities of the Zilla Parishad are likely to be controlled by the authorities in the State capital and the arrangement is far from the ideal of democratic decentralisation. In a State like Assam where different linguistic, ethnic and religious groups' live side by side and where separatist tendencies are open much of the problems could be contained if Zilla Parishad could be developed as vigorous institutions representing local autonomy and fulfilling local aspirations for development.

State Finance Commission

The 73rd Amendment Act, the State Finance Commission has been constituted to suggest measures to strengthen finances of panchayati raj institutions. As per the Assam Panchayati Raj Act 1994 too, the Government of Assam has the power to constitute State Finance Commission to look into the financial aspects of the Panchayati Raj Institutions (PRI) and sharing of taxes, duties, tolls and fees which may be assigned to and appropriated by the PRIs at different levels. The first State Finance Commission in Assam was constituted in 1994 to make recommendations on devolution of funds to the Panchayats for five years from 1996-97 to 2000-01.

The Commission also looks into grants-in-aid to panchayats from the Consolidated Fund of the State. The State Finance Commission consists of a Chairman and two other members appointed by the Governor. The Chairman or a member may resign from office by writing under his hand and addressed to the Chief Secretary to the Government of Assam, but he continues in his office until his resignation is accepted by the government.

State Election Commission

The Assam Panchayati Raj Act of 1994 provided for the constitution of SEC. The Commission is vested with the power of superintendence, direction and control of the preparation of electoral roll for, and the conduct of all election to the panchayats under the provisions of sub-section (1) of Section 114 of the Assam Panchayati Raj Act 1994. On the request of the State Election Commissioner the Government make available to him such staff as may be necessary for the discharge of the functions conferred under this Act. However, the State Legislature may by law make provision with respect to all matters relating to, or in connection with election to the panchayats.

Reservations for Women

The category-wise percentage of elected women representatives is to be ascertained. Details of how many women get elected to non-reserved posts are also to be ascertained. Rotation of offices in all these categories in all three tiers is done once in five years. Seats shall be reserved for women belonging to the SC and the ST from among the seats reserved for the persons belonging to the SC and the ST which shall not be less than one-third of the total number of seats reserved for the persons belonging to SC and ST.

Audit

The audit of accounts maintained by Village Panchayat is done by Director of Local Fund Audit. In respect of Anchalik Panchayats, the audit is done by Local Fund Audit Department. The District Panchayat audit is done by Local Fund Audit Department.

The accounts of Anchalik Panchayats and District Panchayats have been completed upto 2004-05. Audit of accounts have been completed for the year 2001-02, 2002-03, 2003-04 in respect of all 12,618 Village Panchayats, 385 Anchalik Panchayats and 29 District Panchayats.

There is no separate Public Accounts Committees (PACs) for reviewing audit paras of Panchayats. There is no separate Fiscal Responsibility Act for elected local authorities.

Panchayat accounts are maintained by the Panchayat Secretaries. There are a few instances of such responsibilities being outsourced. Details of the extent of automation and computerisation of Panchayat accounts are to be ascertained.

Social Audit

Provisions have been made for the conduct of social audit of Panchayat work by Gaon Sabha. The Village Panchayat and other executing agencies shall make available all relevant documents including the muster rolls, bills, vouchers, measurement books, copies of sanction orders, photos before, during and after the execution of the work and other connected books of account and papers to the Gaon Sabha/External Agencies for the purpose of conducting the social audit.

Standing Committees

Every AP under the Assam Panchayat Act, 1994 constitutes some committees which help it in the performance of its functions.

General Standing Committee performs functions relating to the establishment of local market, communication, buildings, rural housing, relief against natural calamities, water supply and all miscellaneous residuary matters.

Finance, Audit and Planning Committee performs functions with regard to the finance of the AP, preparing budget, scrutinising proposals for increase of revenue, examination of receipts and expenditure statement, consideration of all proposals affecting the finance of the AP and general supervision of the revenue and expenditure of the AP and planning and consolidating the AP plans, co-operation, small saving schemes and any other function relating to the development of AP areas.

Social Justice Committee carries out functions relating to promotion of educational, economic, social, cultural and other interests of the SCs, STs and Backward classes; protecting them from social injustice and other forms of exploitations; amelioration of the SCs, STs and Backward classes; securing social justice to SCs, STs, Women and other weaker sections of the society.

Each Standing Committee consists of the members not exceeding six (6) including the Chairman. Members of the Committees are chosen by the AP from amongst themselves. The President of the AP is the president of the first two Standing Committees and the Vice-President is that of the third i.e., Social Justice Committee. No member of the AP is eligible to serve in more than one Standing Committee and the term of the membership is one year at a time. The Executive Officer of the AP is also the ex-officio Secretary of every Standing Committee, who under instruction of the Committee issue notices and secure the attendance of the of

Autonomous Councils in North-East India and Assam

The Constitution makers recognised the necessity of a separate political and administrative structure for the Hill Tribal Areas of the erstwhile province of Assam by enacting the Sixth Schedule to the Constitution of India. 'In doing so, they were broadly guided by three major considerations:

(1) the necessity to maintain the distinct customs, socio-economic and political culture of the tribal people of the region and to ensure autonomy of the tribal people and to preserve their identities;

(2) the necessity to prevent their economic and social exploitation by the more advanced neighbouring people of the plains; and

(3) to allow the tribal people to develop and administer themselves according to their own genius.'[14]

Article 244(2) of the Indian Constitution provides for the Sixth Schedule, which shall apply to the administration of the tribal areas in the States of Assam, Meghalaya, Tripura and Mizoram. Paragraph 20 of the Schedule provides a list of tribal areas covered by the Sixth Schedule in three Parts – Part I, Part II, Part IIA and Part III. These are given in the following illustration as Table 4.1.

Table 4.1: Autonomous District Council under Sixth Schedule to the Indian Constitution

	Name of District Council	*State*
Part – I	1. The Dima Hasao District Autonomous Council	Assam
	2. The Karbi Anglong Autonomous Council	
	3. The Bodoland Territorial Council (BTC)	
Part – II	1. The Khasi Hills Autonomous District Council	Meghalaya
	2. The Jaintia Hills Autonomous District Council	
	3. The Garo Hills Autonomous District Council	
Part – II A	1. Tripura Tribal Areas Autonomous District Council (TTAADC)	Tripura
Part – III	1. The Chakma Autonomous District Council	Mizoram
	2. The Mara Autonomous District Council	
	3. The Lai Autonomous District Council	

Source: Vijay Hansaria, *'Sixth Schedule to the Constitution'* New Delhi: Universal Law Publishing.

From the aforementioned table, it is clear that Assam has three autonomous councils established under Sixth Schedule.

Structural and Functional Features of Karbi Anglong Autonomous Council (KAAC)

Having given the broad outline of Autonomous Councils in North-East India in the previous section, the present section is devoted to outlining the structural and functional aspects of Karbi Anglong Autonomous Council (KAAC). The United Mikir and North Cachar Hills District was formed on 17th November, 1951 vide Government Notification No. T. A. D. /R 31/50/204 dated 3rd November, 1951. The District was formed by combining partially excluded areas of Nagaon and erstwhile Sivasagar (Mikir Hills Tract), Block-I and Block-II of United Khasi and Jaintia Hills District and North Cachar Hills (excluded area) Sub-Division of Cachar District, on the recommendation of Commission appointed for the purpose. Historically this area was administered by British a bit differently, in the sense that Govt. of India Act, 1919 classified these areas as Backward Tract and Govt. of India Act, 1935 classified them as excluded and partially excluded areas. After independence, Constitution of India also maintained the special status by way of provisions contained in Sixth Schedule. The district of United Mikir and North Cachar Hills district was bifurcated into two separate districts and renamed as "Mikir Hills" and North Cachar Hills district in the year 1970. The Mikir Hill district was again rechristened as "Karbi Anglong District" w. e. f. the 14th October, 1976 vide Govt. Notification No. TAD/R/115/74/47 Dtd. 14-10-1976. Thus, Karbi Anglong came into being as a full-fledged separate district in the map of Assam with its Headquarters at Diphu. The district enjoys autonomy under the provision of Sixth Schedule of the Indian Constitution. It is the largest district of Assam with a total geographical area of 10,434 Sq. Kilometer. The Mikir Hills district was renamed as Karbi Anglong in 1976. Karbi Anglong District Council was renamed as the Karbi Anglong Autonomous Council by an Act of Parliament by incorporating the Sixth Schedule to the Constitution (Amendment) Act, 1995 (42 of 1995) to the Constitution of India granting greater Autonomy to the Council.

The Karbi Anglong Autonomous Council has been entrusted with 30 subjects prominent among them are Industry, Animal Husbandry and Veterinary, Forest, Agriculture, PWD, Sericulture, Education, Panchayat and Rural Development including DRDA, Health and Family Welfare, Engineering, Town and Country Planning, Excise and Finance. The council has 13 departments under its administrative control and some of the important departments are General Administration, Land Revenue, Forest, Primary Education, Taxation, Legislative Transport (Mechanical), Town Committee affairs, Finance, Judicial (Customary Law) and Planning and Development Department.

The Karbi Anglong Autonomous Council (KAAC) consists of 30 (thirty) members, of whom 26 (Twenty Six) are to be elected and the four nominated with a view to provide representation to the minorities who constitute a considerable proportion of the total population of the sub-division.

The tenure of the Autonomous Council is for five years unless it is dissolved earlier. The Autonomous Council has a Chairman and a Deputy Chairman who are elected by the members of the Council in accordance with the provisions of the Assam Autonomous Districts (Constitution of District Councils) Rules, 1951. The Deputy Commissioner functions as the Returning Officer in respect of the elections to Karbi Anglong Autonomous Council.

Paragraph 16 of the Sixth Schedule of the Constitution of India empowers the Governor of Assam to dissolve the Autonomous Council on some specific grounds stated below:

(a) When the Commission appointed to enquire into the administration recommends for the dissolution;

(b) When the Governor is satisfied that the administration of the Council cannot be carried on in accordance with the provision of Sixth Schedule;

(c) After dissolution, the Governor may direct for a fresh general election or reconstitution of the Council. Pending the holding of the general election or the reconstitution, the Governor himself or by person or body authorised by him shall administer the affairs of the Council. But the period of dissolution should be confined to 6(six) months which can subsequently be extended for another period not exceeding 6(six) months.

There is an Executive Committee of the Autonomous Council headed by the Chief Executive Member in addition to a number of members not exceeding one-third of the total number of members of the Karbi Anglong Autonomous Council who are appointed by the Governor of Assam as Executive Member on the advice of the Chief Executive Member. But the Chairman and the Deputy Chairman are not eligible to hold office either as Chief Executive Member or as a Member of the Executive Committee. The Executive committee formulates policy decisions besides discharging of day-to-day functioning and matters of the council. The provision of holding Council Session headed by its Chairman and is also enshrined in the constitution to discuss and consider Acts, Bills, Policy etc. formulated by the Executive Committee of Council. Almost all Development departments within the jurisdiction of council are controlled by the KAAC authority.

In accordance with the provisions laid down in the Sixth Schedule to the Constitution of India the functions and powers of Karbi Anglong Autonomous Council can be divided under three main heads- Legislative, Executive and Judicial.

Legislative Powers

The Karbi Anglong Autonomous Council has the power to make laws with respect to some of the following areas. The allotment, occupation, or use or the setting apart of land other than any land which is reserved forest, for the purpose of agriculture or grazing, or for residential or other non-agricultural purposes likely to promote the interests of the inhabitants of any village or town; The management of any forest, regulation of the practice of Jhum or other forms of shifting cultivation, establishment of village or town committees or Councils, the appointment or succession of chief or headman, the inheritance of property, Marriage, Social Customs, the Autonomous Council has also been empowered to frame laws to regulate and control money lending and trading by persons other than the scheduled tribes.

Though the Karbi Anglong Autonomous Council have the powers to make acts, rules, but the Governor must give his assent to the acts, rules made by the Council. The Governor has the power to suspend or alter any act or resolution of the Council if he is satisfied that it is likely to endanger the safety of India.

Executive Powers

The Autonomous Council may establish, construct or manage primary schools, dispensaries, markets, cattle pounds, ferries, fisheries, road and waterways in the district and in particular may prescribe the language and manner in which primary education should be imparted in the primary schools of the district.

The Autonomous Council has been allotted specific items of revenue for the efficient discharge of its functions and to meet necessary expenses. The following financial power has been vested with the District Councils. The Autonomous Council in respect of all land within the district is vested with the power to assess and collect revenue in respect of such lands in accordance with the principles for the time being followed by the Government of Assam in assessing land for the purpose of land revenue in the State of Assam generally. The Autonomous Council shall have the power to levy and collect taxes on lands and buildings, and tolls on persons residing within such areas.

The council has the power to levy and collect all or any or the following taxes. These are taxes on profession, trades, callings and employment, taxes on entry of goods into a market for sale therein and tolls on passengers and goods carried in ferries, taxes for the maintenance of schools, dispensaries and roads, Licenses or leases for the purpose of prospecting for, or extracting minerals. The Autonomous Council also has the right of sharing the royalties accrued each year from licenses or leases for the purpose of prospecting for, or the extracting of minerals granted by the Government of Assam in respect of any areas within the autonomous district as may be agreed upon between the Government of Assam and the Autonomous Councils.

Judicial Powers

The Part 4 of the Sixth Schedule entitles the Council to constitute Village and Council Courts in the autonomous areas to adjudicate or try cases or customary laws in which both the parties are tribals. However, no case involving offences punishable by death, transportation of life or imprisonment for not less than five years are heard or adjudicated by these courts. The District Council Court and the Regional Council Court are courts of appeal in respect of all suits and cases tried by the Village Council Courts and the Subordinate District Council Courts. No other court except the Assam High Court and the Supreme Court of India have jurisdiction over suits and cases decided by the Council Courts.

Observations with regard to comparative study of Structural and Functional aspects of Panchayats and Autonomous Councils:

(1) The analysis of aforementioned powers and functions of Panchayats and Autonomous Councils shows that Autonomous Councils enjoy extensive legislative, executive and judicial powers in comparison to Panchayati Raj Institutions of Assam.

(2) The Panchayats consists of Gram Sabha and Autonomous Council consists of Village Development Committees which are considered as Social Audit mechanisms. However, a comparison of actual working of these two institutions reveals that Gram Sabhas relatively more active and vibrant institution of people's participation and social audit.

(3) A comparison of the both the institutions reveals that Panchayats are decentralised structures with three tier structure. Although autonomous councils have sub-divisions and village development committees, they are centralised in nature with the authority and powers being concentrated in the top echelons.

(4) The Panchayats have a body called district planning committee to co-ordinate the plans of rural and urban local bodies and to prepare an integrated district plan as a whole. Although autonomous council have town development committee which is an elected body to prepare plans for the towns coming under the jurisdiction of autonomous council, councils do not have

coordinating institution or structure at the lower level to co-ordinate the rural and urban areas.

(5) Autonomus Councils have been endowed with extensive judicial powers. Moreover, Karbi Anglong has its own customary laws and courts to deal with civil issues. In sharp contrast with this, Panchayats especially of Assam do not have any judicial powers. Unlike some states of India which have Nyaya Panchayats, Assam does have such a provision in place.

(6) The panchayats in Assam have a deliberative body known as Gram Sabha, which has a potential to act as social audit body and it could also ensure the accountability of officials and elected representatives to the people. Although the guidelines of Ministry of Rural Development insists on preparing the action plans of most of the flagship rural development programmes and for selecting the beneficiaries by holding gram sabha meetings. Such a body is conspicuous by its absence in the autonomous council areas. In these areas District Collector prepares the actions plans and selects the beneficiaries with the assistance of other lower level officials.

(7) Tripura tribal areas Autonomous District Council (TTAADC) and Autonomous Council of Mizoram established under Sixth Schedule have democratically elected institutions such as Village Committee and Village Council respectively at the grassroot. In this regard the expert committee (Report of the Expert Committee 2006) appointed to review the working of six schedule councils recommended that sixth schedule councils should replicate the democratic institutions established in Tripura and Mizoram. However, till date democratic institutions have not been established in any of the councils.

References

Gassah, L. S. (ed.) 1997. *The Autonomous District Councils,* New Delhi: Omson Publications.

Ghosh, B. K. (ed.) 2011. *The Assam Panchayat Act with Rules,* Guwahati: Assam Law House.

Hansaria, B. L. (revised by Vijay Hansaria). 2005. *Sixth Schedule to the Constitution.* New Delhi: Universal Law Publishing Co.

Moncrieffe, Joy. M. 2001. Accountability: Idea, Ideals and Constraints. *Democratisation,* Vol. 8, No. 3, pp. 26–50.

Paul, Samuel.1992. Accountability in Public Services. *World Development*, Vol. 20, No.7, pp.1047-1060.

Report of the Expert Committee (2006). 'Planning for the Sixth Schedule Areas,' Ministry of Panchayat Raj, Government of India, New Delhi.

Note

1. Gassah, L.S.1997. 'Autonomous District Council,' in L.S. Gassah (ed), *The Autonomous District Council*, p. 3. New Delhi: Omsons Publications.

5

Devolution of Funds, Functions and Functionaries: An Odisha Experience

—*Janmejay Sahu*

Introduction

India initiates several welfare measures for the grassroots people through the local institutions to bring the rural society into the mainstream. The 73rd CAA aims at enabling the panchayats to function as institutions of local self-governments having autonomous in self-planning and implementing schemes for economic development and social justice. Moreover, the 73rd CAA ensures the process of decentralisation of governance with three tiers of institutional set up such as Gram Sabha, Gram Panchayat, Block Panchayat and District Panchayats in India. Over the last 50 years PRIs have emerged as the powerful institutions in bringing about rapid and sustainable development and socio-economic transformation in rural Odisha as Panchayat system was working in Odisha much before the 73rd CAA. Further, this Panchayati Raj system as per the 73rd CCA has given scope to the people at the grassroots to have a direct participation in local governments by electing local government functionaries as well as involving the Panchayat developmental activities and participating in Gram Sabha and Palli Sabha. It also empowers the State government for devolution of adequate powers, functions and functionaries through article 243(G), 243(I) and 243(D) of 73rd CAA to the PRIs for better self-local governance. However, several studies reveal that most of the States in India have not yet transferred all 29 subjects to the panchayats because of political self-interests which is a grave concern even after completion of 23 years of the 73rd CAA. In this backdrop, this study aims at analyzing critically the status of devolution of 3Fs in Odisha.

Devolution and Panchayat Governance

As Saltman (2003) points out that decentralisation is the transfer of authority and power in planning, management and decision-making from higher to lower levels of organisational control. Smith (1985) argues that decentralisation entails the subdivision of a state's territory into smaller areas and the creation of political and administrative institutions in those areas. Decentralisation is a process through which authority and responsibilities for some substantial government functions are transferred to local government.

However, the decentralisation by devolution is that the transferred power should include political power, not just administrative and economic power directed by central governments. The Commission on Scotish Devolution (2008) defines devolution as a process of decentralisation in which power and responsibility is moved outwards and downwards and hence closer to the people. So it can be said that devolution is the transfer of some authority or power from a central organisation or government to smaller organisations or government departments. Moreover, Alok (2012) points out that devolution of responsibility, power and resources is essential for sustainable decentralization. In the context of governance, devolution is concerned with passing on of powers, authority and rights and/or duties and responsibilities or even funds from higher level of jurisdiction to a lower level jurisdiction and making them autonomous in decision making.

In India, the 73rd CAA clearly states that the process of empowering the Panchayati Raj Insitutions is to be through devolution of funds, functionaries and functions in order to enable them to plan and implement their own programmes, economic development and social justice by the means of the laws of the legislatures of the States. Moreover, the article 243H provides the power of panchayats to impose tax and again the article 243G ensures 29 functions through eleventh schedule of 73rd CAA-1992 which needs to be devolved to panchayats. Further, article 243-I states that the constitution mandates setting up of State Finance Commission (SFC) with the objective of reviewing the financial position of the Panchayats. The Report of Tenth Year Plan Working Group (2001) highlights that when the authority and power in respect of certain activity is transferred from the state to the panchayats, the latter should have the prerogative of making 'decisions', in respect of planning and implementation of such activity. In the sphere of devolution of responsibilities to lower levels of governance, some important principles should be kept in view. First, the Principle of 'subsidiary' needs to be given adequate attention. The Principle of subsidiary suggests that any function which can be performed by a lower tier should be handled by that tier alone and not by any higher tier of PRI. Second, the state government should not unilaterally withdraw responsibilities and powers already granted to the panchayat without adequate justification and prior consultation with the latter. Third, responsibilities, authorities and powers granted to the panchayats should be extremely specific, clear and simple in order to be comprehended by the panchayats. Lastly, whenever, functions and responsibilities are transferred to the panchayats, it should be ensured that the necessary funds, functionaries and freedom in decision-making also accompany such transfer. Importantly, Report on Working Group for Panchayati Raj and Rural Governance (2011) has emphasized that matching devolution of funds and functionaries is also required for the PRIs to perform their assigned functions effectively. It also suggests that the role of Centrally Sponsored Schemes (CSSs) and Additional Central Assistance (ACAs) in the devolution of 3Fs upon the PRIs should be given importance through provision of centrality to Panchayat raj institutions with specific roles and functions.

Panchayat Governance in Odisha

The Orissa Gram Panchayat Act, 1948 is the first legislation prescribing constitutional power and functioning of Gram Panchayats in the State of Odisha however the Panchayats were not much vibrant and empowered to function as local self-government. Similarly, in 1961 a three tier PRIs to look at the functions such as literacy, poverty and diseases initiated. The regular conduct of election, financial autonomy and administrative power remained as the key factors affecting the effective functioning of the Panchayats in Odisha. After the introduction of 73rd CCA-1992 three tier Panchayati Raj system, the regular elections are held in 1997, 2002, 2007 and 2012 in PRIs of Odisha. The State Election Commission, State Finance Commission has been set up and District Planning Committees have been constituted however, DPC exists in 30 districts headed by a Minister of Council of Ministers which is not active and not meet regularly. Moreover, the State Government during the Panchayat election of 2012 has increased the reservation for women from 33 per cent to 50 per cent for empowerment of women leadership in panchayats where the important feature of Odisha Panchayat system is that every Chairperson and Vice Chairperson or either of all three tier panchayats will be a women functionary. However, several studies reveal that Odisha has not yet complied fully devolution of 3Fs after 23 years of 73rd CAA.

According to the 2011 census, the rural population constituted 83 per cent i.e. 34970562 of the total population i.e. 41974218 in Odisha. There are total 100872 PRI members which includes 6,235 Panchayat Samiti members and 6236 Sarapanch, 854 Zilla Parishad members and Devolution of Funds, Functions and Functionaries...87547 Ward members in Odisha as per the outcome budget (2012-13) of the Ministry of Panchayati Raj, Government of Odisha. Several administrative and policy decision measures have been taken by the Panchayati Raj Department, Government of Odisha in the recent past to create an enabling environment, to make the Panchayats more vibrant for effective implementation of rural development programmes, to promote grassroot leadership and participatory planning. These includes training and capacity building of the newly elected PRI members on a mission mode, conduct of Palli Sabha and Gram Sabha in a campaign mode, training of officials of Panchayat, Block and district level, devising Job Chart and orientation for the officials engaged in MGNREGS, Odisha Modernising Economy, Governance and Administration (OMEGA), setting up of Panchayat Helpline, Grievance Redressal Cell, Odisha Livelihood Mission and Odisha State Social Audit, Accountability and Transparency (OSSAAT).

Status of Devolution : Odisha Experience

In case of Odisha, Behuria (2012) points out that Biju Pattnaik, former Chief Minister of Odisha was more determined and exhibited sheer self confidence and unremitting zeal to streamline Panchayati Raj. For him "let the people rule themselves, let them check out plans/schemes for the improvement of their respective areas and let them execute their plans" was the hallmarks of Panchayati Raj administration who further had announced that for the first time in the history of Independent India, women will be given 33 per cent reservation in the three-tier PRIs now which is now turned into 50 per cent by 2012 Panchayat election. He was of the view that the goals of Panchayati Raj can not be fructified unless there is proper devolution of financial powers to panchayats. His government made concerted effort for appointment to a Special Finance Commission to look after the domain of devolution of Financial Powers. Misra (2013) suggests that the significance of Panchayati raj is for relieving the administrative burden of the upper layers of government as well as increasing the legitimacy of the system of governance however the lack of proper devolution of powers to local governments is not able to achieve this.

Moreover, out of 29 subjects of the 11th Schedule, only 21 subjects transferred to PRIs relating to 11 departments by Odisha government, specifying general devolution however, devolved subjects like drinking water supply, sanitation, primary education, health, anti-poverty R D Schemes implementation with coordination and cooperation of department of (i) Agriculture, (ii) Food, Supplies and Consumer Welfare, (iii) Health and Family Welfare, (iv) Women and Child Development, (v) Water Resources, (vi) School and Mass Education, (vii) Fisheries and Animal Resources Development, (viii) Co-operation, (ix) Panchayati Raj, (x) Rural Development, and (xi) SC and ST Development. Interestingly, the ground reality of devolution in Odisha as per the findings of Ministry of Panchayati Raj – 3i InfoTech study shows that Odisha is poor in devolution of fund where (i) there're no Panchayat window system, (ii) Partial devolution in 12 out of 29 subjects is done, (iii) Devolution limited to Centrally sponsored or Panchayati Raj Department schemes with little line department's contribution and (iv) the devolved funds are programme bound where there is no scope for need-based work. This findings again indicates about devolution of functions where (i) there are partially 16 out of 29 functions partially devolved, (ii) role is limited to beneficiary selection and monitoring and disbursement of tied up funds etc. However, this study indicates about the devolution of functionaries where (i) the functionaries have no power to appoint or punish, (ii) they are limited to sanction of leave and calling for reports hence limited accountability, and (iii) Concurrent powers of the line Department is in function. In the end this study states that the process of monitoring is not specified, (i) there is lack of role clarity among functionaries, (ii) planning at Gram Panchayat level is not prescribed, (iii) Empowering parallel institutions is a great concern, and (iv) PRI bodies are facing problems such as lack adequate infrastructure, manpower and capacities to carry out devolved functions.

Table 5.1: Devolution Status of Odisha in Devolution Index (2011-12) and Devolution Index (2012-13)

Devolution	*Rank in 2011-12* (among 18 states except North East States and Union Territories)	*Rank in 2012-13* (among 20 states except North East States and Union Territories)	*Remark*
Functions	16	7	increased
Finances	13	8	increased
Functionaries	13	15	decreased

Source: Reports of Devolution to Panchayats in India, 2011-12 and Strengthening Panchayats in India: Comparing Across States, 2012-13, Ministry of Panchayati Raj, Government of India.

As explained in Table 5.1, it is evident from the report of both devolution indices carried out by the ministry of panchayati raj, Government of India for the year 2011-12 and 2012-13 that the rank of Odisha in devolution of functions and finances has increased from 16th to 7th and from 13th to 8th respectively however Odisha ranks below in 2012-13 in comparison to 2011-12 in devolution of functionaries i.e. from 13th to 15th which is a major concern because functionaries are the human power to take up the functions smoothly in panchayats which is lagging behind in Odisha. Moreover, it is agreed by the Minister of Panchayati Raj, Odisha (2015)that huge vacancy from the higher post to lower one in PRIs is seen in PRIs.

Table 5.2: Status of Compilation of Conditions of 13th Finance Commission by Odisha

Sl. No.	*Conditions of 13th Finance Commission*	*Action taken*
1.	The State Govt must put in place a supplement to the Budget document indicating details of transfer of funds to ZP, PS, GPs.	Complied
2.	The State Govt must put in place an Audit System for the 3 tier PRIs. (viii-format data base and viii-format model accounting system)	Audit is being carried out by Local Fund Audit in all PRIs. The C&AG, has also been entrusted to take audit work of 3 tier PRIs. All Collectors and PD, DRDAs have been instructed to extend their cooperation in the matter as and when required. Besides steps have been taken to maintain Accounts of GPs by the Charted Accountants empanelled by C&AG, for Odisha.
3.	The State Govt must put in place a system of Independent Local body Ombudsman at state level.	In this context process has already been started for Amendment of Lokpal & Lokayut Act-1995.
4.	The State Govt must put in place a system for e-transfer of funds to PRIs	Complied
5.	All Rural Local Bodies should be fully enabled to levy property tax on commercial and residential properties.	For imposition of property tax, OGP Act 1964 needs to be amended. In this regard proposal (draft bill) has been sent to the select committee of Odisha Legislative Assembly for placing the same in the next session of OLA.

Source: Outcome Budget of Panchayat Raj Department Odisha, 2013-14.

Table 5.2 shows that Panchayat raj department of Odisha has taken severa; steps to strengthen panchayati raj in compiling with the conditions of 13th Finance Commission, Govt. of India. Importantly, it has pursued to bring an amendment in Odisha Gram Panchayat Act-1964 to fully enable rural local bodies to levy property tax on commercial and residential properties which is an important element of finance devolution to panchayats. It also reveals that Odisha aims at strengthening Panchayat raj institutions through major reforms.

Moreover, the Outcome Budget of Odisha Panchayat Ministry (2013-14) ensures to take the process of devolution and improving the public delivery of service at village level, all attempts shall be made to provide desired physical and human infrastructure at GP and Block level and Various Village level functionaries to be enabled to sit in the GP premises and facilitate convergence of different poverty alleviation programmes in a fair and transparent manner. Also, it ensures to take the process of devolution and improving the public delivery of service at village level, all attempts shall be made to provide desired physical and human infrastructure at GP and Block level. Also, various village level functionaries to be enable to sit in the GP premises and facilitate convergence of different poverty alleviation programmes in affair and transparent manner. Moreover, State Government in its outcome budget for 2013-14 provides funds to PRIs under 3rd SFC in the various major sectors such as (i) Devolution of funds to PRIs, (ii) Untied funds to the PRIs, (iii) Grants to Z P for developmental works, (iv) Grants to GP for Performance linked Incentive, (v) The salary component of field functionaries, (vi) Celebration of PR Divas, (vii) K. L. Grant to PRIs, (viii) Sairat and Cess Grant to PRIs and (ix) Honorarium, Sitting fees to elected PRI members which is shown in the Table 5.3.

Table 5.3: Abstract of the Recommendation of 3rd State Finance Commission for the Period from 2010-11 to 2014-15

Sl. No.	*Sector*		*Amount per annum in Crore*	*Total Amount for 5 years in Crore*
1.	**Devolution of Funds**		181.49	907.45
2.	**Compensation and Assignment**		37.15	185.75
	(a) Sairat	1.00 Crore		
	(b) K L Grant	20.00 Crore		
	(c) Cess Grant	15.00 Crore		
	(d) Minor Forest Produce	1.00 Crore		
	(e) Entertainment Tax	0.15 Crore		
3.	**Untied fund and other Grants-in-Aid**		114.20	571.00
	Untied fund @ '35.00 lakh per Panchayat Samiti for utilisation in their need based requirement of the locality. ('35.00 x 314)	109.90 Crore		
	Incentive	3.60 Crore		
	Celebration of P R Divas	0.70 Crore		
4.	**Grants for Salary, Sitting fee, Honorarium etc.**		251.16	1255.80
	Grand Total		**584.00**	**2920.00**

Source: Outcome Budget of Panchayat Raj Department Odisha, 2013-14.

Here, this Table 5.3 clearly reveals the detail plan for 2011-15 year and status of devolution of funds in various heads to panchayats where annually 181.49 crores is allotted for devolution of funds, 37.15 crores for compensation and assistant, 114.20 crores for Untied fund and other Grants-in-Aid and 251.16 crores Grants for salary, sitting fee and Honorarium of the Panchayat functionaries. Interestingly, it reveals that the State government is allotting the finance to panchayats and controls it as it is the contrary to financial autonomy of the Panchayat raj institutions which lacks to have a Panchayat level budget for well-functioning. However, Pattayat (2013), the Government of Odisha is committed for progressive devolution of funds, functions and functionaries to the Panchayat for effective planning and implementation of different rural development programmes sponsored by the Central and State Government. It has devised the mechanism to position the Gram Sabha at the core Panchayati Raj system for true self-governance and ensuring transparency and accountability of Gram Panchayat.

Major Findings

Though Odisha government is trying best to strengthen the PRIs however, the lack of political will is seen in its parts in transferring of funds, functionaries and functions to the PRIs. The study reveals that only 19 subjects of 11 line department of Government of Odisha is partially transferred to the panchayati raj institutions out of 29 subjects as per the 11th schedule of 73rd CAA which again indicates state government has not yet able to transfer 29 functions fully. It appears that the functionaries of panchayati raj institutions are inadequate who are assigned with multiple assignments which lead towards less possibility of accountability and responsibility among these functionaries. The both studies of Alok (2012 – 2013) on Devolution Index suggests that Odisha has improved in its tally in devolution of finance and function to panchayats but not able to devolve adequate functionaries which is a major concern therefore, it reveals that Odisha Panchayat system is in the process devolving 3Fs to make effective functioning of panchayats.

Moreover, the study points out that no specific budget/fund provision is made so far for the PRIs which is another lacuna in making the local bodies financially autonomous. However, it is revealed that the PRIs are now-a-days getting more funds, functions and functionaries through various State and Union government sponsored programmes and projects which is a remarkable steps mentioned in Budget Outcome of Odisha Panchayat Ministry (2013-14) that leads towards effective functioning of the PRIs however adequate functionaries are not there as many vacancies are noticed in various tiers of panchayats which is again confirmed by Odisha Panchayati Raj Minister too. This study further finds that Odisha Panchayat raj department is taking necessary steps to meet the conditions of 13th Finance Commission to ensure effective functioning of panchayats in Odisha which is a positive indication of Odisha government. Further, it is seen in this study that Odisha government has been initiating various plans, projects and programmes and transferring to the PRIs for its implementations which enables to create necessary infrastructure facilities which indirectly adds to 3 Fs.

Suggestions

Odisha government is yet to do a lot to achieve the main objective 73rd CAA. Accordingly, some of suggestions are emerged from this study for the Odisha government to make the panchayati raj institutions self-reliant, independent, and autonomous in every aspects like finance, administration and governance. The major suggestions such as:

(i) Odisha government should take immediate initiative to devolve rest 10 subjects of 11th schedule to the panchayat raj institutions with the provision for adequate funds and functionaries for easy delivering of projects and programmes;

(ii) Odisha government acknowledges about human resource crunch for PRIs therefore it should immediately fill up the vacancies at various levels of PRIs to ensure proper and effective functioning of Panchayats;

(iii) It should make a specific local government budget for the functioning of PRIs to ensure autonomy in PRI's financial administration despite several schemes;

(iv) The grassroots organisations such as Self Helf Group, Youth Clubs, Non-Government Organisation need to be encouraged by Panchayats to inform people about participation and importance of Palli Sabha and Gram Sabha meetings which will ensure more people's participation;

(v) The Panchayati raj institutions should be revisited for infrastructure as well as manpower development to act independently for the people's welfare which will meet the true spirit of 73rd CAA.

(vi) To ensure proper devolution of 3Fs, there is a need of a local Government List like Union Lists and State Lists. Moreover, a

Concurrent List like Central Concurrent list should be made for both Local and State government.

Conclusion

To conclude, it is clear that devolution of fund, function and functionaries to the panchayats is the backbone of panchayats ensured by 73rd CAA however it is surprised to see that the real objective of panchayat act is not yet attained by the Government of Odisha at the end of 23 years of this act. Due of lack of political will in part of Odisha government; it has not able to transfer all 29 subjects to the panchayati raj institutions fully with necessary funds and functionaries which is a major lacuna however little devolution of 3 Fs is in partial to the line department of the Odisha government. Therefore, it is the need of the hour that the Odisha government must look into the loopholes on the devolution of 3Fs to PRIs and also it must develop a clear roadmap to devolve all the functions with adequate funds and functionaries and necessary support to the PRIs then only these local bodies will be able to act as self and independent local governments for the betterment of the local people and their welfare which will achieve the essence of the 73rd panchayat Act in Odisha.

References

Alok, V. N. (2012). Emperical Assessment on Devolution to Panchayats in India, IIPA, New Delhi.

Alok, V. N (2013). Strengthening Panchayats in India: Comparing Devolution Acros India, Ministry of Panchayat Raj, Govt. of India and IIPA, New Delhi.

Behuria, R. K. (2012). Panchayati Raj in Odisha: An Overview, Odisha Review, Odisha, February-March, 2012.

Burns, D., Hambleton, R. and Hoggett, P. (1994). The Politics of Decentralisation, Macmillan, Basingstoke.

Misra, S. N (2013). Democracy, Development and Decentralisation: Rural Development Through Institutional Intervention, Odisha Review, February – March.

Pattayat, Priyanath. (2013). Strengthening Panchayati Raj System in Odisha: Initiatives and Concern, Odisha Review, Odisha, March, 2013.

Saltman, R., Bankauskaite, V. and Vrangbaek, K. (2003). Decentralisation in Health Care: Strategies and Outcomes. EOHCS, Madrid.

Smith, B. C. (1985). Decentralisation: The Tterritorial Dimension of the State. Allen and Unwin, London.

Government of India (1992). 73rd Constitutional Amendment Act, 1992.

Government of Odisha (2012-13). Outcome Budget, Ministry of Panchayati Raj, Odisha, http://www. odishapanchayat. gov. in/English/Pdf/ OutcomeBudget_ 2012-2013. pdf. accessed on 7th May, 2014.

Government of Odisha (2013-14). Outcome Budget, Ministry of Panchayati Raj, Odisha. http://www. odishapanchayat. gov. in/English/Pdf/ Outcome Budget_2013-2014.pdf, p.6 accessed on 6th May, 2014.

Government of India (2011). Census-2011 report, New Delhi.

Government of India (2001). Report of the Working Group on 'Decentralised Planning and Panchayati Raj Institutions', for the Tenth Five-Year Plan, Ministry of Rural Development, Government of India, New Delhi.

Government of India, Report on Working Group for Panchayati Raj and Rural Governance (2011) http://www. nrcddp. org/file_upload/Report%20of% 20the%20Working%20.

Government of Odisha (2015). Panchayati Raj Minister of Odisha, Sri Arun Sahu's reply to Odisha State Assembly on 2nd December, 2014, PBD Bureau, Bhubaneswar, 3rd December, p.3.

Groupon%20panchayati%20raj%20insti. . pdf, p.19 accessed on 6th May, 2014

6

Local Body Elections and OBC Reservation in Andhra Pradesh

—K. Kondala Rao

Background

"The state shall take steps to organise Village Panchayats and endow them with such powers and authority as may be necessary to enable them to function as units of self-government" is the constitutional directive under Article 40. Though the Panchayati Raj Institutions have been in existence for a long time, it has been observed that these institutions have not been able to acquire the status and dignity of viable and responsive people's bodies due to a number of reasons including –

(1) absence of regular elections

(2) prolonged suppressions

(3) insufficient representation of weaker sections

(4) inadequate devolution of powers and

(5) lack of adequate financial resources

Reform

Under this backdrop national experience of nearly forty years, new part IX, the Panchayats and new part IX-A, Municipalities, with Articles 243, 243-A to 243-O and 243-P to 243-ZG and eleventh and twelfth schedules through 73rd and 74th constitution amendments, 1992, respectively have been inserted into the Constitution of India, essentially with three objectives of –

(1) democratic de-centralisation

(2) greater accountability between the citizens and State apparatus as well as

(3) empowerment of weaker sections 2

and providing for the following:

(1) Three tire hierarchical bodies both for Panchayats and Municipalities

(2) Reservation in seats and officies to SC/ST/OBC/Women categories, by rotation

(3) Five years tenure

(4) Powers and responsibilities of the functionaries

(5) Election Commission, Finance Commission, maintenance of accounts and audit.

The Andhra Pradesh Panchayat Raj Act, 1994 (APPR Act) and the Andhra Pradesh Municipal Corporation Act, 1994 have been enacted and Andhra Pradesh Municipalities Act, 1965 has been amended incorporating these principles. Elections were held thrice so far under these enactments in the State of Andhra Pradesh during 1995, 2001 and 2006. Elections for the fourth time due in July, 2011 have not taken place and the reasons are multifold. The five years tenure of Panchayat bodies constituted in 2006 expired on 21.07.2011.

Art. 243-D and Art.243-T provided for proportional reservations to SC and ST categories in seats and offices at all the three levels in the two categories of local bodies. It also provided for reservation of ***not less than one-third*** of seats and offices at all the levels to women from SC/ST/OBC as well as open categories. But in respect of reservation to OBC category the Constitution did not provide any guidance on identification of OBCs for this purpose or quantum of reservation for them, but left these aspects to the discretion of the legislatures of the respective states under Articles 243-D (6) and 243- T (6) respectively.

Sec. 2 (2) of APPR Act defined "Backward Classes" as any socially and educationally backward classes of citizens recognised by government for the purpose of clause 4 of Article 15 of the Constitution. Secs. 9 (1-A), 15 (2), 152 (1-A), 153 (2-A) and 180 (1-A) of APPR Act provided for 34 per cent of reservations to Backward classes in seats and offices of Panchayats at the three levels. Similar provisions for B C reservations in Municipalities have been made under the corresponding Acts.

Rural population percentage of SC and ST categories from Census-2001 have been adopted for quantifying their respective reservations in

Panchayat Raj bodies, in the previous elections, 2006. According to this data SCs and STs have been provided 18.3 per cent and 8.25 per cent reservations respectively. As per the decision of A.P. High Court percentage of B C voters in the Electoral Rolls have been adopted for computing and allocation of their reservations. The state average of BC voters as computed for 2006 elections was 45.49 per cent, but their reservation is limited to 34 per cent in terms of the APPR Act. Backward classes have been accorded 34 per cent reservations in all the three previous elections in 1995, 2001 and 2006 irrespective of the fact that their population is much more than that.

Judicial Intervention – Supreme Court

As things stand thus, several writ petitions from Karnataka and U. P. States filed in the Supreme Court during 1994 and 1995 came up for hearing in the year 2010. Reservation for Other Backword Classes (OBCs) is the main thrust of challenge by the petitioners, apart from few others aspects. These writ petitions were disposed on 11.5.2010 through a Judgment by constitutional bench of five judges headed by the then Chief Justice of India K. G. Balakrishnan who incidentally happened to be from a Scheduled Caste. This Judgment was delivered just one day before his retirement on 12.05.2010.

The Supreme Court in its Judgment while accepting on one side that the principles that have been evolved for conferring reservational benefits contemplated by Articles 15 (4) and 16 (4) cannot be mechanically applied in the context of reservations enabled by Articles 243-D and 243-T, acted exactly contrary to that in mechanically holding that the upper ceiling of 50 per cent with respect to vertical total reservations in favour of SC/ST/ OBCs should not be breached. The Judgment did not record anything as to why there should be ceiling at all for reservations in local bodies. It also declared that exceptional circumstances for breach of upper limit of 50 per cent in Schedule V areas cannot be invoked for reservation in favour of backward classes for the purpose of local bodies located in general areas.

The Supreme Court further held that the barriers to political participation are not of the same character as barriers that limit access to education and employment; that the identification of "backward classes" under Article 243-D (6) and Article 243-T(6) should be distinct from the identification of SEBCs for the purpose of Article 15 (4) and that of backward classes for the purpose of Article 16 (4) and that the onus is on the executive to conduct a rigorous investigation into the patterns of backwardness that act as barriers to political participation. (Paras 63 and 82 (iii) of the Judgment).

This finding and direction is atleast partially inconsistent with the observation of the court at the end of para 54 of the Judgment which is extracted below:

> "*It is quite conceivable that in some localised settings, backwardness in social and economic sense can also act as a barrier to effective political participation and representation. When it comes to creating a level playing field for the purpose of elections to local bodies, backwardness in the social and economic sense can indeed be one of the criteria for conferring reservation benefits.*"

The local vertical reservations for SC/ST/BC categories in the State of Andhra Pradesh in 2006 elections prior to Supreme Court Judgment on 11.5.2010 were 60.55 per cent (18.3 + 8.25 + 34.0). According to the ceiling of 50 per cent imposed by the Supreme Court Judgment, the backward classes would be adversely affected and their reservations will have to be reduced from 34 per cent to 23.45 per cent to ensure total reservation not to cross 50 per cent. No reduction can be effected in reservation in respect of SC and ST categories since they enjoy constitutional protection as against backward classes whose protection is only of statutory character. The effect of the Supreme Court directions is to unsettle the OBC reservation and the definition of "Backward Classes" and thereby their identification for the purpose of reservation in local bodies settled for over 15 years in all the states throughout the country.

Knowing this position pretty well the Government of A. P. was silent for more than an year after Supreme Court Judgment in May, 2010 without initiating any move to retain 34 per cent BC reservation. Meanwhile the agitation by Backward Classes in the state gained momentum with a warning that they would not allow elections in July, 2011, to take place if any reduction in their 34 per cent reservation is attempted. In such a situation the Government of A. P. issued G. O. Ms. No.128 dated 8.6.2011 ordering total vertical reservation of 60.55 per cent and requesting the State Election Commission to initiate the election process.

Intervention by High Court and Supreme Court

The A.P. High Court (Single Judge) on 14.6.2011 dismissed a Writ Miscellaneous Petition seeking an interim direction to limit total reservation to 50 per cent. A division bench of A.P. High Court on

14.6.2012, while disposing a batch of Writ Petitions as well as PIL petitions ordered among others with the following directions:

(i) For the purpose of present elections, the State shall fix the reservation in favour of Backward Classes at such percentage so that it comes within 50 per cent of total reservation.

(ii) The State shall conduct a detailed investigation with regard to backwardness of the population, collect data, invite objections from the general public, analyse the same and fix reservations in favour of Backward Classes in accordance with the constitutional scheme.

(iii) The State Election Commission shall commence the process of elections immediately and complete the same within a period of three months from the date of finalisation of the reservation percentage by the state.

Meanwhile, the Government of Andhra Pradesh through its G. O. Ms. No.77 dated 7.4.2011 ordered increase of women reservation for all categories of women (i.e.,) SC/ST/BC and open category from the existing one-third to 50 per cent. Already the following seven states have been implementing 50 per cent reservation to women:

(1) Chhattisgarh

(2) Manipur

(3) Uttarakhand

(4) Bihar

(5) Rajasthan

(6) Madhya Pradesh

(7) Himachal Pradesh.

On challenge of orders dated 14.6.2012 of the division bench of A. P. High Court, the Supreme Court of India on 18.02.2013 passed orders as follows:

"As an interim measure all the parties to the above proceedings are agreeable that the State of Andhra Pradesh / Election Commission is to proceed with the election with the existing system. The main issue will be decided at a later stage. In view of the above direction, the directions contained in clauses (i) and (iii) of paragraph 60 of the impugned Judgment of High Court are hereby stayed until further orders."

Careless, Unfair and Fradulent Implementation of Reservations in Andhra Pradesh

Serious damage was caused to the interests of reservational categories particularly BCs and Women due to several factors like careless, unfair, and fraudulent implementation of Reservation to various categories. There are 1097 Mandals in the state. ST, SC and BCs have 8.25 per cent, 18.3 per cent and 34 per cent reservations respectively. The commissioner erroneously calculated their respective share of reserved MPP (Mandal Parishad President) posts as 90, 207 and 371 respectively instead of 91, 281 and 373 respectively in 2006 elections.

Similarly due to violations relating to rules of reservation and rotation BCs could not get reservation in 106 and 167 mandals as ZPTCs (Zilla Parishad Territorial Constituencies) and MPPs respectively out of 373 Mandals to be reserved for them in 2006. Similarly women lost 119 and 272 Mandals as ZPTCs and MPPs respectively out of 366 Mndals to be reserved for them in 2006.

Since BCs have 34 per cent reservations in all the three earlier elections in 1995, 2001 and 2006, it is expected that according to principle of rotation they should have covered all positions in the state by the end of 2006 elections. But due to fraudulent application of rule of reservation they could not get 29 ZPTCs in 11 districts and 42 MPPs in 11 districts.

Observations and Conclusions

(1) There is inequity in the equalising process and BCs are not duly protected in the process of ensuring diversity in empowerment.

(2) BCs are not fairly treated while bringing about 73rd and 74th constitutional amendments. While these amendments unambiguously quantified reservation in respect of SC, ST and women categories, quantum of reservation to OBCs is left to the discretion of State legislature and their reservations are accorded only statutory protection as against constitutional status accorded to other reservation categories.

(3) With the result when a ceiling of 50 per cent on reservations is imposed by the Judgment of Supreme Court BCs are sought to be made exclusive victims.

(4) The reservation ceiling of 50 per cent contemplated after Supreme Court Judgment in 2010, had thrown OBC reservations to depend on the combined population of SC and ST categories. If the combined population of SC/STs is considerably more, OBC reservation will become marginal irrespective of their high population and need.

Examples

(i) As per electoral rolls, 2006, BCs population is 45.5 per cent
Muslim groups – 15 Nos. added to BC list (2007) 6.3 per cent
31 new castes added to BC list (2008-09) 5.3 per cent
Total BCs constitute 57.1 per cent

BCs in AP irrespective of their population of more than 50 per cent will have to content with only 23.45 per cent reservation.

(ii) BCs of Rajasthan with 43 per cent population will have to content with 16 per cent reservation since SC/ST constitute 33.4 per cent population.

(iii) BCs in UP with about 59 per cent population will have to content with 27 per cent reservation because of 23 per cent of SC/ST population.

(5) While 50 per cent ceiling rule is ensuring proportional opportunities to SC/ST and even open categories, it is adversely targeting only BC categories.

(6) Reservations are in principle accorded to those categories who have been denied access to political power. There are no reservations to BC/OBCs in seats in State Assemblies and Parliament. With the result, in States like AP, they could never enjoy proportional opportunities either in the State Assembly or Parliament.

(7) While proportional opportunities are ensured to SC/ST categories in local bodies, who have also been enjoying proportional opportunities in both Assemblies and Parliament, it is nothing but unfair that BCs are not ensured proportional opportunities atleast in local bodies.

(8) For ensuring equity and substantial social justice to BCs Article 243-D (6) and 243-T (6) need to be amended to ensure proportional opportunities to BCs.

(9) Caste census are a must to work out proportions.

7

Democratic Decentralisation and Political Participation of Backward Castes in Andhra Pradesh: Pros and Cons

—Gooru Sreeramulu

Introduction

Without understanding the Indian society—its nature, social structure, pattern of land holding, caste structure, the problem of rural villages—it may not be possible to understand the working of local governments in rural India. Since the social structure of Indian society is based on caste system, social inequalities existed in the villages and have continued for centuries. The reasons may be several. For example, the people from higher social strata had received education, took up high-income-earning-activities, controlled and managed land. On the other hand, the lower strata people were not only denied education, but they were also deprived of their right to manage and control land. They were forced to take up low-income-earning-activities. In the villages, particularly, the lower strata people took up supportive works such as carpentry, blacksmith, leather work, and labour for the people who had taken up agricultural activities (Rajesh Kumar, 2006: 457).

Due to above-mentioned reasons and consequent social inequality, the people from higher social status only could easily enter into the process of administration, directly or indirectly; the marginalised became the weaker sections of the society. Under these circumstances, soon after independence, the concept of social justice figured in the Indian Constitution. The Constitution of India made an attempt to provide equal social opportunities for the overall development of all the people in the society without any discrimination based on caste, sex or race (S. N. Singh, 1996:28).

After Independence, India was one of some countries to go for social and economic transformation of their rural population. Rural development, as a condition, became a preferred strategy for improving the rural poor's living conditions. The Government of India—by giving greater attention to the rural poor's empowerment—made efforts to solve problems such as poverty, ill health, illiteracy, and backwardness of varied nature prevailing in rural areas. Further, because of their socio-economic deprivation in a traditional society like India, the marginalised sections i. e., SCs, STs and OBCs have become an important component in defining the development policies.

However, political involvement of the upper castes is still more in institutions like State Assemblies and the Parliament. In State Assemblies and the Parliament, reservation of seats was restricted to 15 per cent; and, even in this small space, there was no representation of a larger section of BCs. As a result of this, at present, political participation in India is limited to a few upper castes only as they manage and control the political system and land pattern. The upper caste people did not bother to formulate and execute welfare and developmental policies intended for the weaker sections; it can be seen in the failure of several programmes such as Community Development Programme (CDP), National Extension Programme (NEP) etc (Syamala Devi, D. and G. Lakshmi, 2005: 77). These programmes were implemented in favour of the upper caste people in the rural areas.

Democratic Decentralisation and Backward Castes in India

Balwant Rai Mehta Committee Report: In 1957, a study team was appointed under the chairmanship of Balwant Rai Mehta. The purpose was to evaluate the functioning of CDP. While reviewing the functions of CDP, the committee anticipated the Panchayati Raj system. The committee recommended a three–tier system of the Panchayati Raj. The thrust was on Panchayat Samiti—to be established at block level—known as block level body. It is a statutory and executive body, comprehensive in its functions, equipped with necessary authority and in possession of adequate resources.

The committee further felt that the Panchayat Samiti must not be put under too much control of the government agencies. It is important to note that the committee had given importance to Panchayat Samiti and had neglected the other two systems of the PRIs. The most important reason was that the committee wanted to implement rural developmental programmes very effectively and without interference from political parties and groups.

Thus, the creation of Panchayati Raj system in India is an intellectual contribution of Balwant Rai Mehta Committee (Ashok Bajpai and M. S. Verma, 1995:47-48). Panchayati Raj system was launched in India on 2nd October 1959 in Rajasthan, Andhra Pradesh, Tamil Nadu, Kerala, Madhya Pradesh, Orissa, Uttar Pradesh, Bihar, West Bengal, Himachal Pradesh, Gujarat, Assam, and in some Union Territories. The basic purpose of creating the Panchayati Raj system was to meet the local problems and to implement the developmental programmes.

Ashok Mehta Committee Report: In 1977, an important committee appointed by the new government at the centre was the Ashok Mehta Committee (The 73rd Constitutional Amendments Act, 1992: 148). It was appointed to enquire into the working of the PRI's and to suggest measures to strengthen them to "enable a decentralised system of planning and development to be effective." The committee recommended reform and revitalisation of the Panchayat Raj system based upon the central premises of "linking institutions of democratic decentralisation with socially motivated economic development" in rural areas.

From the above discussion, it becomes clear that both the committees attempted to bring about rural development by recommending either three or two tier system of the PRIs. However, they could not achieve the specified motives to a large extent due to ignorance of the people, non-involvement of weaker sections—for the benefit of whom the schemes were launched. The upper caste and dominant people of the villages intentionally diverted the schemes. Thus, the attempt of the PRIs in developing the weaker sections has remained limited to the records only.

In view of these issues, the Constitutional Amendments Act of 1992, known as the 73rd Constitutional Amendments Act, came into effect in 1993. As per the Act, due share has been given to the OBCs for ensuring their political participation, welfare plans and programmes. However, the 73rd Amendments offered several opportunities only to a small number of people—with better agrarian resources—among BCs. This is why the developmental programmes are not reaching to the lower strata categories among BCs, they still remain underdeveloped.

Objectives of the Study

The study has the following objectives:

- Assess the representation of BCs in the PRIs in relation to social background in the three regions of Andhra Pradesh.
- Examine the welfare of BCs in terms of political participation of their representatives in the three regions of Andhra Pradesh.
- Examine the pros and cons of reservation provisions of BCs after the 73rd Amendments in the three regions of Andhra Pradesh.
- Assess the role of caste, social status and agrarian resources in capturing various positions in the PRIs in the three regions of Andhra Pradesh.
- Examine whether people belonging to higher social categories within BCs are capturing positions in the PRIs.

Democratic Decentralisation and Backward Castes in Andhra Pradesh

In Andhra Pradesh, the panchayat system was working before the 73rd Amendments. The Andhra Pradesh Gram Panchayat Act, 1964, and the Andhra Pradesh Mandal Praja Parishads, Zila Praja Parishad and Zila Abhivrudhi Sameeksha Mandals Act, 1986 were in force. The attempt made by the Act of 1986—providing reservations to BCs in the PRIs—is significant in the history of Andhra Pradesh. This Act is considered as the most significant in the process of political participation of low social categories. Political participation of low social categories began after the 73rd amendments.

Andhra Pradesh passed a subsequent Act known as the Andhra Pradesh Panchayat Raj Amendment Act, 1994. The state adopted a uniform pattern of three-tiered Panchayati Raj system: Gram Panchayat at Village level; Mandal Parishad at Mandal level; and, Zila Panchayat at District level. Further, the Act also provided for the constitution of a Gram Sabha for every village. Besides, the Act also facilitated reservation provisions for the people belonging to certain depressed classes such as SCs, STs, OBCs, and women in all the three-tiers of the PRIs. As per the Act, 33 per cent of the total seats are to be reserved for OBCs in all the PRIs with a determined vision of developing these sections of the society.

In spite of the Constitutional provisions, the people belonging to weaker sections are unable to work in the PRIs independently.

Among several factors, the social system and the structure of caste in Andhra Pradesh have been predominant over activities of the people from BCs. Thus, caste has long been an important dimension of social articulation and political mobilisation in the state. In the domain of electoral politics, caste assumed an active role as the basis of political grouping and mobilisation of electoral support in the state. In terms of caste structure and articulation, three regions i.e. Telangana, Andhra and Rayalaseema display significant variations. The Brahmins—comprising a meager percentage of the population, ritually placed at the top of the caste pyramid—have historically dominated social, cultural, and economic life. It is only in the early decades of the twentieth Century that we find a serious challenge to their supremacy—manifested in the form of specific caste articulations (Overseas Development Institute, 2002: 27).

Political Participation of Backward Castes after the 73rd Amendments: Perceptions and Problems

In a developing society like India where forces of caste and kinship influence the social life, and acute disparities—related to sub-culture and the standard of living—among various groups and regions are existing (N. K. Singhi, 1974: 55), a study of the socio-economic conditions of BCs would help in revealing their significant political, sociological, and economic dimensions. Knowledge of socio-economic background of a community is an indispensable prerequisite in understanding thought or behaviours of its members. This holds good for all human communities, and more so in the case of SC/ST and OBC communities which are more traditional in their structure. As Geraint Parry observes, 'it is a wide spread assumption of political sociology that social background and upbringing of a decision-maker will influence his attitudes and policies (1969: 264).

The socio-economic conditions play an important role in characterising the social life and behaviour of an individual. The socio-economic status of an individual affects the patterns of interaction in the society. It is widely believed that the analysis of age, education, caste, family structure, occupation, income, land holding, party affiliation, etc. are important elements in determining the nature of leadership. The socio-economic, educational, and political background of the leaders would also enable us to anticipate as to what they are capable of, what we should expect from them, and how well they are equipped to discharge their responsibilities towards the electorate (Sashilata Puri, 1978: 31). It is therefore, essential to analyse the socio-economic background of the relationship between the leader and the environment.

Methodology, Techniques of Data Collection, and Analysis

Analytical, descriptive, and normative methods have been employed in the study. In view of the objectives, need, and importance of the present study, the required data have been collected by using different methods of scientific techniques. Particularly, different methods of social enquiry were adopted. A special tool (questionnaire)—based on the scientific process—was used by the investigator. The questionnaire consists of items spread over behavioural areas, the personal data i.e. name, sex, age, social, economic, political, and educational background of the respondents. Further, the collected data have been analysed with the help of computer-based quantitative analysis programme. The data were assigned codes and the analysis was made with the help of single variable and multivariable tables. Statistical tools such as average, percentage, mean, correlation, cross-sectional, and SES has been measured.

Analysis of Data

The data relating to the socio-economic background of elected respondents of the PRIs were collected to get an insight into the emerging pattern of rural leadership with reference to BCs in East Godawari district of Andhra Pradesh. Based on the data collected from the field work, a detailed analysis in relation to the impact of the 73rd Constitutional amendments on the political participation of BCs is discussed below. Given below are a total 12 tables representing BCs' awareness and opinion on various issues. The analytical discussion proceeds according to the contents of each of the tables.

The Purpose of the PRIs: The Table 7.1 represents opinion regarding the purpose of the PRIs. The opinion of the respondents of BCs in East Godawari District shows that 62.90 per cent out of the total 62 respondents belonging to the category 'A' are aware of the PRIs. This is followed by 66.67 per cent of the respondents belonging to the category 'B', 53.06 per cent of the respondents belonging to the category 'C', and 62.16 per cent of the respondents belonging to the category 'D'.

In the developed region of Andhra Pradesh, i.e., Andhra region, 29 respondents belonging to category 'B' and 22 respondents belonging to category 'D' are participating in PRIs. The table reveals that majority of respondents i.e., 16 belonging to category 'A' are not participating in the activities of PRIs.

Table 7.1: Opinion about the Purpose of the PRIs in East Godawari District

		Categories of Backward Castes			
		A	*B*	*C*	*D*
S.No.	*Opinion*	*Frequency*	*Frequency*	*Frequency*	*Frequency*
1.	Yes	10(38.46)	29(72.50)	13(81.25)	22(57.89)
2.	No	16(61.54)	6(15.00)	6(37.5)	15(39.47)
	Total	**26(100.00)**	**40(100.00)**	**16(100.00)**	**38(100.00)**

Source: Compiled from the data collected from field work.
Figure in the Brackets shows the percentage.

Participation in the Meetings of Gram Sabhas: The Table 7.2 represents respondents' opinion regarding attending the meetings of Gram Sabhas. The table reveals that in East Godawari District, majority of the respondents (61.29 per cent and 55.56 per cent) belonging to the categories 'A' and 'B' are *participating* in the meetings of Gram Sabhas. It is also observed that majority of the respondents belonging to category the 'C' (22.45 per cemt) are not attending the meetings of Gram Sabhas.

Table 7.2:Opinion about Attending the Gram Sabha in East Godawari District

		Categories of Backward Caste			
		A	*B*	*C*	*D*
S.No.	*Opinion*	*Frequency*	*Frequency*	*Frequency*	*Frequency*
1.	Yes	17(68.00)	14(56.00)	14(53.85)	27(67.50)
2.	No	8(32.00)	11(44.00)	12(46.15)	13(32.50)
	Total	**25(100.00)**	**25(100.00)**	**26(100.00)**	**40(100.00)**

Source: Compiled from the data collected from field work.

It is found that in East Godawari District, the majority of respondents i.e., 27 belonging to category 'B' and 18 belonging to category 'D' are attending the meetings of grama sabha. 46.15 per cent of respondents belonging to category 'A' and 32.50 per cent of respondents belonging to category 'B' are not attending the meetings of gram sabha.

Non-participation in the Meetings of Grama Sabhas: The Table 7.3 represents respondents' opinion regarding reasons for not attending meetings of Gram Sabhas. In Anantapur District, from the category 'A', 37.10 per cent of respondents are not attending the meetings of Gram Sabhas due to casteism. This is followed by 33.87 per cent due to faction, 19.35 per cent due to ignorance, and only 9.68 per cent due to politics. It is clear from the table that 33.33 per cent of the respondents belonging to the category 'B' are not attending Gram Sabhas due to ignorance.

Reasons for not attending Grama Sabhas include faction, casteism, ignorance, and politics (Kiran Saxena, 2000: 87). Nearly 38.78 per cent respondents belonging to the category 'C' are of the opinion that they are not attending due to casteism. Respondents belonging to the category 'D' are not attending meetings due to casteism and politics.

Table 7.3: Opinion regarding Reasons for not Attending Meetings of Gram Sabhas in East Godawari District

		Categories of Backward Caste			
		A	*B*	*C*	*D*
S. No.	*Opinion*	*Frequency*	*Frequency*	*Frequency*	*Frequency*
1.	Faction	10(40.00)	6(24.00)	6(23.08)	20(50.00)
2.	Casteism	7(28.00)	7(28.00)	7(26.92)	7(17.50)
3.	Ignorance	3(12.00)	5(20.00)	6(23.08)	3(7.50)
4.	Politics	5(20.00)	7(28.00)	7(26.92)	10(25.00)
	Total	**25(100.00)**	**25(100.00)**	**26(100.00)**	**40(100.00)**

Source: Compiled from the data collected from field work.

It is observed that casteism is the obstacle in the working of Gram Sabhas. It is also observed that most of the BCs are affected by casteism and faction. It is important to note that the higher castes within BCs are not participating due to politics and particularly due to the involvement of lower castes. The lower castes are able to participate in the PRIs only due to the provisions of reservation for BCs. The lower castes are involving due to political compulsions and they are in need of political support as many criminal cases are filed against them.

Table 7.4: Opinion about Questions in the Meetings of Gram Sabhas in East Godawari District

		Categories of Backward Caste			
		A	*B*	*C*	*D*
S. No.	*Opinion*	*Frequency*	*Frequency*	*Frequency*	*Frequency*
1.	Yes	16(61.54)	32(80.00)	9(56.25)	24(63.16)
2.	No	10(38.46)	8(20.00)	7(43.75)	14(36.84)
	Total	**26(100.00)**	**40(100.00)**	**16(100.00)**	**38(100.00)**

Source: Compiled from the data collected from field work.

Questions in the Meetings of Gram Sabhas: The Table 7.4 represents respondents' opinion regarding the question whether questions are asked or not asked in the meetings of Gram Sabhas.

In East Godawari District, 10 respondents belonging to category 'A', eight respondents belonging to category 'B', seven belonging to category 'C' and 14 belonging to category 'D' are not asking any questions in the meetings of gram sabhas.

Powers of the PRIs: The Table 7.5 represents distribution of the respondent's awareness about the powers of the PRIs in the study area. The table reveals that in Ananthpur District, 75.81 per cent of the respondents belonging to the category 'A' and 37.04 per cent of the respondents belonging to the category 'B' are not aware of powers of the PRIs.

Table 7.5: Awareness of BCs about Powers of the PRIs in East Godawari District

		Categories of Backward Caste			
		A	*B*	*C*	*D*
S. No.	*Opinion*	*Frequency*	*Frequency*	*Frequency*	*Frequency*
1.	Yes	16(64.00)	10(38.46)	30(75.00)	10(62.50)
2.	No	9(36.00)	16(61.54)	10(25.00)	6(37.50)
	Total	**25(100.00)**	**26(100.00)**	**40(100.00)**	**16(100.00)**

Source: Compiled from the data collected from field work.

The highest number 61.54 per cent of respondents belonging to category A are not aware of powers of panchayat raj institutions. Whereas the highest number i.e. 75 per cent, 62.50 per cent and 60.53 per cent belonging to category 'B', 'C' and 'D' are aware of the power of panchayat raj institutions.

Table 7.6: Opinion about Officials' Co-operation in the Working of the PRIs in East Godawari District

		Categories of Backward Caste			
		A	*B*	*C*	*D*
S. No.	*Opinion*	*Frequency*	*Frequency*	*Frequency*	*Frequency*
1.	Yes	12(46.15)	28(70.00)	8(50.00)	21(55.26)
2.	No	14(53.85)	12(30.00)	8(50.00)	17(44.74)
	Total	**26(100.00)**	**40(100.00)**	**16(100.00)**	**38(100.00)**

Source: Compiled from the data collected from field work.

Official's Co-operation in the Working of the PRIs: The Table 7.6 represents the respondents' opinion about official's cooperation in the working of the PRIs.

The table reveals that in East Godawari District the respondents belonging to category 'B' and 'D' are getting cooperation from the official. On the other hand respondents belonging to category 'B' in more number are not getting cooperation from the officials.

Contest of Election: The Table 7.7 represents opinion about contest of election. It is clear from the table that in East Godawari District majority of the respondents are not contesting elections in the PRIs. It is observed that majority of the respondents belonging to the category 'A' are not contesting elections in the PRIs.

Table 7.7: Opinion about Contest of Election in East Godawari District

		Categories of Backward Caste			
		A	*B*	*C*	*D*
S. No.	*Opinion*	*Frequency*	*Frequency*	*Frequency*	*Frequency*
1.	Yes	18(69.23)	30(75.00)	14(87.50)	31(81.58)
2.	No	8(30.77)	10(25.00)	2(12.50)	7(18.4
	Total	**26(100.00)**	**40(100.00)**	**16(100.00)**	**38(100.00)**

Source: Compiled from the data collected from field work.

Causes of Dominant BCs' Election in the PRIs: The Table 7.8 represents the respondents' opinion regarding the question as to why dominant among BCs get elected in the study area.

Table 7.8: Opinion regarding the Question to why Dominant BCs get elected

		Categories of Backward Caste			
		A	*B*	*C*	*D*
S. No.	*Opinion*	*Frequency*	*Frequency*	*Frequency*	*Frequency*
1.	Agricultural Resources	8(30.77)	18(45.00)	7(43.75)	12(31.58)
2.	More Number of Caste	5(19.23)	9(22.50)	3(18.75)	7(18.42)
3.	Higher Social Status	5(19.23)	5(12.50)	3(18.75)	10(26.32)
4.	Party Support	8(30.77)	8(20.00)	3(18.75)	9(23.68)
	Total	**26(100.00)**	**40(100.00)**	**16(100.00)**	**38(100.00)**

Source: Compiled from the data collected from field work

It is observed from the table that in East Godawari District, the majority of the respondents are of the opinion that due to agricultural resources and numerical strength of the caste, the dominant castes among OBCs are being elected. It is found that agricultural resources and numerical strength of the castes and also the social status of the caste within BCs are important factors for occupying positions in the PRIs.

Non-involvement of Weaker Sections in the PRIs: The Table 9 represents the respondents' opinion regarding reasons for the non-involvement of weaker sections in the PRIs. In East Godawari District illiteracy and low economic conditions and dominant of upper castes are the factors, which are preventing the weaker sections in capturing the political power. The majority of respondents from all the categories of BCs are not able to involve in the PRIs due to illiteracy and low economic conditions.

Table 9:Opinion about Reasons for the Non-involvement of Weaker Sections in the PRIs

		Categories of Backward Caste			
		A	*B*	*C*	*D*
S. No.	*Opinion*	*Frequency*	*Frequency*	*Frequency*	*Frequency*
1.	Illiteracy	8(30.77)	17(42.50)	7(43.75)	10(26.32)
2.	Economy	6(23.08)	10(25.00)	3(18.75)	9(23.68)
3.	Dominance of Upper Castes	4(15.38)	6(15.00)	2(12.50)	9(23.68)
4.	Conspiracy of Upper Castes	8(30.77)	7(17.50)	4(25.00)	10(26.32)
	Total	**26(100.00)**	**40(100.00)**	**16(100.00)**	**38(100.00**

Source: Compiled from the data collected from field work.

It is found that the weaker sections are not able to capture political power due to illiteracy, low income, and the dominance of upper castes.

Reservation and Welfare of BCs: The Table 7.10 represents respondents' opinion regarding utility of reservation for the welfare of BCs. In East Godawari District, the respondents belonging to category 'A' have negative opinion and other categories have positive opinion. They expressed that the reservation provision in the PRIs have not achieved its goals. On the other hand, the upper castes within BC's such as the categories of 'B', 'C' and 'D' are of the opinion that the reservation provision are helpful in achieving the welfare of their categories. It observed that in East Godawari District, as far as welfare is concerned, reservation provisions have been helpful for welfare of the categories of 'B', 'C' and 'D' people;

on the other hand, these provisions have not been helpful for welfare of the category 'A'.

Table 7.10: Opinion regarding Reservation and Welfare of BCs

		Categories of Backward Caste			
		A	*B*	*C*	*D*
S. No.	*Opinion*	*Frequency*	*Frequency*	*Frequency*	*Frequency*
1.	Yes	10(38.46)	31(77.5)	10(62.50)	31(81.58)
2.	No	16(61.54)	9(22.5)	6(37.50)	7(18.42)
	Total	**26(100.00)**	**40(100.00)**	**16(100.00)**	**38(100.00)**

Source: Compiled from the data collected from field work.

Involvement in the PRIs and Crimes: The Table 7.11 represents opinion regarding the question whether involvement of BCs in the PRIs lead to crimes.

Table 7.11: Opinion regarding Involvement in the PRIs and Crime

		Categories of Backward Caste			
		A	*B*	*C*	*D*
S. No.	*Opinion*	*Frequency*	*Frequency*	*Frequency*	*Frequency*
1.	Yes	10(38.46)	31(77.5)	10(62.50)	31(81.58)
2.	No	16(61.54)	9(22.5)	6(37.50)	7(18.42)
	Total	**26(100.00)**	**40(100.00)**	**16(100.00)**	**38(100.00)**

Source: Compiled from the data collected from field work.

It is observed that in East Godawari District in Andhra region the respondents belonging to category 'C' are not facing any criminal charges by involving in the working of PRIs. And other category respondents i.e., 61.54 per cent belonging to category 'A', 75.00 per cent belonging to category 'B' and 63.16 per cent belonging to category 'D' are facing the criminal charges.

It is the important finding of the study that in all the regions the majority of respondents belonging to most backward categories are facing the criminal charges. The policy-makers have to think this aspect very seriously.

Political Economy of BCs' Elected Representatives in the PRIs: The Table 7.12 represents respondents' opinion regarding the question whether rich in BC's are able to capture positions in the PRIs. The table reveals that in East Godawari District, majority of the respondents from all the categories are of the opinion that the castes with high economic resources within BCs are capturing positions of power in the PRIs.

Table 7.12: Opinion regarding Influent BC's Political Participation in the PRIs

		Categories of Backward Caste			
		A	*B*	*C*	*D*
S. No.	*Opinion*	*Frequency*	*Frequency*	*Frequency*	*Frequency*
1.	Yes	21(80.77)	29(72.50)	10(62.50)	28(73.68)
2.	No	5(19.23)	11(27.50)	6(37.50)	10(26.32)
	Total	**26(100.00)**	**40(100.00)**	**16(100.00)**	**38(100.00)**

Source: Compiled from the data collected from field work.

It is found that in the study area, the positions such as ward member, presidents, MPTC, ZPTC and chairpersons from Mandal and Zilla Panchayats under reserved categories for BCs are captured and controlled by rich people within BCs. Though there are reservation provisions for BCs, economically poor people within BCs are not able to enter in the PRIs.

Conclusion

Based on the findings of the study, it is observed by the researcher that the 73rd Constitutional Amendments have caused BCs' involvement in the democratically decentralised PRIs. But the reservation provisions in these institutions have adversely affected some of the BCs. In a faction prone district like East Godawari, people belonging to lower castes within BCs have suffered economically; lost their lives and belongings due to rivalries within blood relations and are facing criminal cases. The positions such as, ward member, presidents, MPTC, ZPTC and chairpersons of Mandal and Zilla Panchayats, reserved for BCs, are captured and controlled by rich, dominant and higher status people within BCs. Despite reservation provisions, economically poor people among BCs are not able to enter in the PRIs.

References

Singh, S. N. *Reservation Policy for Backward Classes*, Rawat Publications, Jaipur, New Delhi, 1996, p. 28.

Rajesh Kumar, "Political Empowerment of Weaker Sections: A Study of Municipal Bodies in Haryana", *Indian Journal of Political Science*, Vol. LXII, No. 3 July-Sep., 2006, p. 457.

Syamala Devi D. and Lakshmi. G. "Political Empowerment of Women in Indian Legislature: A Study", *Indian Journal of Political Science*, Vol. LXVI, No.1, Jan-March 2005, p.77.

Bajpai, Ashok and M. S. Verma. *Panchayati Raj in India: A New Thrust*, Sahitya Prakashan: Delhi, 1995, pp. 47-48.

GOI. The 73rd Constitutional Amendment Act, Government of India, 1992, pp. 148.

ODI. *Caste, Class and Social Articulation in Andhra Pradesh*, India: Mapping Differential Regional Trajectories, Overseas Development Institute, 01-Nov-2002, p. 27.

Singhi, N. K. *Bureaucracy: Positions and Persons*, Abhinav Publications: New Delhi, 1974, p. 55.

Puri, Sashilata. *Legislative Elite in an Indian State: A Case Study of Rajasthan*, Publications: New Delhi, 1978, p. 31.

Parry, Geraint. *Political Elites*, London: George Allen and Unwin Ltd., 1969, p. 264.

Saxena, Kiran. *Women and Politics*, Gyan Publishing House: New Delhi, 2000, p. 8.

8

Democratic Decentralisation and Religious Minorities: A Case Study of West Bengal

—*Sk. Abdul Matin*

Introduction

Democratic decentralisation, *Panchayati-Raj* institution, local self-government etc. play a very important role in the deepening of democracy especially in a highly unequal society like that of India. Democratic decentralisation is not only about people's participation at all the levels of governance from decision-making to implementation but also the all-round development of the citizens in general and the deprived or marginalised sections in particular.

Reorganisation of the system of local government was one of the most important institutional changes brought about by the Left Front government in West Bengal.[1] In the process, West Bengal has created a history of participation of the common people through the process of decentralisation, which is unique in India. A system of democratic elections to local bodies at block and district level was instituted: *gram panchayats* at the village level, *panchayat samitis* at the block level and *zilla parishads* at the district level.

West Bengal is the only State in India to have had regular elections to local bodies every five years for the past 30 years. The aim has been to provide a substantial share of fiscal resources of the state to the local bodies. West Bengal was the first state in the country to make a serious effort at devolving funds from the state government level to the lower tiers of administration. The *panchayats* have also been assigned a large and substantial range of responsibilities that were earlier seen as under the purview of the district-level bureaucracy. The *panchayats* perform civic duties and undertake developmental activities like construction and maintenance of hospitals, schools and libraries; promotion of agriculture, cooperatives and cottage industries; child welfare activities etc. They play an important role in the local-level planning and implementation of government schemes. *Panchayats* in West Bengal have played an important role in activities like mobilising cooperation for improving agricultural production, management of local resources, and identification of beneficiaries for housing, poverty alleviation and social security programmes. This has made the *panchayats* a critical institution of local governance in the West Bengal countryside.[2]

Muslims constitute the second largest religious community and single largest minority community in West Bengal, comprising more than 27 per cent of the total population. The Muslim population is scattered almost all over West Bengal but is mostly concentrated in the districts of Murshidabad, Maldah, Birbhum, Nadia, North Dinajpur, South 24 Parganas, North 24 Parganas, Coochbehar, Burdwan, East Medinipur, Bankura, Hooghly, Howrah, Kolkata etc. Out of the nineteen districts in West Bengal, twelve fall under the list of Muslim Concentrated Districts as notified by the Government of India and the socio-economic status of Muslims there is well below the national average.[3]

Right from the Dr Gopal Singh Committee to the recent Sachar Committee (a Prime Minister's High Level Committee) constituted to enquire into the socio-economic and educational status of Muslims in India, Muslims have been found to be the most under-developed and under-represented among all religious communities in India, in terms of social, economic, educational and political development. The condition of the Muslim community in India is more abject than that of the presently notified backward classes.[4]

In the case of West Bengal, the scenario is worse with the Bengali Muslim community falling below the national average for Muslims in the socio-economic, educational and political contexts. In the aftermath of the publication of the Sachar Committee Report in 2006, several Muslim organisations came into existence in West Bengal, which started questioning the CPI(M)-led Left Front government that had been ruling the state for more than three decades.

Bengali Muslims have a unique history and legacy due to double partitions- one in 1905 (the partition of Bengal) and another in 1947 (the creation of East Pakistan under the Two Nation theory)- which has affected the community in terms of economy, politics, culture and leadership.[5] Unlike many others states where Muslims mostly reside in urban pockets, around 80 per cent of the Muslims of West Bengal are concentrated in rural areas and engaged in agriculture. As Richard Eaton has rightly pointed out, Islam in Bengal is the religion of the plough.[6]

In my paper I would like to raise three important issues. First, why is it that even after three decades of democratic decentralisation in West Bengal the rural poverty of Muslims is 33 per cent, which is the fourth highest in India? Second, is there any significant role played by the Panchayati Raj institutions in West Bengal toward the socio-economic development of Muslims? Third, what is the contribution of Left parties, the champion of democratic decentralisation, in the development of the Muslim community in West Bengal?

Panchayati Raj Institution in West Bengal

The PRI plays an important role in West Bengal because more than seventy per cent of the people in West Bengal reside in rural areas which come under the purview of Panchayat. The West Bengal Panchayat Act was enacted in 1956 and it was subsequently modified to form the West Bengal Zilla Parishad Act which came into existence in 1963. This Act provided for a four-tier structure consisting of Zilla Parishad, Anchalik Parishad, Anchal Panchayat and Gram Panchayat. This Act was further modified in 1973 and a consolidated legislation called "West Bengal Panchayat Act" was enacted. This Act provided for a three-tier Panchayati Raj system as in the case with other states along the lines of the national model: Zilla Parishad at the district level, Panchayat Samity at the block level and Gram Panchayat at the village level. The Act provided for a direct election to each tier of PR system i.e. Zilla Parishad, Panchayat Samity and Gram Panchayat.

The elections to the Panchayat bodies on party lines were first held in 1978 one year after the Left Front government came to power in West Bengal.[7] In pursuance of the 73rd Constitutional Amendment, West Bengal Panchayat Act was further amended in 1992 in order to provide reservation to women for not less than one-third of the total seats. Presently women's reservation has further gone up to 50 per cent of the total seats. West Bengal has 17 Zilla Parishads, 332 Panchayat Samities and 3343

Gram Panchayats. The PR bodies provide 664 seats for Zilla Parishad, 9516 seats for Panchayat Samities and 61,396 seats for Gram Panchayats.[8]

The PRI undertakes a wide range of activities in the state such as healthcare, irrigation, small scale industries, cottage industries, roads, culverts, non-farming activities, community development initiatives, education etc.

Muslims in West Bengal

As stated earlier, Muslims make up more than 25.2 of the total population of West Bengal. There are more than 88 Blocks in West Bengal where Muslim population is between 40 to 50 per cent and there are more than 28 Blocks where the population of Muslims is beyond 60 per cent of the total population.[9] Government of India has identified 90 minority concentrated districts in India based on the substantial minority population and socio-economic underdevelopment. Out of 19 districts in West Bengal, 12 falls under the minority a concentrated district to address the development deficit of minority concentrated areas by creating socio-economic infrastructure and providing basic necessities.

Table 8.1: District-wise Muslim Population in West Bengal

Sl. No.	*District Name*	*Total Population*	*Total Muslim Population*	*Percentage of Muslim Population*
1.	Murshidabad	5866569	3735380	63.67
2.	Malda	3290468	1636171	49.72
3.	Uttar Dinajpur	2441794	1156503	48.18
4.	Birbhum	3015422	1057861	35.18
5.	South 24 Parganas	6906689	2295967	34.07
6.	Dakshin Dinajpur	1503178	361046	28.02
7.	Nadia	4604827	1170282	25.41
8.	Howrah	4273099	1044313	24.44
9.	Cooch Behar	2479155	600911	24.24
10.	North 24 Parganas	8934286	2164058	24.22
11.	Kolkata	4572876	926769	20.27
12.	Burdwan	6895514	1364133	19.78
13.	Hooghly	5041976	76347	15.14
14.	Purba Medinipur	4098181	540490	13.19
15.	Jalpaiguri	3401173	369195	10.85
16.	Paschim Medinipur	4086264	443352	09.46
17.	Bankura	3192695	239722	07.51
18.	Purulia	2536516	180694	07.12
19.	Darjeeling	1503178	85378	05.31

Source: Census of India, 2001.

Socio-economic Status of Muslims in West Bengal

The socio-economic condition of Muslims in West Bengal is abysmally poor even after the 34 years of Left rule in the state. The rate of poverty (both urban and rural), unemployment, malnutrition, child mortality, illiteracy, school drop-out rates etc. are extremely high among the Muslims of West Bengal. The representation of Muslims in government employment, education, bureaucracy, judiciary, executive, legislative etc. is very low and grossly out of proportion with the community's population figures in the state.

Mohd Sanjeer Alam argues that in West Bengal the condition of Bengali Muslims is very poor in spite of huge population and sharing the same language, food habit, life style etc with the non-Muslim majority. But he further mentions that the large size of minority population is linked to underdevelopment. He has undertaken a field study of various districts like Birbhum, 24 Parganas South and North, Hooghly, Nadia etc. where majority of the Muslim-concentrated villages do not have proper schools, post offices, banks, health centres or electricity etc.[10]

Educational status

Education is pivotal to the development of any society. The literacy rate is considered one of the most important indicators of social development and help in the improvement of the quality of life. The literacy rate among the Muslims in West Bengal is abysmally low and dropout rates very high. The state of higher education is much more vulnerable, with the representation of Muslims in higher education, either as students or staff, being almost negligible. As far as literacy rate of female is concern it is absolutely dismal.

Table 8.2: Literacy Rates among the Various Religious Communities in West Bengal

Religious Communities	*Persons*	*Male*	*Female*
All Religions	68.64	77.02	51.61
Hindus	72.44	81.12	63.09
Muslims	57.47	64.61	49.75
Christians	69.72	77.20	62.30
Sikhs	87.19	91.37	81.98
Buddhists	74.73	83.09	66.22
Jains	92.81	96.46	88.87
Others	51.53	68.63	34.24
Religion not stated	-	71.52	54.84

Source: Census of India, 2001, Government of India.

Table 8.3: Educational Level Differentials in West Bengal, 2001 and 2007-8

	Muslim		*SCs/STs*		*Others*	
	2007-08	*2001*	*2007-08*	*2001*	*2007-08*	*2001*
Matriculation & above	15	12	17	13	39	38
Middle	50	26	52	30	62	58
Primary	85	50	90	54	93	80

Source: (i) Estimated by Dr Abusaleh Shariff from the unit level records of the 64th Round NSSO (ii) Census of India 2001.

Economic Status

The economic condition of Muslims in West Bengal is extremely poor. The poverty rate as well as unemployment and underemployment rate among Bengali Muslims is quite alarming. According to the Sachar Committee Report, the rural poverty rate of Muslims in West Bengal is 33 per cent, which is higher than the corresponding rates in Kerala, Assam, Karnataka, Maharashtra, Andhra Pradesh etc. Per capita income, consumption and standard of living among Muslims are quite low as compared to other backward communities.

The work participation rates among Muslims in West Bengal are lower than the national average. Many people migrate out of the state in search of jobs, especially to Hyderabad, Kerala, Delhi, Mumbai, Gujarat etc. In terms of sectoral employment, the share of Muslims in wage-earning employment in manufacturing and industrial enterprises is relatively higher than Hindus but the long-term trend shows reduction in total employment due to closure and modernisation of industry. Most of the labour force in the state is self-employed. A staggering 55 per cent of the state's Muslims fall into this category with almost no links to modern markets.[11]

The situation of Muslims in State government employment is worse, with only 2.1 per cent of Muslims being State government employees. Rural poverty among the Muslims in West Bengal is very high in comparison to other states as well as the national average.

Table 8.4: Share of Muslims in State Government Employment

States	*Muslim population (per cent)*	*Total Number of Employees*	*Share of Muslims in State Employment (per cent)*	*Education Department*	*Health Women and Child Welfare Dept.*	*Home Department*	*Transport Dept.*	*Other Dept.*
West Bengal	25.2	134972	2.1	-	1.0	7.1	-	2.4
Kerala	24.7	268733	10.4	12.3	10.5	10.7	9.2	10.2
Uttar Pradesh	18.5	134053	5.1	-	5.6	9.8	4.2	5.0
Bihar	16.5	78114	7.6	12.3	2.6	6.9	10.9	7.6
Assam	30.9	81261	11.2	-	10.8	11.3	11.8	11.7
Jharkhand	13.8	15374	6.7	-	3.4	7.4	-	7.0
Karnataka	12.2	528401	8.5	11.9	5.0	4.2	7.5	7.0
Delhi	11.7	135877	3.2	7.2	1.7	2.2	1.1	0.9
Maharashtra	10.6	915643	4.4	4.7	2.8	4.2	-	3.8
Andhra Pradesh*	9.2	876291	8.8	7.9	6.4	14.6	10.0	8.9
Gujarat	9.1	754533	5.4	4.5	1.5	5.6	16.3	5.3
Tamil Nadu	5.6	529597	3.2	5.5	3.5	2.5	2.4	2.2
Sum of States	15.4	4452851	6.3	6.5	4.4	7.3	6.5	6.0

*Does not provided for group ABCD employees, only Total Employees and Muslim employees is provided.

Source: Sachar Committee Report p. 370, Government of India.

Table 8.5: Rural Poverty among the Indian States

State	*All*	*Hindu All*	*Hindu SC/STs*	*Hindu OBC*	*Hindu General*	*Muslims Muslims*	*Other Minority*
India	22.7	22.6	34.8	19.5	9.0	26.9	14.3
West Bengal	25	21	27	16	14	33	N. A
Kerala	9	9	19	7	4	11	4
Uttar Pradesh	28	28	39	26	10	33	40
Bihar	35	34	56	29	13	35	33
Assam	18	12	14	16	7	27	20
Karnataka	14	14	21	14	7	18	N. A
Andhra Pradesh	8	8	16	6	2	7	4
Tamil Nadu	17	17	23	14	14	10	18
Gujarat	14	15	24	14	3	7	6
Madhya Pradesh	30	31	45	22	6	25	2
Punjab	6	4	4	7	3	4	6

Source: Sachar Committee Report, 2006, GoI.

Health and Nutritional Status

Health and nutritional status are the two important and interlinked aspects of human development which also plays crucial role in the economic growth.[12] As far as health and nutritional condition of Muslims are concern the situation is very alarming both at the all India level as well as state level. As Sachar Committee observed that the Muslim child experiences a greater risk of being underweight or stunned than a child belonging to other socio-religious communities and Muslim children are at a slightly higher risk of child malnutrition than 'other Hindu' children.[13] The highest number of Infant Mortality Rate (IMR), malnutrition, underweight, under nutrition, chronic diseases etc are found mostly among SCs followed by STs and Muslims in the state of West Bengal.[14]

The public health system in West Bengal in general is poor and especially at the Muslims and Scheduled Castes concentrated areas. The primary health system specially at the rural areas where majority of Muslims and other marginalised communities lives are not functions properly due to lack of funds, unavailability of doctors, nurses, medicine and other necessary apparatus.[15]

For examples, the situation of rural public health system is extremely poor in most of districts such as Murshidabad, Malda, Dinajpur, South and North 24 Parganas, Nadia, Birbhum, East Medinipur, Purulia etc where majority of the population belongs to Muslims, Dalits and Adivasi community. It is not possible for the poor Muslims or Dalits/Adivasi to get treatment from private clinic because of huge expenditure. One has to travel more than hundreds kilometer from South Bengal districts and more than 300 kilometers for non-southern districts to get better treatment in Kolkata, because almost all the important public hospital such as Chittaranjan Hospital, SSKM, Nilratan Sarkar Hospital etc are located in the city of Kolkata.

Representation of Muslims in Panchayati Raj Institution in West Bengal

West Bengal has created a history of participation of the common people through the process of decentralisation, which is unique in India. It is the only state in India to have had regular elections to local bodies every five years for the past 34 years. The aim has been to provide a share of the fiscal resources of the state to the local bodies, and the panchayats (at various levels) have also been assigned a large and substantial range of responsibilities, that were earlier seen as being under the purview of the district-level bureaucracy. In addition, the composition of the panchayats has reflected the caste, class, occupation and gender composition of local society, (even if not completely) more faithfully than panchayats anywhere else in the country. There has been substantial representation of the rural poor and of socially deprived groups, as well as women, in the elected bodies. All this has helped to change the power equations in rural society as well as encouraged the social and political empowerment of women and social groups that were earlier marginalised.[16]

There is no data available categorically for Muslim representation in the PRI elections, although careful analysis of the election results reveals that at the Gram Panchayat level the representation of Muslims, SCs, STs etc. is quite substantial but decreases considerably when it comes to Panchayat Samity and Zilla Parishad levels. It is found that at the policy-making level the representation of Muslims is quite low whether it is Panchayat Samity or Zilla Parishad.

The total number of Sabhadhipatis (President of Zilla Parishad) and Saha-Sabhadhipatis (Vice-President of Zilla Parishad) is 34 and out of that only six belong to the Muslim community, whereas it is supposed to be 10 for the figure to be in proportion with the community's population.

Role of PRI and Development of Muslims in West Bengal

Apart from political participation and decentralised governance, PRI is supposed to play an important role in the socio-economic development of the people in general and various marginalised communities in particular. Therefore an all-round holistic developmental approach is an important feature of a decentralised government or PRI.

The Human Development Index Report of West Bengal published in 2004 clearly pointed out the material and socio-economic condition of Muslims in the state. The highest rates of illiteracy, malnutrition, under-nutrition, child mortality etc. are found in the districts of Malda, Murshidabad, Birbhum, Dinajpur, South 24 Parganas etc. which are Muslim-concentrated districts.

There are various reports and findings which show that the funds allocated for Minority Development under various schemes of the Government of India are utilised in the non-minority concentrated villages or areas. There had been no targeted policy initiated by the PRI in West Bengal for the Minority community, before the Sachar Committee recommendations came out.[17] The participation of Muslims in various livelihood schemes such as MGNREGA, SGSY, SJSRY etc. are very low in West Bengal compared to other social or religious groups. There are instances where the village health centre, schools, skills-development centre, proper roads under PMGRY etc. were set up in non-minority dominated village or blocks to the disadvantage of the Minority community.

Conclusion

In spite of the three-tier Panchayati System, the historical land reforms programme or Operation Barga (which directly and indirectly helped deprived communities) and three decades of Left rule in the state (which makes it the longest-serving elected government in the world), the condition of various marginalised communities in West Bengal such as Muslims, Tribals, SCs etc. is below par in all walks of life. The Panchayati raj has made very insignificant impact on the development of Muslims in West Bengal. There has been a serious malfunctioning in the PRI in West Bengal which needs to be investigated further very carefully in order to understand the loopholes in the system. There were no such targeted schemes or programme for the welfare of minority community until Sachar Committee Report in 2006. Whatever little development schemes are being implemented for the welfare of minority are the impact of Sachar Committee report and large scale Muslim mobilisation to overcome the 'development deficit' in the post-Sachar scenario. This very same issue of minority mobilisation against the incumbent Left Front government was also an important factor that led to the downfall of the CPI (M)- led Left Front government in the 2011 State Assembly election.

References

Banerjee, Partha Sarathi, 'The Party and the Panchayats of West Bengal', *Economic and Political Weekly*, June 14, 2008, pp.17-19.

Banerjee, Sumanta, 'West Bengal's Next Quinquennium, and the Future of the Indian Left', *Economic and Political Weekly*, June 4, 2011, Vol. XLVI. No. 23.

Bardhan, Pranab, Sandip Mitra, Dilip Mookherjee, Abhirup Sarkar, 'Local Democracy and Clientelism: Implications for Political Stability in Rural West Bengal', *Economic and Political Weekly*, February 28, 2009, Vol. XLIV, No. 9.

Basu, Dipankar, 'The Left and the 15th Lok Sabha Election' *Economic and Political Weekly,* May 30, 2009, pp.10-15.

Basu, Amrita, 'Parliamentary Communism as a Historical Phenomenon: The CPI(M) in West Bengal' in *"Party and Party Politics in India"* edited by Zoya Hasan, OUP, 2002.

Bhattacharya, Dipankar, 'For a Left Resurgence', *Economic and Political Weekly*, November 19, 2011, Vol. XLVI, No. 47.

Bhattacharya, Dwaipayan, " Party Society, its consolidation and crisis: Understanding political change in West Bengal", in *Theorizing the Present: Essays for Partha Chtterjee,* edited by Anjan Ghosh, Tapati Guha-Thakurta and Janaki Nair, OUP, 2011.

Bhattacharya, Dwaipayan, "Left in the Lurch: The Demise of the World's Longest Elected Regime?" *Economic and Political Weekly*, January 16, 2010, Vol. XLV, No. 3.

Bhattacharya, Dwaipayan, "Making and Unmaking of Trinamool Congress", *Economic and Political Weekly*, April 3-10, 2004, pp.1529-1537.

Bhattacharya, Dwaipayan, "Of Control and Faction: The Changing 'Party-Society' in Rural West Bengal" *Economic and Political Weekly*, February 28, 2009, Vol. XLIV, No. 9.

Bhattacharya, Dwaipayan, 'West Bengal: Permanent Incumbency and Political Stability', *Economic and Political Weekly*, December 18, 2004, pp.5477-5483.

Bhattacharya, Dwaipayan and Kumar Rana, "Politics of PDS Anger in West Bengal", *Economic and Political Weekly*, February 2, 2008, pp. 63-69.

Bhattacharya, Dwaipayan, "Politics of Middleness: The Changing character of the CPIM in Rural West Bengal (1977-90)" in Ben Royal, Barbara Harris-White and Sugato Bose (ed) *Sonar Bangla? Agricultural Growth and the Agrarian Change in West Bengal and Bangladesh*. Sage Publications, New Delhi, 1999.

Chakrabarty, Bidyut, 'The Left Front's 2009 Lok Sabha Poll Debate in West Bengal, India: Prospective Causes and Future Implications', *Asian Survey*, Vol. 51, No. 2 (March/April 2011), pp. 290-310.

Chakrabarty, Bidyut, 'The 2011 State Assembly Election in West Bengal: The Left Front Washed Out!', *Journal of South Asian Development*, 2011 6:143.

Chatterjee, Partha, *The Present History of West Bengal: Essays in Political Criticism*, OUP New Delhi, 1997.

Chatterjee, Jyotiprasad and Suprio Basu, 'West Bengal: Mandate for change' *Economic and Political Weekly*, September 26, 2009.

Chatterji, Joya, 'Bengal divided: Hindu Communalism and Partition 1932-1947', Cambridge University Press, 1994.

Costa, Dia Da, 'Tension of Neo-liberal development: State discourse and democratic opposition in West Bengal',*Contributions to Indian Sociology*, 2007, 41:287.

Dasgupta, Avhijit, "On the Margins: Muslims in West Bengal", *Economic and Political Weekly*, April 18, 2009.

Dasgupta, Rajarshi, "The CPI (M) Machinery in West Bengal: Two Village Narratives from Kochbehar and Malda", *Economic and Political Weekly*, February 28, 2009.

Desai, Manali, 'Party formation, Political Power and the Capacity for Reform: Comparing Left Parties in Kerala and West Bengal', *Social Forces*, Vol.80, No.1 (September, 2001), pp. 37-60.

Eaton, Richard M, 'Rise of Islam and the Bengal Frontier, 1204-1760', Berkeley; University of California, 1993.

Franda, Marcus, 'Radical Politics in West Bengal' The M. I. T Press, 1971.

Ghosh, Buddahadeb, 'The Subaltern and Politics at the Grassroots', *Economic and Political Weekly*, August 9, 2008.

Guha Roy, Samir and Kasturi Sen, 'Patterns of Healthcare Utilisation and expenditure: A household survey in an Indian state, West Bengal, 1999', Indian Statistical Institute, Kolkata, 2002.

Gupta, Monobina, 'Left Politics in Bengal: Time Travels among Bhadrolok Marxists', Orient Blackswan, Hyderabad, 2010.

Hasan, Zoya, *Politics of Inclusion: Castes, Minorities and Affirmative Action*, Oxford University Press, New Delhi, 2009, Second Impression.

Hussain Nazmul, 'Muslims of West Bengal: An Analysis of the Educational Status of a Minority Community in India', *Journal of Muslim Minority Affairs*, 29:2, pp. 249-260.

Kohli, Atul, 'The State and Poverty in India: The Politics of Reform', Cambridge University Press, 2006.

Majumdar, Manabi, 'Democracy in Praxis: Two Non-Left Gram Panchayats in West Bengal', *Economic and Political Weekly*, February 28, 2009, Vol. XLIV, No. 9.

Neilson, Kenneth Bo, 'In Search of Development: Muslims and Electoral Politics in Indian state', *Forum for Development Studies,* 38:3, pp. 345-370.

Neilson, Kenneth Bo, 'Four Narratives of a Social Movement irl West Bengal', *Journal of South Asian Studies,* 32:3, pp. 448-468.

Nigam, Aditya, 'How the Sickle Slashed the Left', *Tehelka*, May 30, 2009.

Osgood Field John and Marcus Franda (Ed), *Electoral Politics in the Indian states: The Communist Parties of West Bengal,* Manohar Book Service, New Delhi, 1974.

Raychaudhuri, Diptendra, 'Understanding CPI (M): Will the Indian Left Survive?, Vitasta Publishing Pvt Ltd, New Delhi, 2010.

Roy, Dayabati and Parthasarathi Banerjee, 'Left Front's Electoral Victory in West Bengal: An Ethnographer's Account', *Economic and Political Weekly.*

Roglay, Ben, Barbara Harris-White and Sugata Bose, eds. *Sonar Bangla? Agricultural growth and agrarian change in West Bengal and Bangladesh,* Sage, New Delhi, 1999.

Ruud, Arild Engelsen, 'Talking dirty about politics: a view from a Bengali village', V. Benei and C. Fuller, Eds. *The Everyday state and society in India,* Social Science Press, New Delhi, 2000.

Ruud, Arild Engelsen, 'The Indian hierarchy: culture, ideology and consciousness in Bengali village politics', *Modern Asian Studies* 33, 3 (pp. 689-732).

Rudd, Arild Engelsen, *Poetics of Village Politics: The Making of West Bengal Rural Communism,* Oxford University Press, New Delhi.

Yadav, Yogendra, 'How West Bengal Voted', *The Hindu*, May 16, 2011.

Documents, Reports, Resolutions, Manifestos etc

Human Development Index Report, Government of West Bengal, 2004, Kolkata.

Sachar Committee Report, Prime Minister's High Level Committee, Social, Economic and Educational Status of the Muslim Community of India, Government of India, New Delhi, 2006.

Statistical report on the General Election of the West Bengal Legislative Assembly, 2006 and 2011, Election Commission of India.

Ranganath Mishra Commission Report, 2007.

"Promises to Keep: *Investigating Government Responses to Sachar Committee Recommendations*" A report prepared by Centre for Equity Studies under the supervision of Harsh Mander, 2011.

Communist Party of India (Marxist) Review of the 15th Lok Sabha Elections adopted by the Central Committee meeting held on June 20 and 21, 2009.

Notes

1. Report published by the Government of West Bengal after completion of 30 years of their government.
2. Report published by the Ministry of Minority Affairs, Government of India, in 2008.

3. See Sachar Committee Report, the Prime Minister's High Level Committee to enquire the Social, Educational and Economic Status of Muslims in India, published in 2006.
4. See Zoya Chatterji, 'Bengal Divided: Hindu Communalism and Partition, 1932-1947'.
5. See Richard Eaton, The Rise of Islam and the Bengal Frontier 1206-1760.
6. A Study on Health through Panchayats in West Bengal by Institute of Social Studies Trust, New Delhi, p. 3.
7. Report of the West Bengal State Election Commission, Kolkata.
8. Census of India, 2001.
9. Mohd Sanjeer Alam, 'Is Relative Size of Minority Population linked to Underdevelopment', *Economic and Political Weekly*, November 28, 2009, Vol. XLIVI, No. 48, pp. 17-21.
10. Abusaleh Shariff, *India Today*, 2009.
11. Human Development Report, West Bengal 2004.
12. See Sachar Committee Report, pp. 43-44.
13. HDI Report West Bengal 2004.
14. Guha Roy, Samir and Kasturi Sen (2002); 'Patterns of Healthcare Utilization and expenditure: A household survey in an Indian state, West Bengal, 1999, Indian Statistical Institute, Kolkata.
15. Human Development Index Report of West Bengal, 2004, Government of West Bengal.
16. 'Promises to Keep: Investigating Government Response to Sachar Committee Recommendation' a report prepared by the Centre for Equity Studies, New Delhi, under the guidance of Harsh Mander.

9

Empowerment of Women through Reservations in Panchayati Raj Institutions: An Analysis

—*Shriram Yerankar*

Introduction

The 73rd Constitutional Amendment Act passed by Parliament in December 1992 and enacted in 1993 was a historic act since it institutionalised decentralisation and grass-root political participation and empowerment, thus seeking to deepen democratic polity. In the context of socially and politically disadvantaged groups, the Act assumes special importance as it sought to empower these groups, viz. Scheduled Castes, Scheduled Tribes and Women. The Act has been hailed by many as the most significant measure for encouraging the participation of women in political processes and leadership formation.

India has a long tradition of Gram Panchayats but the institution has had a fairly chequered development in the post-independence period. The continued and continuing evolution of the role and function of the Panchayati Raj Institution reflects the pursuit of political goals and values by the government of the day. Closely intertwined with this is also the changing perception of the role of women in the Indian polity. Through the Panchayati Raj Institutions it is possible to trace the path of women's political empowerment and the attempt to redress gender injustices.

The main issues dealt with in this paper are evolution and growth of Panchayati Raj System in India, implications of 73rd Constitutional

Amendment Act, women's representation in Panchayati Raj Institutions and to trace the obstacles to women's empowerment through PRIs.

Evolution and Growth of Panchayati Raj System in India

The Rig Veda, one of India's oldest sacred books and historical source mentions about the existence of village communities across the sub-continent that were self-governing and serving as the main interface between the predominantly agrarian village economies and their higher authorities. Such councils or assemblies called "sabhas" slowly assumed the form of the "Panchayat" (an assembly of five respected elders). These panchayats in north and south India became the pivot of administration, the focus of social solidarity and the principal forum for the dispensation of justice and resolution of local disputes. During the medieval and Mughal periods these characteristics of the village panchayats remained unchanged.

In 1870, Lord Mayo, Governor General-in-Council secured the passage of a resolution for the decentralisation of power aimed at bringing about greater administrative efficiency in meeting the demands of the people but primarily designed to augment imperial finances. At about the same time, a significant first step towards reviving the traditional village panchayat system in Bengal was taken through the Bengal Chowkidari Act, 1870, which empowered District Magistrates to set up Panchayats of nominated members in the villages. The Ripon Resolution of 1882 provided for rural local boards with two-thirds of membership to be composed of elected, non-official representatives and presided over by a non-official chairperson. Actual progress in implementation was slow but the role of rural local administration was elevated and the term "self-government" gained currency. In 1907, the government constituted a six-member Royal Commission on Decentralisation with Shri Ramesh Chandra Dutt as the only Indian member. The Report of the Royal Commission on Decentralisation, released in 1909, elaborated the principles enunciated in the Ripon Resolution and recognised the importance of Panchayats in the governance of India. The Montagu-Chelmsford Reforms of 1919 brought local self-government under the domain of Indian Ministers in the provinces. To make local self-government both fully representative and responsible, the Montagu-Chelmsford reforms suggested that there should be, as far as possible, complete popular control in local bodies and the largest possible independence for them from outside control. The Government of India Act, 1935 and the inauguration of provincial autonomy under it marked another crucial stage in the evolution of Panchayats. With popularly elected governments in the Provinces, almost all provincial administrations enacted legislation for further democratisation of local self-government institutions, including the village Panchayats.

India has a long tradition of village Panchayats but the institution has had a fairly chequered development in the post-Independence period, coinciding with national and international imperatives. Although the issue of establishing panchayats was hotly debated in the Constituent Assembly, it did not find a mention in the Draft Constitution. Its advocates, however, eventually succeeded in inserting Article 40 that was finally included in the chapter of Directive Principles of State Policy. It declares that "The state shall take steps to organise village panchayats and endow them with such power and authority as may be necessary to enable them to function as units of self-government." (Kashyap, 2011:352). The Lukewarm response to creating Panchayati Raj Institutions at the time can be traced to the anxiety over creating a stable and united India. Hence the emphasis at the time, given the experience of partition, was on creating a strong centre even while adopting a federal parliamentary structure.

Consequently, nothing was actively undertaken by the government to promote decentralisation till the early 1950s in the context of Community Development Programme for improving economic and social conditions in rural areas and increasing agricultural production. These programmes were not delivering consequently, the Balwantrai Mehta Committee was set up by the Planning Commission in 1957 to study this issue. The Committee in its report recommended that " Public participation in community works should be organised through statutory representative bodies" since community development can only be real when the community understands its problems, realises its responsibilities, exercises the necessary powers through its chosen representatives and maintains a constant and intelligent vigilance on local administration. (Mathur, 2006:126).

The report further proposed the co-option of two women interested in working amongst women and children at the village Panchayat and samiti levels of the three tier system recommended by it. Subsequently, the National Development Council endorsed the basic principles of democratic decentralisation enunciated in the Balwantrai Mehta report and laid on States the duty of working out the structures suitable to each state. It was during this period that the term "Panchayati Raj" gained currency as a process of governance. In 1959, Prime Minister Jawaharlal Nehru inaugurated Panchayati Raj on 2 October, 1959, at Nagaur in

Rajasthan. By the mid-60s, Panchayats had been established in several States all over India in accordance with local state legislations. However, these were differently empowered by these legislations. Women were not given any special representation through reservation in Panchayat bodies. Elections to these bodies were not held regularly and state governments often superseded them prematurely and placed them under administrators.

However, politics continued to be a male domain with women still excluded from decision-making, and women's representation in the Panchayats being at best a token presence. In 1971, in response to the UN initiative, the Government of India set up a committee on the Status of Women in India (CSWI), which submitted its report Towards Equality: Report of the Committee on the status of women in India in 1975. With regard to Panchayati Raj and rural development, the report highlighted the fact that although women contributed substantively to the rural economy, yet their role and contribution went unacknowledged and development plans and policies were not informed by their perspectives. The CSWI also questioned the principle of co-option, alleging that this would create patronage by dominant social and political groups ensuring the perpetuation of gender, caste and class inequalities to the detriment of the empowerment of women and of social transformation. The CSWI, therefore, strongly recommended the setting up of autonomous statutory women's panchayats at the local level linked to Panchayati Raj Institutions and with sufficient resources for pursuing development programmes (Sharma, 1998:31). It further pointed out, "Women's ability to produce an impact on the political process has been negligible because of the inadequate attention paid to their political process has been negligible because of the inadequate attention paid to their political education and mobilisation by both political parties and women's organisations" and went on to add that, "rights guaranteed by the Constitution have helped to build an illusion of equality and power, which is frequently used as an argument to resist special protective and accelerating measures to enable women to achieve their just and equal position in society." This was further underlined by the remark that, "though women constituted a numerical majority, they were acquiring the features of a minority group because of inequality of status and political power." The report recommended broadening the political elite structure through the inclusion of women (Sharma, 1998:27).

However, the institution of Panchayati Raj stagnated from the mid-sixties to the late seventies due to various anomalies such as irregular elections, excessive bureaucratic control, lack of political will and financial resources etc. The Janata Government appointed the Ashok Mehta Committee in 1977 to review the Panchayati Raj Institutions and to suggest measures to strengthen them. In its report submitted in 1978, the committee recommended a two tier Zilla Parishad and mandal panchayat with elections fought by political parties but it did not go into the issues of women's representation raised by the CSWI. In keeping with the spirit of the Ashok Mehta Committee recommendations, some States including West Bengal, Karnataka and Andhra Pradesh revisited their respective Panchayati Raj systems and undertook several new initiatives to endow local bodies with more powers. In 1985, in the wake of Ashok Mehta Committee's recommendations, Karnataka became the first State to introduce reservation for women in the PRIs even before the enactment of the 73rd Amendment. The Act of 1985 provided for 25 per cent reservation for women at the district and mandal panchayat levels. West Bengal and Andhra Pradesh were the other two states where reservation for women in PRIs existed prior to the enactment of the 73rd Amendment. In 1988, the National Perspective Plan for Women addressed the issue of political participation and under-representation of women at all levels and keeping in mind the experiences of the States that had introduced reservation for women in panchayats, they recommended "30 per cent reservation for women in local bodies with a higher representation of dalits/tribals and women of weaker sections" (Sharma, 1998:27).

73rd Constitutional Amendment Act and its Implications

In May 1989, the Union Government introduced the Constitution (64th Amendment) Bill, which proposed constitutionally-sanctioned Panchayati Raj. Although both the 64th and 65th amendments (the latter dealing with Nagarpalikas) Bills received the required two-thirds majority with at least half the members present and voting in the Lok Sabah on 13 October 1989, the Bills failed by a handful of votes in the Rajya Sabha. In 1991, the Union government introduced the 72nd (Panchayats) and 73rd (Nagarpalikas) Constitution Amendment Bills, based substantially on the earlier Bills moved in the Eighth Lok Sabha but also incorporating some changes. Both the Lok Sabha and Rajya Sabha passed both bills on the 22 and 23 December 1992 respectively. By then, their sequence changed to the 73rd and 74th amendments respectively. Following their ratification by more than half the State Assemblies as required under the Constitution, the President of India gave his assent and the Acts came into force as the Constitution (Seventy-third Amendment) Act,1992 on 24th April 1993 and the Constitution (Seventy-fourth Amendment) Act,

1992 on June 1, 1993, adding two new Parts to the Constitution, namely, Part IX titled "The Panchayats" and Part IXA titled "The Municipalities."

Basic Features of the Act

The basic features of the 73rd Constitutional Amendment are:

- Panchayats are given a Constitutional status and uniformity provided by making the three-tier system a permanent feature.
- Panchayats are to be constituted in every State at the village, intermediate and district level, except States with a population not exceeding 20 lakh.
- A Gram Sabha is to be established in each village, exercising powers and performing functions at the village level, as the State may provide by law.
- Members of Panchayats are to be elected at all levels through direct elections. Chairperson at the intermediate and district level is to be elected through indirect elections.
- Seats are reserved for SCs and STs at all levels according to their population. Not less than one-third of the seats are to be reserved for women.
- The office of chairperson will also be subject to this provision.
- Panchayats have been granted a uniform five-year term and in case of dissolution, elections are to be held within six months of the date of dissolution.
- Panchayats are entrusted with (a) preparing plans and implementing schemes for social justice and economic development; and (b) matters listed in the Eleventh Schedule.
- State legislature authorises the panchayats to levy, collect and appropriate suitable local taxes. The government can make grant-in-aid to the panchayats from the Consolidated Fund of the concerned State.
- Review of the financial position of the panchayats will be undertaken by a Finance Commission, which shall be constituted to ensure free and fair elections to the panchayats. (Kaushik, 2005:84)

This Act for the first time sought to empower women and SCs and STs through the provision of reservation. Moreover, one-third of the offices of Chairperson in the Panchayats had in future to be women.

Following the enactment of this amendment, all States except Jharkhand have conducted at least one election to the Panchayats at all levels. About 28 lakh Panchayat representatives have been elected to 2,39544 PRIs (all three levels included). Of these 10.39 lakh representatives are women.

Reservation of Seats in the Panchayats for Women

Since 1993, when the 73rd Constitution Amendment came into force, women have moved forward and demonstrated their capacities and abilities to hold such positions and fulfill the mandate of their constituency. With every succeeding Panchayat election, women have been able to enlarge their representation beyond the minimum 33 per cent prescribe by the Constitution. Of the total 28 Lakh elected Panchayat representatives, more than 10 lakh are estimated to be women. This takes the overall presence of women in Panchayats to approximately 36.7 per cent (as on 1.12.2006), thus, changing the profile of rural leadership. In Bihar, while 50 per cent of the Panchayats seats and leadership positions are reserved for women, roughly 55 per cent of elected seats at the Gram Panchayat level are occupied by women. In Maharashtra, the representation of women in panchayats is nearly 34 per cent. In April 2011, the Maharashtra Assembly approved 50 per cent reservation for women in PRIs. In Karnataka, it is around 43 per cent. The data regarding the number of panchayats and elected women representatives in all the three tiers of Panchayats in States/ UTs as on 2006 is given in Table 9.1.

Table 9.1: No. of Panchayats and Elected Representatives in the Three Tires of Panchayats in States/ UTs as on 1-12-2006

Sl. No.	*State/UT*	*No. of Panchayats*	*General*	*SC No.*	*SC per cent*	*ST No.*	*ST per cent*	*Total*	*Women No.*	*Women per cent*
	States									
1.	Andhra Pradesh	22945	172136	34025	15.2	17842	8.0	224003	74019	33.0
2.	Arunachal Pradesh	1789	0	0	0.0	8260	100	8260	3183	38.5
3.	Assam	2431	23206	1344	5.3	886	3.5	25436	9903	38.9
4.	Bihar	9040	109767	19440	14.9	884	0.7	130091	70400	54.1
5.	Chhattisgarh	9982	76013	17540	10.9	66833	41.7	160386	54102	33.7
6.	Goa	192	1500	0	0.0	0	0.0	1500	453	30.2
7.	Gujarat	14068	83982	7970	7.0	22235	19.5	114187	38068	33.3
8.	Haryana	6325	54508	14965	21.5	0	0.0	69473	24994	36.0
9.	Himachal Pradesh	3330	16793	8724	32.0	1753	6.4	27270	9128	33.5
10.	Jharkhand	3979								
11.	Karnataka	5856	67920	17859	18.6	10311	10.7	96090	41210	42.9
12.	Kerala	1165	16246	2005	10.8	232	1.3	18483	6515	35.2
13.	Madhya Pradesh	23412	222836	61103	15.4	112938	28.5	396877	134368	33.9
14.	Maharashtra	28302	176877	25268	11.0	27565	12.0	229710	77118	33.6

(Contd...)

15.	Manipur	169	1684	43	2.4	41	2.3	1768	646	36.5
16.	Orissa	6578	56576	16910	16.8	27376	27.1	100862	36086	35.8
17.	Punjab	12605	62680	28376	31.2	0	0.0	91056	31838	35.0
18.	Rajasthan	9457	73030	25364	21.2	21410	17.9	119804	42402	35.4
19.	Sikkim	170	639	57	5.7	309	30.7	1005	384	38.2
20.	Tamil Nadu	13031	91958	23653	20.3	877	0.8	116488	39364	33.8
21.	Tripura	540	3914	1509	26.3	310	5.4	5733	1986	34.6
22.	Uttar Pradesh	52890	578984	191950	24.9	727	0.1	771661	299025	38.8
23.	Uttarakhand	7335	44450	11077	19.3	1973	3.4	57500	21517	37.4
24.	West Bengal	3713	37177	17158	29.2	4314	7.3	58749	21428	36.5
UTs										
25.	A&N Islands	75	856	0	0.0	0	0.0	856	296	34.6
26.	Chandigarh	19	153	34	18.2	0	0.0	187	62	33.2
27.	D&N Haveli	12	7	3	2.4	115	92.0	125	49	39.2
28.	Daman & Diu	15	71	4	4.1	22	22.7	97	37	38.1
29.	Lakshadweep	11	1	0	0.0	100	99.0	101	38	37.6
30.	Puducherry	108	784	237	23.2	0	0.0	1021	370	36.2
	Total	**239544**	**1974848**	**526618**	**18.6**	**327313**	**11.6**	**2828779**	**1038989**	**36.7**

Source: Third Report of Committee on Empowerment of Women, Parliament of India, 2010, p. 53.
Note: General (Non-SC/St) categories, Males and Females SC: Scheduled Caste Males and Females
ST: Scheduled Tribe Males and Females **Women:** Combined SC, ST and General Categories.

This table also contains the data relating to the distribution of reserved categories, i. e. SCs, STs and OBCs in States/ UTs. As greater representation of the other weaker sections of the society viz. Scheduled Castes (SCs) and Scheduled Tribes (STs) would enhance their voice in democratic bodies and promote inclusive governance which is critical to inclusive growth, the vital role played by panchayats in this regard is laudable. Interestingly, at the national level the representation of women remains below one-third of the total seats. This is supposed to represent the 'critical mass' that is to say this proportion is required for women to be able to make an impact on policy making? In contrast to this, at the local level, elections to the PRIs between 1993 and 2006 have resulted in women's representation exceeding the mandatory 33 per cent in some states, such as Bihar with 54.1 per cent, Karnataka with 42.9 per cent, Uttar Pradesh with 38.2 per cent and Kerala with 35.2 per cent.

The Amendment has been instrumental in making women visible at the level of local governance. By 2006, 10,38,989 women had entered the political fray due to the PRIs and there was a major shift in the numbers of women participating in political activity pre and post the amendment. Earlier there were only about four to five per cent women engaged in political participation, after the amendment the number of women was in the range of 33-54 per cent. Women's participation has not only made a quantitative difference, there is also a qualitative difference as the women's perspective now informs the manner in which issues are addressed. Women have brought their "experience in governance of civic society" to bear upon the "governance of State" and in so doing have made the "state sensitive to issues of poverty, inequality and gender justice." (Kaushik, 2005:158).

Since further enhancement of reservation in PRIs would lead to more women entering the public sphere, the Constitution (One Hundred and Tenth Amendment) Bill, 2009 for enhancing reservation for women in Panchayats at all tires from one-third to 50 per cent in the total number of seats was moved in Parliament on 26th November by the Minister of Panchayati Raj. Thereafter the said bill has been referred to the Parliamentary Standing Committee on Rural Development for examination and Report. The proposed amendment would increase reservation for women in (i) the total number of seats to be filled by direct election, (ii) offices of Chairpersons and (iii) in seats and offices of chairpersons reserved for Scheduled Castes (SCs) and Scheduled Tribes (STs) to 50 per cent in all tiers of Panchayats. Reservation for women in the third tier of governance including in leadership positions in PRIs was itself a unique innovation in the governance area. Enhancement of the reservation for women in PRIs to 50 per cent will further accelerate this process and make PRIs uniquely inclusive institutions. With the proposed Constitutional Amendment, the number of elected women representatives is expected to rise to more than 14 Lakhs from the present 10 lakhs. States such as Bihar, Chhattisgarh, Madhya Pradesh, Maharashtra, Rajasthan, Himachal Pradesh, Uttarakhand, Odisha, Tripura, Jharkhand, Himachal Pradesh and Kerala have already amended their legislation and reserved 50 per cent of the seats for women. In Sikkim, reservation for women is 40 per cent.

Obstacles to Women's Empowerment through PRIs

However, there are many obstacles to the realisation of the PRIs transformative potential. There are many social constrains to women's political participation:

1. **Patriarchal ordering of society** often results in surrogate representation and tokenism, whereby the dominant male member of either the family or the community actually exercises power through the person of the women. Her agency is totally suppressed and her will is not considered-neither at the time of being put up as a candidate nor as an elected member of the PRIs. In this connection, if a woman does try to nevertheless

assert herself, often her illiteracy, ignorance of procedural matters and inexperience in dealing with public matters and possible lack of familiarity with male modes of discourse is taken advantage of. Men thus either view her as a threat to their privileges or a source of status enhancement.

2. **Familial resistance practiced by the Male** is often the bane for the women member of the PRIs. Frequently "women are involved in a daily struggle against authority patterns and powerlessness in the sphere of the family to play their new socio-political role. The familial structures now embody dual patterns of subservience and resistance, strength and submission that forms part of the paradoxical nature of women's experiences. (Sharma, 1998:37)
3. **Proxy Participation of male members related to EWRs in Panchayat meetings** –It is a cause of concern that relatives of elected women representatives interfere in the official activities of women EWRs. Though in some cases the relatives of newly elected representatives play a role in nurturing, encouraging and leading support to women elected representatives, in many cases male relatives even participate in official proceedings on behalf of women, a practice that can never be approved.
4. **The 'two-child' norm** that had been introduced in some States disqualifying persons having more than two children after a certain cut-off date from seeking an elected office also discriminated against women. Since very often they had no choice in the matter reflecting the fact women more often than not to do not have control over their bodies. Moreover the legislation is a violation of the reproductive rights of the women as well as the right to make an informed choice.
5. **Rotations of Seats reserved for women**- The provision for the rotation (between Constituencies) of the reserved seats means that those change from one election to the next. This general works to the detriment of women and their opportunity to craft a political career as even if they have performed effectively in their first term they are unable to reap the benefits of these achievements in the next election, when they are generally sidelined by men who are eager to come back to power.
6. **Illiteracy** is the most pertinent hurdle that prevents the entry of rural women into mainstream politics. The AC Nielsen

ORG-MARGA study commissioned by the Ministry of Panchayati Raj among elected representatives of PRIs showed that about one-fifth of them were illiterates. The study showed that the educational attainment of elected women representatives is generally up to middle school. It is also observed that among the female Pradhans 11.4 per cent and among female Ward Members 26.6 per cent are illiterates. (Third Report CEW, 2010:27).

7. **Low self-esteem and paucity of funds are** further constrains in the political participation of women at the local level. The political culture is also not conducive to women's active participation- incentives given for garnering votes often take the form of distribution of alcohol or money. Rampant corruption and the criminalisation of politics are said to be other deterrents to women's political participation.
8. **Violence** often violence is perpetrated against women candidates to discourage them from participating in elections-in itself an exercise in power and domination resulting in coercive exclusion.
9. **Loss of Income-** A major constraint faced by women from poor families is the lack of time as they have to work for long hours as wage earners. It may not be fair to expect them to devote time to Panchayat work sacrificing their income earning opportunities. Though remuneration in terms of honorarium, monthly/daily allowances, sitting fees, TA/HRA, etc. are payable to all elected representatives as provided by different States, there is no provision for payment of separate honorarium to EWRs.

Caste positions often caste positions also constrained women from participating politically- occasionally it created barriers in interaction between high and low caste women. In the case of high caste women, their caste position additionally imposed restrictions on their mobility and interaction with male colleagues and members of their constituency.

PRIs and Women's Empowerment

Despite the above-mentioned challenges and obstacles to women's political participation, women's reservation in the PRIs has also been transformative to an extent, it has

1. created a bonding and solidarity among women going beyond the domestic; it has generated self-confidence and political

awareness. Women have succeeded in bringing important social issues; on the agenda of local self-government-these are issues such as drinking water, ponds and wells, construction of roads, primary health centres, schools, housing programmes, daycare centres and construction of public toilets.

2. It has generated an awareness of the necessity to become literate and build capacities with regard to planning and budgeting and accounting. It has highlighted the need for deliberative action-the need to justify and therefore to provide explanation for decisions taken and in so doing create transparency and accountability.
3. Women's reservation has helped women assert control over resources. It has compelled them to interact with officials and also in some instances to challenge men. It has made them aware that qualitative strength lies not in numbers alone but rather in acquisition of knowledge, skills and literacy.
4. PRIs have given women a better understanding of the working of politics, in particular the importance of political parties although initially they sought the assistance of their male family members to overcome their functional difficulties.
5. Learn to deal in a socially effective manner with social evils such as the menace of alcoholism, domestic violence etc. Have also gained an insight into the functioning of corruption and have sought to overcome it.

Progress Made in Qualitative and Quantitative Terms

In order to document the progress made in qualitative and quantitative terms with regards to the participation of Elected Women Representatives (EWRs), the Ministry of Panchayati Raj commissioned AC Nielsen ORG-MRG to carry out a nationwide survey in the States. Its finds inter alia showed:-

- As many as four-fifth of the elected representatives did not have anyone in their family affiliated with politics.
- Around 86 per cent of EWRs were first timers in politics. Around 14 per cent were elected more than once at the Gram Panchayat level. Reservation played a significant role in their first entry into politics.
- Sizeable proportion of elected women representatives perceive enhancement in their self-esteem (79 per cent), confidence (81 per cent) and decision-making ability (74 per cent).

- A large proportion (72 per cent) reported having been actively involved in providing civic amenities.
- Sixty two per cent of EWR said that they made efforts in increasing enrollment and mitigating domestic violence. (MoPR Annual Report, 2011-12).

The performance of EWRs had greater positive correlation with three factors:

1. When they were elected for second time,
2. When they had received training for capacity building, and
3. When they were educated beyond school level.

Conclusion: Empowerment of Women, a Myth or Reality

Empowerment of women through reservation in PRIs is not a complete myth but much still remains to be done for it to really become a reality. The enactment of the 73rd Amendment has set in motion the awakening of the latent power of women at grass-root level and must certainly be oriented towards achieving a social transformation, otherwise why would there be such a strong opposition to the women's reservation in parliament. Where it has yet to make inroads is in certain states where it has been captured by the elites and hence social structures of power and dominance remain unchanged. Even where the fall out has been positive from the point of view of developmental activities, issues of social equity and social justice have not been adequately addressed. But reservation has certainly provided women with a platform to learn about the public sphere and administration and to channel this knowledge as a first step towards material development of the village and eventually to build on this and usher in a genuine transformation of the power structure.

The experience of women and PRIs has been varied- there are some commonalities, which have been broadly listed and discussed in the foregoing but successful empowerment has been different in different regions and PRIs. A beginning has been made and to sustain the transformative process that is a serious challenge, it is necessary to go beyond providing technical support. Women's solidarity needs strengthening by forging closer ties amongst women's organisations and elected bodies. Access to information that would enhance the quality of women's lives is essential. For empowerment to be real –enabling conditions must be evolved and developed. One of these is the eradication of poverty. The quest for equality will only succeed if all groups are represented and have access to equality of opportunity. Existing political institutions and structures must be further reformed to facilitate broader representation and its translation into political power for those currently marginalised.

For women's empowerment at the grass-root level to become a reality, it is necessary that the PRIs themselves become truly autonomous by providing them with sufficient powers and resources, which they lack currently and for women to move beyond welfare and development programmes to innovatively shape the practices of good governance and to evolve a truly egalitarian system, which would herald the crumbling of the existing system of power relations.

Suggestions

Committee of Empowerment of Women, Parliament of India has made following important recommendation in its third report which is presented to Lok Sabha in May, 2010. These are:-

1. **50 per cent Reservation of Seats in PRIs for Women**

   To further enhancing the participation of women in the public sphere and making Panchayats more inclusive institutions, the government moved the Constitution (One hundred and Tenth Amendment) Bill, 2009 in Parliament on 26th November 2009 for enhancing the reservation for women in Panchayats. This Amendment to Article 243 D of the Constitution envisages 50 per cent reservation for women in the total number of seats to be filled by direct election in the offices of chairpersons and in seats/offices of chairpersons reserved for SCs and STs in all tires of PRIs. However, after introduction, the said bill has been referred to the Parliamentary Standing Committee on Rural Development for examination and report. The Constitution Bill, 2009 providing for 50 per cent reservation for women in the third tier of governance should be expeditiously enacted as a law on priority basis without much delay.

2. **Need to enhance training facilities and capacity building programmes of EWRs**

   The elected representatives of the people, especially women, need training to enable them to discharge their duties because of their lower literacy levels and limited exposure to public affairs. Though the MoPR has some training modules under schemes like Panchayat Mahila Evam Yuva Shakti Abhiyan (PMEYSA) and Rashtriya Gram Swaraj Yojana, there is no separate scheme exclusively for the capacity building of women. Therefore, a separate and exclusive training programme based on the principle of continuous and comprehensive training for women representatives should be devised.

3. **Steps to ward off proxy participation of male members related to EWRs in panchayat meetings**

   In many States, the relatives of elected women representatives interfere in the official activities of EWRs. Though in some cases the relatives of newly elected representatives might play a role in nurturing, encouraging and lending support to her, in many cases male relatives even participate in official proceedings on behalf of women sidelining them, a practice that can never be approved of. The answer might be in changing mindsets, particularly of men through counselling and promoting the confidence of women in negotiating the space and independence they need their official tasks.

4. **Need to extend the rotation cycle of reserved seats for women to two terms**

   The provision for the rotation (between constituencies) of the reserved seats means that these change from one election to the next. This generally works to the detriment of women and their opportunity to craft a political career. Even if they have performed effectively in their first term, they are unable to reap the benefits of these achievements in the next election, as the constituency they nurtured in the first term gets de-reserved and the women candidate may have to shift to another constituency. A study among the EWRs in PRIs shows that a large proportion (83.4 per cent) of those interviewed have contested only one election in their career while only a small proportion (12.4 per cent) have attempted a second and third round (4.2 per cent) of elections. The main reason cited by female respondents for not contesting elections for a second time was the de-reservation of their seats. The rotation cycle of reservation of seats for women may be extended to two terms and the same methodology may be followed by all States.

5. **Special Additional honorarium for Elected Women Representatives**

   A major constraint of women from poor families in devoting time to panchayat activities is lack of time as they have to work for long hours as wage earners. It may not be fair to expect them to devote time to the Panchayat activities sacrificing their income earning opportunities. To encourage active participation of women in panchayat activities, special additional honorarium equal to minimum daily wages should be given to women representatives.

6. **Disincentives in the population policies of States**

   It is find that the disqualification mentioned in the Representation of the People Act, which are applicable to the Panchayat members. The States of Andhra Pradesh, Maharashtra, Odisha and Rajasthan at present have laws that disqualify persons having more than two children from becoming the members of Panchayayts. This norm has been particularly bars on women as they rarely have a say in matters relating to number of children that they bear. This provision may also encourage sex selective abortions. Hence, the Ministry of Panchayati Raj should pursue the matter with those States having such provisions in their Panchayati Raj Acts and get them withdrawn at the earliest.

7. **Special adult literacy programmes for Elected Women Representatives**

   Illiteracy is the most important hurdle that prevents the entry of rural women into mainstream politics. Education being an important detriminant of good performance, the EWRs is made literate by reviving adult education centres and make knowledgeable through information sharing process in such a way that they could perform their duties confidently and efficiently. The regular meetings between women sarpanches and panchayat secretary are arranged to enhance women's understanding and knowledge about the functioning of panchayats.

8. **Involvement of NGOs and local women's groups in strengthening EWRs**

   Ignorance about the role, responsibilities and rights play a major role in preventing women representatives from performing the decision-making roles they are supposed to fulfill. Many States are involving NGOs to some extent in the Training/ Capacity Building of elected representatives as well as in carrying out need assessment and preparing participatory plans at the panchayat level. However, the involvement of local women's groups and NGOs are required in an extended level to help the women, particularly from poor households to come out into the mainstream, overcome their limitations and contribute to grass root level development process. Pamphlets and booklets in local language can be used in community mobilisation and awareness generation.

9. **Strengthening of Gram Sabhas**

   As Gram Sabha occupies a central place in the entire scheme of local governance by providing an opportunity to the individual villager to be part of the local decision-making process, the real strength of local governance is in strengthening Gram Sabhas. Though the Gram Sabha is supposed to meet twice a year, effective and vibrant governance at the local level can be realised only through more regular and meaningful meetings of Gram Sabhas. Gram Sabhas are endowed with a lot of powers including social welfare, development, and village management and monitoring. Social Audit is the most powerful tool that can make Gram Sabha more energetic and transparent in its functioning. All out efforts should be made to empower Gram Sabhas through proper guidelines. This should include at least one meeting in two months; authorising Gram Sabhas with powers to identify project and beneficiaries; conduct of social audit and making mandatory the presence of government officials at the meeting of Gram Sabha.

References

Kashyap, Subash (2011), 'Our Constitution', National Book Trust, New Delhi.

Kaushik, P. D. (2005), "Panchayati Raj Movement in India: Retrospective and Present Status" in Bibek Debroy and P. D. Kaushik (ed.) *Energising Rural Development through Panchayats*, Academic Foundation, New Delhi.

Mathur, Kuldip (2006), 'Empowering Local Government: Decentralisation and Governance in India': Social Development Report, OUP, New Delhi.

Ministray of Panchayati Raj, GOI, Annual Report, 2011-12.

Parliament of India, Committee on Empowerment of Women, Third Report (2009-10).

Sharma, Kumud, (1998), 'Transformative Politics: Dimensions of Women's Participations in Panchayati Raj. In *Indian Journal of Gender Studies*, 5(i) p. 75.

10

Panchayat Extension to Scheduled Fifth Areas-An Assessment of its Implementation

—*Mahi Pal*

Introduction

Provisions of the Panchayat (Extension to the Scheduled Areas) Act (hereafter referred to as PESA) is an important piece of legislation to bring not only the control of *jal*, (water), *jungle* (forest) and *Jamin* (land) in the hands of tribals, but also give supremacy to them in settling their disputes in their own traditional and cultural way. The terra firma on which, PESA based is gram sabha (village assembly). States of Himachal Pradesh, Rajasthan, Madhya Pradesh, Chhattisgarh, Jharkhand, Odisha, Maharasthra, Andhra Pradesh and Gujarat are covered under Fifth Scheduled of the Constitution.

Present paper focuses on provisions about powers and authority contained in the PESA and to examine as to what extent these provisions have been interwoven in the State Panchayat Acts in the 5th Scheduled Areas States of the country. Paper also focuses on as to what extent conformity legislations of the States have been amended to give effect of the provisions of the PESA.

Salient Features of the PESA

Before giving salient features of the PESA, let us give a short background as how this Act could see light of the day. Although

Article 243(1) of the Constitutions prohibits extension of provision of the 73rd Constitutional Amendment Act 1992 to tribal areas and Scheduled Areas referred in Article 244 Clause (1) and (2) of the Constitution, Article 243M(4)(b) empowers the Parliament to make laws to extend the provisions of the Act to these Areas subject to certain conditions. But without making a law by the Parliament, the states like Andhra Pradesh, Himachal Pradesh and Rajasthan have extended 73rd Amendment Act to the Scheduled Areas. This was an unconstitutional step on the part of the states. Tribal leaders considered it another step by the state against the autonomy of the tribal people. They mobilised tribals around this issue. The matter was also taken up with the Andhra Pradesh High Court by the tribals and by some activists, which had termed State Act ultravirous to the Constitution. Keeping in view of the agitation by the tribals and judicial verdict of the Andhra Pradesh High Court, a need was felt for extending the provisions of part IX of the Constitution to the Scheduled Areas by enacting a law in the Parliament. This resulted in constituting of a high level committee under the chairmanship of Mr Dileep Singh Bhuria with the purpose to recommend as to how the Scheduled Areas could be recovered under the provision of the 73rd Amendment Act. Accordingly, in view of the recommendations of this committee a Bill was introduced in the Parliament and passed on December 19, 1996 which subsequently, after getting President's assent on December 24, 1996, extended 73rd Amendment Act to the Scheduled Area mentioned under Clause (2) of Article 244 of the Constitution, It became mandatory on the part of the states to amend their existing Panchayat Acts in conformity with the PESA within a year. Following are the salient features of the Act:

(1) Every legislation on the panchayats in 5th Scheduled Area be in conformity with the customary law, social and religious practices and traditional management practice of the community resources.

(2) Gram Sabha has been vested with following powers:
   (a) Ownership of minor forest produce.
   (b) Approval of development plans and programmes.
   (c) Selection of beneficiaries under various programmes.
   (d) Prior consultation on land acquisition matter.
   (e) Management on village markets.
   (f) Control money lending to STs and prevention of alienation of land.
   (g) Control on institutions and functionaries in all social sectors.

(h) Giving of utilisation certificate of funds used for the projects and programmes of social and economic development etc. to the village panchayats.

(i) Prior recommendation for granting licence or mining lease for minor minerals.

(3) Reservation for the scheduled tribes shall not be less than half of the total number of seats at all tiers (i.e. Gram Panchayat, Panchayat Samiti and Zila Panchayats) of Panchayati Raj System and reservation for other communities mentioned in Part IX of the Constitution shall be on the basis of proportion to the population of these communities.

(4) The chairpersons at all levels of the panchayats shall be reserved for STs.

(5) In case of STs they have no representation at intermediate or district level panchayats, the state government shall nominate such underrepresented Scheduled Tribes but such nomination should not exceed one-tenth of the total elected members of that panchayat.

(6) State legislatures while devolving powers and authority to panchayats to enable them to function as institution of self-government, it should be ensured that the panchayats at the higher level do not assume the powers and authority of any lower level panchayats or the Gram Sabha.

(7) The state legislatures shall follow the pattern of the Sixth Scheduled areas to the Constitution while designing the administrative arrangement for the panchayats at district level.

Thus, the PESA has given an important legislative framework for the tribal to have their control and rights over natural resources and conserve and preserve their identity and culture in participatory manner through the institution of Gram Sabha.

The state legislatures should keep in mind the following aspects while amending their respective Panchayat Acts.

(a) Gram Sabha should be made a corner stone of entire scheme of decentralised governance, planning and development by way of awarding independence in managing, protecting and preserving natural resources and formulation of socio-economic development programmes, projects and schemes for tribal people.

(b) Relationship between the Gram Sabha and panchayat should be similar to the one existing between legislatures and the government. In the other words, panchayats should take approval of the Gram Sabha in all matter effecting rural economy and society.

(c) The underlying spirit of the Act is on devolution of powers and authority (rather than delegation of powers) to the Gram Sabha which represents participatory democracy rather than empowering representative decentralised democracy in the form of gram panchayats and higher tiers of Panchayati Raj System. And while devolving powers and authority on panchayat or Gram Sabha, state legislature should ensure that panchayats at higher level do not assume the powers and authority of any panchayat at lower level or of the Gram Sabha. In other words, principle of subsidiary is to be followed i.e. the function which can be performed better should be given to that tier of the government and not to the other tiers of it. Such provisions are not contained in the 73rd Amendment Act.

A Critique of State Panchayat Raj Acts

As the tribal societies are homogenous and monolithic and have the cultural and tradition to work collectively, the participatory democracy through the Gram Sabha is very appropriate for them. Keeping in view of the participatory culture of tribal the Bhuria Committee has recommended making the Gram Sabha the corner stone of entire scheme of decentralised governance. In view of above, let us examine as to what extent the conformity legislations contained this philosophy of decentralised governance for these areas.

Table 10.1 presents state-wise details whether the provisions of the State Panchayat Acts have been legislated in conformity with the Act. As per Section 4(d) of the Extension Act every Gram Sabha (GS) shall be competent to safeguard and preserve the traditions and customs of the people, their cultural identity, community resources and the customary mode of disputes resolution. Secondly, as per Section 4(e) of the Act GS approve the plans, programmes and projects for social and economic development. Thirdly, as per Section 4(f) of the Act every panchayat at village level shall be required to obtain utilisation certificate of the work done in the areas from the GS. It may be seen from Table 10.1 that these provisions have been made in the State Panchayat Acts.

Table 10.1: Compliance of State Panchayati Raj Act with Section 4 of Extension Act

State	*(d) Gram Sabha's competency for safeguard*	*(e) GS's Approval plans etc. and identification of benefi-ciaries under Poverty Allevi ation Programmes*	*(f) Utilisation Certificate from Gram Sabha*	*(i) Consultation with Gram Sabha for acquisition of land for Development Projects and before re-settling or rehabilitating persons affected*	*(k) Recommendation of Gram Sabha prior to grant of Licence or minimum Lease for minor minerals*
Andhra Pradesh	Yes	Yes	Yes	Yes	Yes
Chhattisgarh	Yes	Yes	Yes	No	No
Gujarat	Yes	Yes	Yes	Yes	No
Himachal Pradesh	Yes	Yes	Yes	Yes	Yes
Jharkhand	Yes	Yes	Yes	No	No
Odisha	Yes	Yes	Yes	Yes	Yes
Maharashtra	Yes	Yes	Yes	Yes	Yes
Madhya Pradesh	Yes	Yes	Yes	No	No
Rajasthan	Yes	Yes	Yes	Yes	Yes

Source: Annual Report (2011-12) of the Ministry of Panchayati Raj.

Section 4(i) of the PESA says that GS or Panchayats at appropriate level shall be consulted before making the acquisition of land in the Scheduled Areas for development projects. This is very important provision of the Act as issue of land is involved, which is very important for the point of view tribal. It may be seen from table that this provision has been provided in all the State Acts except Chhattisgarh, Jharkhand and Madhya Pradesh States. Section 4(k) of the Act says that recommendation of the GS or the Panchayat at the appropriate level shall be made mandatory prior to grant of prospective licence or mining lease for minor minerals in these areas. About this, the table shows that States of Chhattisgarh, Gujarat, Jharkhand and Madhya Pradesh have not enacted these provisions in their Panchayat Acts.

Section 4(m) of the PESA says that while endowing Panchayats in Scheduled Areas, State Legislature shall ensure that the Panchayats at the appropriate level and the GS are endowed with powers enumerated in Para 2 under salient features of the Extension Act. Table 10.2 depicts state- wise status of these powers to GS. It may be seen from the table that enforcement of prohibition has not been provided in the States of Chhattisgarh, Gujarat, Jharkhand and Madhya Pradesh. Ownership of minor forest produce has been endowed in GSs in all the States except Chhattisgarh and Madhya Pradesh. Another important power is prevention of alienation of land. Out of nine States, this provision has been provided only in four States namely, Andhra Pradesh, Odisha, Maharashtra and Rajasthan. Power of managing village markets has been given to GS in all the states except Maharathara. Power of control over money lending to GS has not been provided in the State Acts of Chhattisgarh, Jharkhand and Madhya Pradesh. The power of control over institutions and functionaries in all the social sectors has been given to the GS in all the States except Gujarat.

Making provisions is important for enabling the GSs to control over resources in their respective jurisdiction. But more important is as whether the respective state legislations have been conformed to the State Panchayat Acts. For example, consultation with the GS is mandatory for any land acquisition in the area as per the State Panchayat Act. But to make this provision effective and operational, the respective State Acquisition Act should be conformed with the State Panchayat Acts. In other words, the power relating to land acquisition mentioned in the State Acquisition Act must be deleted otherwise it may create an environment of confusion which lead to no empowerment of GS and their members about taking decisions regarding land issues.

Table 10.2: Compliance of State Panchayati Raj Act with Section 4 (Para M) of Extension Act

State	*(i) Enforce prohibition by Gram Sabah*	*(ii) Ownership of minor forests produce by Gram Sabha*	*(iii) Prevent alienation of land by Gram Sabha*	*(iv) Manage Village Markets by Gram Sabha*	*(v) Control money lending by Gram Sabha*	*(vi) Control over institutions and functionaries by Gram Sabha*
Andhara Pradesh	Yes	Yes	Yes	Yes	Yes	Yes
Chhattisgarh	No	No	No	Yes	No	Yes
Gujarat	No	Yes	No	Yes	Yes	No
Himachal Pradesh	Yes	Yes	No	Yes	Yes	Yes
Jharkhand	No	Yes	No	Yes	No	Yes
Odisha	Yes	Yes	Yes	Yes	Yes	Yes
Maharashtra	Yes	Yes	Yes	No	Yes	Yes
Madhay Pradesh	No	No	No	Yes	No	Yes
Rajasthan	Yes	Yes	Yes	Yes	Yes	Yes

Source: Annual Report (2011-12) of the Ministry of Panchayati Raj.

Table 10.3: Compliance of Conformity Legislations of the States with State Panchayati Raj Acts in reference with the Section 4 (Para M) of Extension Act

(i) In force prohibition	*(ii) Ownership of minor forests produce*	*(iii) Prevent elimination of land*	*(iv) Manage village markers*	*(v) Control money landing*	*(vi) Control over institutions and fund*
No	No	No	No	No	No
Yes	Yes	No	Yes	No	No
No	N. A.	No	No	No	No
Yes	No	No	Yes	No	No
No	No	No	No	No	No
No	Yes	Yes	Yes	No	Yes
No	No	No	No	No	No
Yes	Yes	No	Yes	Yes	Yes
No	No	N. A.	Yes	No	Yes

Source: Annual Report (2011-12) of the Ministry of Panchayati Raj.

In above context, let us examine as to what extent the important subject laws having bearing with Extension Act have been compliance with by the States.

Table 10.3 depicts such status across States in the country. It may be seen from this table that in case of land acquisition, State Acts of Andhra Pradesh, Gujarat, Jharkhand, Odisha, Maharashtra and Rajasthan have not been compliance with. In case of excise, State Acts of Andhra Pradesh, Himachal Pradesh, Jharkhand, Maharashtra, and Rajasthan have not been compliance with. In case of forest produce, the situation is very bleak as except Odisha, none of the state made any progress this regard. In case of mines and minerals situation is not encouraging as table indicates. Interestingly, in case of agricultural produce and market, except Madhya Pradesh none of the States has made any progress in this regard. Almost, similar is the position in case of moneylenders across the States.

Above analysis of the Acts shows that not much interest has been shown by the States in putting in practice of the Act in letter and spirit for improving self-governance.

On behalf of the Ministry of Panchayati Raj, IRMA had carried out an independent assessment of the functioning of the panchayats across the States. Some of the states which come under 5th Scheduled Areas have also been covered. Based on the findings of this assessment, an evaluation has been done about the grassroots realities. In case of Andhra Pradesh, although several mandatory provisions of the Extension Act have been incorporated in the state Act, actual implementation lacking. In case of Himachal Pradesh, in practice, most of the functions are handled by the States. In some States as Chhattisgarh some of the provisions such as enforcement prohibition, control over moneylending are not clearly stated. In case of Rajasthan, conditions have not been created in the tribal areas to give effect of provisions of the Act at the ground level. This might be on account of deficiencies in the legal framework and due to inability of tribal to seize the opportunities of the Act for their empowerment and self-governance.

Conclusion

It was desired that the PESA would further strengthen participatory democratic culture among tribals by way of making their functioning in self-governing mode and there by instrumental in establishing Gram Swaraj as envisaged by Father of Nation. But it could not be realised due to lack of political will and administrative support at different levels of governance in the country. Secondly, due to lack of awareness about the potential of the PESA, tribal could not seize this opportunity to assert for the implementation of the provisions of the Act in letter and spirit. Further, it may be said that the areas where this Act is applicable, are suffered from Left Wing Extremism. Ineffective implementation of the provisions of this Act might be one of the main reasons of discontent among tribals leading to extremism in these areas. Hence, there is an urgent need to implement the provisions of this Act in letter and spirit in the country.

The plan of action to put in practice the provisions of the Act, among others, includes removing of deficiencies from the State Panchayat Acts, amendment of conformity legislations making Panchayat Acts more effective and build up the capacity of functionaries implementing the PESA.

References

Provision of the Panchayats (Extension to Scheduled Areas) Act, 1996.

Annual Report of the Ministry of Panchayati Raj, (2011-12), Government of India, New Delhi.

Mahi Pal (2000), Panchayats in Fifth Scheduled Areas, *Economic and Political Weekly*, May 6, 2000.

State of Panchayats Report (2008-09), Independent Assessment, IRMA (sponsored) Ministry of Panchayati Raj, Government of India.

11

Governing the Scheduled Areas: Appraising the Decentralisation and Self-Rule in Adilabad District of Telangana

—*Jadhav Prathap Singh*

The state and non-state actors have been engaging in the governing of tribal areas and in arena of tribal development since independence. As developing the tribals is a constitutional obligation, but the contestation on their development and how should they be governed still remains a debated question among policy practitioners, civil society and in the academia. Indeed, the tribal communities themselves are ascribing and consolidating identity and asserting their identity to counter the imposed governance or centralised tendencies. Consequently, giving imputes to contestation which draws inspiration from mainly two reasons, which are- Firstly, the normative aspect of tribal question that provides prerogatives to tribal communities, and the second is constitutional obligation which needs to be fulfilled. These aspects become sources to unresolved problem of the tribal communities in India because the conflict question, on the one hand based on normative claims and legitimate ground for the tribal rights and on the other hand the sovereign subject over them. These aspects invoke intricate questions who should rule and how should they be governed? These questions are carrying more weight in recent times, when there has been growing realisation and acceptance of the fact that tribals living in the resource rich regions have been the worst victim of the model of the political governance, state apparatus and the development strategy pursued especially in the post-colonial state (Sharan and Singh, 1999).

From the last two decades of the twentieth century onward, governance has centred into the dominant discourse of development so vigorously that it become a buzzword in the mainstream public sphere. But, the procedural law of the land has been providing a distinct framework and procedure to govern tribal communities and their areas. However, still there is disillusionment among the tribals toward the state and its activities in their areas and perquisite seems futile. Thus, it is interesting to explore the governing philosophy and process that is taking place in Scheduled/ tribal Areas and in specific Scheduled Areas of Adilabad District, which is inhabited by cultural and spatial communities. So, there is need to examine the tribal community's role in the governance process and how the decentralisation process is giving space for 'Self-rule' as purported by the tribals. During the colonial and post-colonial state, most of the tribal resistant, revolt and movement stood on the bedrock theme of 'Self-Rule', given the importance on it, dialect on governing the tribal areas has been viewed within the purview of Self-Rule. Since the colonial period both tribals and the state have been arguing from their point of view to govern the tribal areas. In this process the common jargon that has been used is 'Self-Rule' which is being seen as devolution and delegation of power. Nonetheless, the interface between the state and tribal communities engendered the binary on the governing of tribal areas/ Scheduled Areas. As one comes from the communities themselves, and the other is from the state itself.

In order to understand the governing process and larger Adivasi political questions, this paper attempts to unravel the underlying patterns of decentralisation carried within the governance process from the state as well as communities point of views. This paper is divided into three sections. First section highlights on the philosophical defense of decentralised governance in the tribal areas. The second section examines the state policies to ensure tribal rights and understanding efforts of state in governing the tribal areas. The third section projects the views of people from scheduled areas of Adilabad District and provides conclusions. To understand above aspects the research is based on primary and secondary sources of data. The primary data is derived from ethnographic study and interviews with the people in this region. The field work was carried in five Scheduled Mandals which includes Sirpur (U), Jainoor, Jannaram, Utnoor and Tiryanai of Adilabad District in Telangana State. The secondary sources include books, articles, government Acts and internet sources.

Through the policies and actions by the state as it purport to carry decentralisation, and the tribal communities claims for decentralised 'self-rule' could be understood from their resistance to the state in Adilabad district. In this district, tribals constitutes a predominant number, as there are major four tribal communities- The Kolams, the Gonds, the Lambadas and the Naikpods, who have been living in the same forest area for generations. Geographically these areas are located in the central part of the district, which is vastly covered by the forest and mostly inhabited by these tribal communities. Due to cultural and spatial distinctness, tribal areas in the district are recognised as a Scheduled Área from 1950s. But the same region has been declared as a 'Tiger Reserve' (named as 'Kawal Tiger Reserve') (GOAP, 2012) on 10 April 2012 by the erstwhile Andhra Pradesh (AP) government by issuing a Government Order (G. O) No. 27. Thus, this new legal identity to areas brought conflagration in the region for mainly two reasons. The first is declaring Scheduled Areas without the knowledge and consent of the tribal communities. The second, there is no evidence of Tiger existence in the forest, even Forest Department didn't find the evidence for it. This larger reasons peeved them, resultantly vehement opposition raised from all the tribal communities against the declaring their area as Kawal Tiger Reserve. They have been actively protesting, taking rallies, dharnas and it gradually become a movement to resist the state action in the region. This phenomenon by the state in the region certainly makes them to ponder on decentralisation and claims Self-Rule.

The state which is supposed to protect the rights of tribal communities is alienating their rights (Xaxa and Nathan, 2012; Munshi, 2012), it occurs by violating the procedure which alienate their political, social and survival rights, rather bizarre the state claims that it is the sole protector and stand for the tribal rights. This the process by which the state establish and exercise its hegemony over the people. On the other hand tribal communities are struggling with the state to get their rights to govern themselves, because they see the state as the source of exploitation of their rights, in the sense they are seeking for decentralisation. The common theme that both are trying to legitimatize is governing the tribal society, i.e. subject of their rule. The state claims that it is giving all possible means for tribals to govern themselves, whereas tribal groups say that they are not being allowed to govern themselves. This dialect has been taking place whenever the state tries to enter into the tribal areas in the pretext of developmental activities, ecological and wildlife conservation. Thus, there is need to see how historically the governance and decentralisation philosophy developed or debated with regard to tribal/ scheduled areas.

Debating Governance

There are various policies and Acts made to protect the rights of the tribal communities which were the result of the protest and resistance movements by tribals. These movements came with slogan and framework of decentralised autonomy or Self-Rule. As during the colonial and early decades of independence, anthropologists, philanthropists, policy-makers, administrators and activists viewed on the subject of governing the tribal areas that has been discussed in the following section. But in the recent decades the source to tribal resistance are derived from the existing Acts and policies and also by critiquing them if these were not meet with demand for decentralisation. Most of the demands emerge from the Scheduled Area point of view, because the tribal Self-Rule is discussed in the Panchayat Extension Scheduled Area (PESA) Act 1996 AP PESA Act 1998 and the Forest Rights Act 2006. Thus, since independence, there has been debate on the governing the tribal communities and their areas.

The philosophical defense for self-rule or decentralisation came from different points of view. Jawaharlal Nehru had proposed the '*panchsheel'* principles to guide the development policies towards tribals. The five principles are first, people should develop along the lines of their own genius and state should avoid imposing anything on them. We should try to encourage in every way their traditional art and culture. Second, tribal rights in land and forests should be respected. Third, we should try to train and build up a team of their own people for the work of administration and development. Some technical personnel from outside will, no doubt, can be needed, especially in the beginning. But we should avoid introducing too many outsiders into tribal territory. Fourth, we should not over-administer these areas or overwhelm them with a multiplicity of schemes. We should rather work through and not in rivalry to its own social and cultural institutions. Fifth, we should judge results not by statistics or the amount of money spent, but by the quality of human character that is evolved (Nehru, 1957). These principle remained basic structure for governing the tribal areas in which Nehru was against to any kind of imposition on tribals. Nehru said 'that we desire that your customs, traditions and religion should not be interfered with. I want such arrangement that you should decide for yourself how you would like it to be' (cited in Doshi, 1997:99). Nehru's understanding and sense developed from the tribal revolts and resistance to colonial state. He also opposed assimilationists like N. K. Bose who and G S Ghurye's view that tribals are backward Hindus and they are aspiring people so they should be assimilated into the mainstream and governed with them.

Another prominent personality and an anthropologist who worked for tribal development was Varrier Elwin who adhered the 'isolationist' approach. In this approach he envisage that the tribals living in the forest of the country had a 'happy-go lucky life' and are away from the evils of civilised society. Elwin (1941) viewed that 'if tribals were allowed to break their isolation and begin to mix with the non-tribal society or mainstream plain, they would suffer from loss of their nerve'. They should be left in the forest so that they would remain in their primordial traits, thus, this approach is called as a 'national park' approach. However, there were criticisms on Elwin approach on the ground that it will keep tribal primitive. But his was concern for the tribal autonomy and protecting their identity with the natural development. Austrian Anthropologist Haimendorf (1982) views that tribal should be allowed to govern themselves but for these essential facilities has to be provided by the state'.

In the constitutional assembly the normative claim and base for tribal self-rule emerged from the two exploitative aspects and occurrences: one is exploitation suffered by tribals from non-tribal and the colonial rulers. But the very nature of their living and lifestyle and their identities give them the legitimate rights over their claim of self-rule, however, their historical experiences with state and mainstream gave impetus to their claim and narration for self-rule.

Apart from these scholars and administrator, 'The UN declaration of 1994-2004 as Decade of Indigenous People' and 'people right to self-governance and self-determination' as a basic human right, recognising the right of people to determine their political status and fully pursue their economic, cultural and social development in the broad framework of national unity and territorial integrity of member nations' (Choudary and Patnaik, 2008). Thus, the declaration gives substantive base to tribal for claim over the Self-Rule through procedural decentralisation.

Historically tribes have been living in separate geographical areas, later, many establishments of feudal and modern state occurring political power or were absorbed into regional political systems, which left them with considerable autonomy in the management of their affairs and control of resources. It is also well established that there were linkages between tribes and other producing societies (Munshi, 2012: 1). The production relation which is not completely modernised, equal access to water resources, forests, pastures land; a sense of community defined by the reorganisation of a common ancestor within the larger kinship, shared rituals and religions dominated by nature and spirit, language, culture practices and political-social organisations to manage the affairs of the community, which give them their distinctiveness. Therefore, legislations have been framed to protect the rights of the tribals, because 'their diversified economic and social formation coupled with varied ethos and style of life' (Choudary and Patnaik, 2008).

Meanwhile, several regulations were passed in mid-nineteenth century with the object of protecting and regulating forest for citing various reasons, especially the imperial purpose. Law related to the management of forest and forest produce were subsequently consolidated in the Indian Forest Act of 1927, it laid the foundation to establish and control over the forests of the state. Munshi (2012: 6-7) says 'over all, notwithstanding the regional differences, one could suggest that creation of large areas of reserved forest in India under control of the state, supervised and managed by the Forest Department resulted in the restriction of the customary rights of the forest communities endangering their survival. These communities suffered great hardships at that even a minor breach of regulation was treated as crime'.

The scientific management of forests introduced by the British also resulted in the enhanced commercial values of the forests, and opened up an important source of revenue for government. The main intension behind this was to earn revenue (Guha, 2012: 18), the surveillance and policing by the state apparatus inevitably led to more and more crimes and offences being committed by Forest Department (Munshi, 2012). The Forest Department's colonial legacies of treating tribals/ adivasis as the enemies of forest, hold them responsible for its destruction. The scientific arrogance, economic compulsion and sheer callousness towards the basic needs of the poor have largely guided the working of the Forest Department (ibid).

The Forest has been major source of food, socio-economic purposes. The major disruption has been caused by the larger political entity, i.e. the state. As Xaxa (cited in Munshi, 2012: 6) pointed out reason about bring tribal land and forest under the state control. The first one is 'introduction of the administrative system by colonial rulers and which continue in post-colonial state as well. The second is not recognition of the shifting cultivation of these communities' control or village control'. Later period the legitimacy of tribal community's rights has been questioned. In this process the creation of national parks and wild life sanctuaries further excluded these communities from their survival base (ibid). While debate between forest, wildlife supporters and Adivasi rights continue to dominate. The new forest policies envisage and give rights to people to participation and involve. But it has not been implemented by the FD and other state apparatus. This is primarily because of their ignorance about the forest laws and the restrictive and insensitive attitudes of their vigilant guards and forest officials who question them for any activities in the forest (Gaur and Patnaik, 328). The natural life of the tribal communities becomes criminaliz life due to colonial state policies. It is the first political entity which alienated and marginalised tribals in very modern ways and mechanisms like regulation through its power.

The same legacies have been carried by the post-colonial state as well in different ways. But uses different pretexts like development, forest and wildlife conservation to enter and colonialise the tribal areas (Guha, 2006: 92-93). In this process, thus there is paradox, when the context come it has been put on suspended the community interest by the state for its own gain. Therefore, there have been questions coming from tribal communities on various laws like forest and wildlife protection policies.

The state and tribal rights policies

The persistent struggle of tribal communities and also due to the covenant, they have been guaranteed certain rights over their socio-cultural, political and regional affairs. There are various acts and laws which empower them to govern themselves. Acts like Scheduled Areas Act, PESA Act, Forest Right Act 2006; these are the Acts which also give power to them over their region and areas. These Acts give power to tribal communities to govern and decide their own affairs without any influence from the outside. If any activity or action government wants to carry out it has to go through the people's approval and agreement. The government has to take decision with people's participation and consent.

While making the GO No. 27 (Government of AP 2012), AP Government did not consider the PESA Act of 1996, which categorically state that 'the State legislations that may endow Panchayats with powers and authority as may be necessary to enable them to function as institutions of self-government shall contain safeguards to ensure that Panchayats at the higher level do not assume the powers and authority of any Panchayat at the lower level or of the *Gram Sabha*' (Government of India (GOI) 1996). The GO No. 27 thus, issued against to this philosophy of self-government by not involving them in the whole process of declaring tiger reserve. The *Panchayats* or decentralised level governance did not involve in the part of issuing the GO or its content. In this case state legislation does not recognise the village level governance and their rights so it is one kind of state of exception. It is complete the procedural exception has been done by the state to create Tiger Reserve in the Scheduled Areas of Adilabad.

Other exception that of PESA Act 1996, Section 4 (1) say that 'State legislation on the *Panchayats* that may be made shall be in consonance with the customary law, social and religious practices and traditional management practices of community resources'(GOI, 1996). The law recognises that the village management goes according to their community customs and tradition within their region and PESA act recognises these aspects. Therefore, state government can't make laws or issue order which is incompatible with above aspects. But in this case state with its authoritative power issued the GO while neglecting the above aspects. Thus, this process is leading to the sheer denial of their socio-cultural rights.

The PESA Act 1996 empowers the *Gram Sabha* to protect their interest, rights and identity and manage their affairs and in this regard the state supposed not to intervene in their areas. The Act says 4 (d) 'every *Gram Sabha* shall be competent to safeguard and preserve the traditions and customs of the people, their cultural identity, community resources and the customary mode of dispute resolution' (GOI, 1996). It is the *Gram Sabha* that has governing power over their area, rather than the state or forest bureaucracy, but by declaring this areas itself is the violation done by the exceptional measure and the tribal people's rights of self-determination is questionable once the areas made under the tiger reserve. The very important aspects of 1996 PESA Act are by nature, it empowers the people and gives them all rights like political, socio-cultural and economic and allow them to do their self-rule. It also makes mandatory that if any project effect on the tribal people they must be consulted and consent must be taken from them.

The FRA 2006 Act states that historical injustice has been done to the tribal and forest communities of India, so recognise their rights over forest land, resource and their areas (GOI, 2006a). When all these acts give rights and empower the tribal communities for self-rule in their region in reality the tribals don't enjoy these rights. The significant thing of this Act is it also mentions in Section 2(b) about the creation of 'Critical Tiger Habitat' or 'Core Area', should be established on the basis of scientific and objective criteria, after open process of consultation by an expert committee which must consult to the people of the area and region (*ibid*). To recognise or declare the tribal region as tiger reserve the Forest Department alone can't take the decision. The expert committee must be constituted by different people from tribals to ecologists. They must study how human and wildlife conflict exist and what are the wildlife and people problem. This mention process didn't take place in the establishment of the Kawal Tiger Reserve. Therefore, the Forest Department doesn't have authority to recognise the region as Tiger Reserve without consultation and participation of the people. Hence, not following and implementing these Acts as acts of state of exceptional act done by the Forest Department. In order to recognise the reserve the state arbitrarily decided the boundaries of Core and Buffer Areas. Indeed this contrary to the Wildlife (Protection) Act, 2006 Section V (ii) which 'says that Core and Buffer Areas wherein the limits of such areas are determined on the basis of scientific and objective criteria in consultation with the concerned Gram Sabha and an Expert Committee constituted for the purpose (GOI, 2006b). This Act Section 38V (5) states that no Scheduled Tribes and other forest dwellers shall be resettled or have their rights adversely affected for the purpose of creating inviolate areas for tiger conservation unless; (ii) the concerned agencies of the State Government, in exercise of their powers under this Act, establishes with the consent of the Scheduled Tribes and such other forest dwellers in the area, and in consultation with an ecological and social scientist familiar with the area, that the activities of the Scheduled Tribes and other forest dwellers or the impact of their presence upon wild animals is sufficient to cause irreversible damage and shall threaten the existence of tigers and their habitat'(*ibid*).

Adding to this, Scheduled Area Act 1950 states that 'if any act goes against the tribal communities' interest then the Act can be nullified by the concerned state governor. Even the Tribal Advisory Committee also has suggestive role to play if governor refers to it' (GOI, 1950). But in the whole tribal establishment process governor of AP did not make any such acts, though he was approached by the tribal leader and civil society members. Not acting when you have to act is also an exceptionalism of power.

In the Kawal forest the situation created by the Forest Department with the support of Non-Governmental Organisation (NGO) called Hyderabad Tiger Conservation Society (HYTICOS)(perhaps this NGO played significant role) that there is no evidence of tiger but still the area is declared as Tiger Reserve based on moral element of wildlife conservation. Whatever the government has done it is neither fact nor right. This view can be drawn from the ongoing conflict between tribal communities and the state apparatus. Hence, in this process without following the principle of decentralisation while taking decision and implementing the decision, but the state is trying to centralise with the assistance of NGO.

The state in this case is not only fail to protect but also disregarding the people's rights through Forest Department represent it, so this process represent and reflect the state version of governing the tribal areas. To become more sovereign and dilute the devolution of power to communities, apply stringent laws which not only disregard the tribal rights but also negate the Adivasi identities over the areas/region through hegemonic procedure. The Wildlife (Protection) Amendment Act 2006 creates the Critical Tiger Habitat or Core Area which should be kept inviolate and people should be displaced and not allowed to enter this area, while in Buffer area people are allowed to stay with restricted rights and under controlled supervision. The Clause of this same Act 38Z(1)&(3) says about 'No alteration in the boundaries of a Tiger Reserve shall be made except on a recommendation of the Tiger Conservation Authority and the approval of the National Board for Wild Life'. If the boundaries are altered by the people they will be punished' (GOI, 2006b). The Wild Life (Protection) Amendment Act, 2002 precisely states in a Section 54(1) 'The Central Government may, empower the Director of Wild Life Preservation or any other officer not below the rank of Assistant Director of Wild Life Preservation and in the case of a State Government in the similar manner, empower the Chief Wild Life Warden or any officer of a rank not below the rank of a Deputy Conservator of Forests, to accept from any person against whom a reasonable suspicion exists that he has committed an offence against this Act, payment of a sum of money by way of composition of the offence which such person is suspected to have committed' (GOI, 2003). One could question that with these stringent laws do the communities really exercise their rights to self-rule?

All the Acts made by the state like Wildlife (Protection) Act 1972, Wildlife (Protection) Amendment Act 1999, Wildlife (Protection) Amendment Act 2002, Biological diversity Act 2002, Wildlife (Protection) Amendment Act 2006, create bureaucratic structure for the regulation and control people of the region. It gives power to operate on the people under the guise of reasonable suspicious. On the one hand it gives power to FD and creates its own power structure in the region and on the other it gives abysmal rights to the people. Henceforth, this phenomenon leading to centralisation and alienating people rather than the decentralisation and govern themselves, so the tribal communities have been suspicious toward the state activities in the region and resisting the state.

Tribal's Dissension in the Decentralisation

Tribal people are dissenting against the process where procedural decentralisation becoming weak. With this activities of the state, perception of the local communities being framed. So demonstrates that they are no longer a mute, inarticulate lot, recognition of their identity and they also called for amendment of forest acts (Chaudhary and Patnaik, 2008). Their assertion comes from their basic survival, culture and political aspects, because they 'had to suffer the exploitative structure of governance symbolised in policies, exercise and Forest Department, exploitative market structure, rural stagnation and mass poverty pauperisation' (Saran and Singh, 1999).

Guha (2012) says the process whereby an introduction of forest policy, management and regulation, the customary rights of the forest community has been progressively curtailed. The colonial policies were guided by the colonial interest for raw material for railways and world war, in post-independence times has been commercial and industrial interest. In spite of lip-services paid to the need of the forest communities in the policy documents, the forest communities have experienced progressive loss over their habitat (Guha, 2012: 26-33). Bringing them under the larger political identity, within the guise of legitimate rights and power of the state is hegemonic process through which general causes like development and wildlife protection fulfilled, certainly this process goes against the rights of tribals.

The assault on the tribal land resource in the decades preceding the twentieth and twenty first century was mainly through private land grabbing and demarcation of forest reserves (Doshi, 1997:96). The colonial government had converted large tracts of forests into state forests, notwithstanding mute, semi-articulate and violent tribal protests affirming their paramountcy. The government/state attitude could be understood by looking at 'our new forest policy is more callous to the tribal and hold them responsible for present forest decay. Most of the futile land has been usurped by the non-tribals. This has reduced to the level of marginalisation and small peasant. The tribal lot, therefore, in an era of development is depressed because of loss of their land and forest' (Doshi, 1997: 1). There has been no letup in these processes because traditional skills and aptitudes have not equipped them to participate in modern evocations except as unskilled labour, administrative process have resulted in expropriation of tribal land without the knowledge of their tradition. Their identity and culture is rooted in their land and around the natural setting they live in. It is this relationship, which constitutes the unique feature of Adivasi culture. Their societies are community-based. Land is owned commonly. Community life is cooperative and based on reciprocity. Any decision is taken by jointly through consensus. Their society is considered as classless and egalitarian. On the hand, the societies around them are often highly exploitative, stratified, centralised, individualistic and anti-nature, tribal see land as mother and valuable thing (Guha, 2006: 221-224).

All the communities have maintained their cultural continuity through social heritage consisting of myths, legends, folk tales, proverbs, and stories and historical evidences pertaining to community towards their customs, traditions, values etc. The community cohesiveness is maintained through the channels of communication through religious, social and political networks. They have a deep attachment with the region and area. These are the common aspects which are helping these communities to build a strong unity and identity in the region. The traditional *Panchayats* are very effective among all the tribal communities. In this situation they came to react against the issue and there is unity among all the communities to resist against the state intervention into their areas. There is a lack of space for tribal communities to represent, negotiate and bargain, though they have given power and rights, still they are struggling to given rights. This is uniqueness of the problem and puzzle of the story.

The Gond community has special importance for the place and region. They have kept their clan's name after places and they identify themselves with space and region. Tradition and cultural have a greater role to play in the life of the tribal communities of the region and the tendency to preserve the traditions and culture rooted in the space which form the base of their identity is reflected in the social and cultural perceptions. For example, although the Gond chief and community lost political power two centuries ago but still they feel that they have cultural and social authority over the region. Reflecting this tendency, Somu (Interviewed: 13 December 2013) a 85 years old man belonging to the Gond community and a resident of the Zamuldhar village of Sirpur (u) Mandal which falls under the core area of Tiger Reserve says that 'our grandfather and our community ruled the forest, the rivers and also other community people. Everyone was happy under them. Once we lost our rule, the problem started getting into our life and now we want to protect our community rights and culture'. This narration reflects the inherent demand for decentralisation and self-rule.

The tribals experience and their attachment with the forest and unique worshipping style make them to be more attached with region. Bheemu (Interviewed: 13 December 2013) a 65 years old man of the Kolam Guda who belongs to the Kolam community says that 'cannot imagine us without the forest, it is everything for us. The restrictions or regulations on our movement in the forest are suffocation for us; please leave us to live our life. We have been here for generations, we neither harm to forest nor to animals. We live the life of forest; we know which tree produce what? We live in our *gudam* forest; it is our God. So forest is life we will not leave the forest and will not tolerate any regulation on us because this forest is ours. We lived with tigers and despite having various problems with tigers we did not kill them. Tigers lived in this area but gradually have disappeared from this region the reasons for their disappearance are not known to us. But now the *Sarkar* (government) has declared the tiger zone without involving us which resulting difficult for us to sustain, so we are opposed to this decision of the *sarkar*. In this whole of his narration, he is attaching with history, culture and their identity with the region.'

Patte Posakka, (Interviewed: 8 June 2013) a 75 years old women from Dongapally village which is inhabited by the Naikpod community says 'the FD is consistently asking them to leave their village but we have our God Bhimna Devudu in the forest. When we went to the office of the FD, they told the same word that if we do not leave then they will not allow us to worship our God and will take us to police station'. This indicates how people of the region terrorized by the state via FD. Thus, the people's self-rule envisaged living in the forest without fear from outside element.

This narration could be derived from the people resistance to state and their protest and dissent. Everywhere, Adivasi struggle are taking place to protect their resources and livelihood. Prabu (cited in Munshi, 2012: 11) views that the state is primary responsible for denial of Adivasi rights to their survival resources, and that tribal struggle shows sift from resistance to resurgence'. The perspective that emerging in tribal movement is 'affirming of tribal-self, recapturing the control over resources, reclaiming political domain and redefining political development' (*ibid*). But, the dream to enjoy complete rights over forest remained unfulfilled, which torments the tribal till today (Gaur and Patnaik, 2008: 324).

The demand for the self-rule is coming for several reasons. These includes: First, mainstream mobility into tribal areas and their exploitation, in order to prevent this and keep their area protected and intact so that would stop the process of their marginalisation and alienation. The Second, is atrocities by the Forest Department and it prejudice: 'tribals being the forest dwellers, are the first enemy of the forest who destroy the forest (Patel, 1994: 106). One of the basic objectives of the forest policy of 1988 was to meeting the requirement of fuelwood, fodder, minor forest produce and small price of timber for the rural and tribal population. However, the preconceived notion still prevail which doubt the intension of the tribals (*ibid*). The Wild Protection Act 1972 (GOI, 1972) has made forest dwellers more prone to displacement and devoid of userfructary right in forest and forest produce. Conflict arises because on the one hand industry-revenue oriented policies of the state governments and on the other hand unwillingness on the plays in the Forest Department to understand vital role forest play in the tribal economy. Third, tribal communities attachment with the region and their apprehension toward the centralised state and its apparatus, that their rights would be violated. Finally, various Acts empower the tribal to exercise their rights over the region and they are entitled to do so. These are the aspect which provokes them to demand for the decentralised Self-Rule where they can decide their activities by themselves.

Conclusion

It could be argued that state of exception and exclusion is the predictable outcomes, since the structure of bureaucracy at all levels is a colonial inheritance and their insensitive to the cultural complexity of the region. The nature and quality of governance and change in their area should be left to the tribal communities itself. The crux of the matter is that tribal has to be the arbiter of his destiny. They should ask themselves i.e., what type of change and development they aspire, then only it will fulfill the democratic dreams. As the community sense emanated from village and also guides their social life. Thus, tribal community life is both democratic and open, as deliberations were always open and everybody had to voice his/her grievances. 'Nature, environment and ecology play the most important role in the tribal life. They have built up their social, economic and religious lives around nature.

The consensual and participatory democracy in the tribal societies and areas are perhaps more democratic than the representative democracy. But in reality, claim of state on self-rule of tribal communities in Scheduled Areas are without self, it is rule, i.e. dominant, exploitative and oppressive rule. To challenge this tribal communities are seeking for their decentralised self-rule where they are free from all the state oppressive activities. Therefore, all the communities resisting the state with the slogan of decentralisation and Self-Rule, as in the indigenous Gondi tribal language *Mava Nate Mava Raj* (our village and our rule) and '*Jangal Jamin Jaal Hamara Hai'* (Forest, Land and Water belong to us).

References

Chaudhury, K. Sukant and Soumendra Mohan Patnaik ed. (2008): *Indian Tribes and the Mainstream*, (New Delhi: Rawat Publications).

Doshi, S. L. (1997): *Emerging Tribal Image*, (Jaipur: Rawath Publication).

Elwin, Varrier (1941): *Loss of Nerve*, (Wagle Press: Mumbai).

Government of India (GOI)[32] (1950): "Scheduled Area Act 1950", (New Delhi: Ministry of Tribal Affairs Publication), accessed on 21 March 2013, (http://tribal. nic. in/Content/DefinitionofScheduledAreasProfiles. aspx).

______(1972): "The Wildlife (Protection) Act1972", (New Delhi: Ministry of Environment and Forests Publication), accessed on 21 March 2013, (http://envfor. nic. in/legis/wildlife/wildlife1. html).

______ (1996): "Panchayaths Extension to Scheduled Areas (PESA) 1996", (New Delhi: Ministry of Tribal Affairs Publication), accessed on 21 March 2013, (http://tribal. nic. in/WriteReadData/CMS/Documents/2012112-90242170976562pesa6636533023. pdf).

______(2003): "The Biological Diversity Act 2002", (New Delhi: Legislative Department), accessed on 21 March 2013, (http://bamu. ac. in/dept/zoology/3. per cent20The per cent20biological per cent20Diversity per cent20act, per cent202002. pdf).

______(2006a): "The Scheduled Tribes and other Traditional Forest Dwellers (Recognition of Forest Rights) Act, 2006", (New Delhi, Ministry of Law and Justice Publication), accessed on 21 March 2013, (http://tribal. nic. in/WriteReadData/CMS/Documents/201211290332077861328File1033. pdf).

______(2006b): "The Wildlife (Protection) Amendment Act 2006", (New Delhi: Ministry of Environment and Forests Publication), accessed on 21 March 2013, (http://www. moef. nic. in/sites/default/files/WildLifeAmedment Act2006 per cent20. pdf).

Government of Andhra Pradesh (1998): "Andhra Pradesh Panchayaths Extension to Scheduled Areas (PESA) 1998", (Hyderabad: Panchayath Raj and Rural Development Department Publishers), accessed on 21 March 2013, (http://www. Panchayath. gov. in/documents/10198/348968/AP per cent20PESA per cent20Rules per cent20_2011. pdf).

______(2012): "Kawal Tiger Reserve: Forest Department-Government Order-27)", (Hyderabad: Forest Department) accessed on 1 September 2012, (http://goirarchive. ap. gov. in/).

Guha, Ramachandra (2006): *How Much Should a Person Consume?: Environmentalism in India and the United States*, (California:University of California Press).

Guha (2012) in Indra Munshi (ed.): *The Adivasi Question: Issues of Land, Forest and Livelihood*, (Hyderabad: Orient Black Swan).

Gaur, Mokshika and Mohan Soumendra Patnaik (2008): "Struggle for Azadi: Adivasi Movements in Chhattishgarh" in (ed) Sukant K. Chaudhury and Soumendra Mohan Patnaik (ed.): *Indian Tribes and the Mainstream*, (New Delhi: Rawat Publications), pp. 320-336.

Haimendorf, Christoph von Furer (1982): *Tribes of India: The Struggle for Survival*, (California: University of California Press).

Jayal, Gopal Niraja and Sudha, Pai. ed. (2001): *Democratic Governance in India: Challenges of poverty, development and identity*, (New Delhi: Sage Publication).

Munshi, Indra (ed.) (2012): *The Adivasi Question: Issues of Land, Forest and Livelihood*, (Hyderabad: Orient Black Swan).

Nathan, Dev and Virginius Xaxa (ed.) (2012): *Social Exclusion and Adverse Inclusion: Development and Deprivation of Adivasis in India*, (New Delhi: Oxford Publications).

Nehru (1957): "Forward' in Elwin: *A philosophy for NEFA*, (New Delhi: Gyan Publishing House).

Sharan, Ramesh and Amar Kumar Singh (1999) 'Bhuria Committee Report and Tribal Self-Governance in Jharkhand Region of Bihar' *Social Change*, September-December: Vol. 29 Nos. 3 and 4, pp. 302-315.

12

Rural Development, Local Governance and Implementation of MGNREGA

—E. Venkatesu

Introduction

Public policies and institutions are important instruments in building of social, human, natural, physical and finance capital for the reduction of poverty. The International Fund for Agricultural Development (IFAD)[1] report on rural poverty found that the poverty is a multi-dimensional one and tackling of the poverty requires multi-dimensional interventions. The multi-dimensional interventions to reduce the level of poverty are supposed to be the five capitals endowment as referred above. The State policies and institutions are also supposed to work in favour of building the capital framework. Specifically, the institutions are supposed to play the pro-active role in terms of planning, convergence, monitoring, transparency, accountability and evaluation of the initiatives to reduce the poverty in rural areas.

According to Amartya Sen democratic institutions are prerequisite to achieve the concept of development as freedom. He points out that the use of democratic institutions is conditioned by our values and priorities and the use we make of the available opportunities of articulation and participation.[2] In rural development, the social and human development are the inbuilt aspects, therefore, in the words of PR Panchamukhi the social sector, which contribute to the human capital and human development, includes education, health and medical care, water supply and sanitation, equality of economic opportunities, housing conditions etc. He also refers that the term social sector value system of the economy such as values of freedom, gender equality, decentralisation, democratic federalism, inter-regional equalities, nationalism, values of prudence and abstinence, habit of saving, control on consumption, long-term perspective and components of social sector are supposed to promote the values both at the individual level and macro societal level.[3]

In post-independent period, during planning era through five years plans and NITI Aayog the state has been making several policy initiatives for the rural development. In the contemporary period about 15 flagship programmes are being implemented in the rural areas for the social and human development, while focusing on, broadly, infrastructure development, service delivery, capacity building, livelihoods etc.

Mahatma Gandhi National Rural Employment Guarantee Act is an important one among flagship programmes. The Act made several provisions for making institutional arrangements as an instrument for facilitating the community to participate. It has almost about to complete a decade of its implementation, therefore, it is appropriate time to examine the question of whether the constitutional bodies such as Panchayati Raj Institutions playing the role of enabling the community for effective participation in implementation of MGNREGA?

In India, Panchayati Raj Institutions are the indigenous historical institutional legacy, which has got constitutional status two decades ago. Similarly, Mahatma Gandhi National Rural Employment Guarantee Act, which has got legal status a decade ago, is the biggest state sponsoring social security programme in the history of human civilisation. At the time of drafting of the Constitution, both of them were in part four i.e., Directive Principles of State Policy, which are not supposed to be enforced by law. Second observation is that two of them operating at the grassroots level in the rural India for the empowerment of the community and assured 100 days employment opportunities for those people who are ready to do the physical labour. Two of them were introduced in the context of globalisation and post-globalisation. Before going to analyse the role of Panchayati Raj Institutions in the implementation of Mahatma Gandhi Rural Employment Guarantee Act, it would be appropriate to give a brief historical account about the evolution of social sector programmes, which are essential for the economic development, social justice, to improve the standard of living, quality of life, enhance the capabilities etc.

The analogy for the genesis of rural development programmes in India can be traced back to the impact of political and social movements, which took place before independence such as (a) anti-colonial Indian national movement led by Congress and Gandhi, (b) anti-caste movement by Mahatma Jyothiba Phule, Ambedkar, and others and (c) anti-feudal movement by the Communists, which set the agenda of social sector for post-independent India. Second is the incorporation of the political philosophy and ideology in the form of Fundamental Rights and Directive Principles of State Policy of the Constitution. Therefore, the origin of rural development programmes in India can be traced to part three and four of the Indian Constitution.

Constitution and Rural Development: Part-III and IV of the Indian Constitution are basis for evolving the rural development programmes, while focusing on social sector as they are ensuring the rights and entitlements of the citizens. The Fundamental Rights are defined as the basic human rights of citizens. These rights are defined in the part three of the Constitution and apply irrespective of race, place of birth, religion, caste, creed and sex. They are enforceable by the courts, subject to specific restrictions. The Directive Principles of State Policy are guidelines for the framing of the laws by the government. These provisions, set out in Part IV of the Constitution, are not enforceable by the courts, but the principles on which they are based are fundamental guidelines for governance that the State is expected to apply in framing and enacting the laws.

Directive Principles of State Policy: Directive Principles of State Policy have been grouped into four categories. These are:

(1) the economic and social principles, (2) the Gandhian principles, (3) Principles and Policies relating to international peace and security and (4) miscellaneous. Here only the economic and social principles and the Gandhian principles are discussed to understand the nature of social sector policy of the state in India.

(1) The economic and social Principles: The state shall endeavour to achieve Social and Economic welfare of the people by: (1) providing adequate means of livelihood for both men and women, (2) reorganising the economic system in a way to avoid concentration of wealth in few hands, (3) securing equal pay for equal work for both men and women, (4) securing suitable employment and healthy working conditions for men, women and children, (5) guarding the children against exploitation and moral degradation, (6) making effective provisions for securing the right to work, education and public assistance in case of unemployment, old age, sickness and disablement, (7) making provisions for securing just and humane conditions of work and for maternity relief, (8) taking steps to secure the participation of workers in the management of undertakings etc., (9) promoting education and economic interests of working sections of the people especially the SCs and STs, (10) securing for all the workers reasonable leisure and cultural opportunities, (11) making efforts to raise the standard of living and public health and (12) providing early childhood care and education to all children until they complete the age of six years.

(2) The Gandhian Principles: There are certain principles, based on the ideals advocated by Mahatma Gandhi. These Principles are (1) to organise village Panchayats, (2) to promote cottage industries in rural areas, (3) to prohibit intoxicating drinks and drugs that are injurious to health, (4) to preserve and improve the breeds of the cattle and prohibit slaughter of cows, calves and other milch and drought animals.

Evolution of Rural Development Programmes: With the change of the character of the State from colonialism to independence, democracy, socialism, secularism, social and economic equality before the law, subsequently, the ideas, which have been inserted in the Constitution, became the guiding principles of the State to introduce rural development programmes. The basic aim of these programmes in India are (1) increasing opportunities of all urban/rural people in respect of knowledge, health, skill development, participation in decision-making. (2) Creating conducive environment in reducing social and economic inequalities and (3) bringing all present and future potential resources to optimum use, conservation, development and protection.

Broadly there are two approaches in the implementation of the rural development programmes. (1) re-distribution with growth for increasing the productivity, income and output of low income groups, maximising the growth of Gross National Product, re-directing investment to poverty groups and transfer of assets to poverty ridden groups and (2) Basic need approach targeting and addressing the food, housing and health of the poor.

Broadly, there are five phases in the evolution of rural development programmes. The phase of welfare programme in 1950s, developmental initiatives in 1970s, empowerment of the community with special emphasise on women component plan in all the sectors in 1990s, participatory developmental processes from 2000 onwards while emphasising on engender and rights based approach and demand driven Acts from 2005 onwards. These policies can also be classified into two categories (1) rural development programmes since independence to pre-globalisation and (2) rural development programmes in post-globalisation period. During the first category i.e. post-independent period to pre-globalisation, the rural development programmes were guided by the nationalism, constitution and social-welfare, but the policies were highly centralised by the dominant party politics, Planning Commission and implemented by the steel framed colonial legacy of bureaucracy.

While taking into account the experiences of Gurgaon experiment by FL Brayne, 1920, Marthandam experiment by Spencer Hatch, 1921, The Sriniketan experiment by Tagore, 1920s , Sewagram experiment by M. Gandhi, 1933, Etawah Pilot project experiment by Albert Mayer, 1948, Experiments by social reformers, missionaries, religious institutions and government departments and Grow More Food campaign Launched in 1943 in the wake of Bengal Famine, and evaluation by VT Krishnamachari, the Community Development Programme was launched in 1952.[4] One of the constraints that was emerged in the process of implementation of the Community Development and National Extension Service programmes was the lack of institutional support for the participation of the community in the post-independent developmental process. Therefore, Balwant Rai Mehta Committee, which was constituted for the evaluation of Community Development Programme by the Planning Commission, recommended for the three-tier Local Bodies for the effective participation of the community in the developmental processes.

Following Balwant Rai Mehta Committee, a series of Committees were appointed to make Panchayati Raj Institutions as the most viable community centric institutions.[5] After Balwant Rai Mehta Committee recommendations, some of the State governments adopted three-tier and two-tier local bodies and series of rural development programmes were introduced for the social and economic development in the country. These programmes were implemented by the highly centralised and top-down administrative arrangements and until the 73rd and 74th Constitutional Amendment Acts 1992, there was no uniformity in the Panchayati Raj system, regular elections, and proper representation to the marginalised groups of the society.

The decade 1990s stands for two important radical changes in India one was providing constitutional status to the indigenous historical institutional legacy for the deepening of democracy, planning for the economic development and mechanism for conflict resolution and second was the introduction of neo-liberal economic policies for the structural adjustment and privatisation of the public sector economy in the process of globalisation.

Globalisation, increasing crisis and demand for rights and entitlements based policies

The process of globalisation was started in 1990s for the structural adjustment and liberalisation. The prominent economists who assessed the impact of neo-liberal policies for ten years (1990-2000) have come to a conclusion that the new economic policies produced the adverse impact on the social, economic and political life of the people. The findings of the studies are (1) *Panchamukhi*[6] study of the social sector before and after reforms made two important observations that (a) the relative allocations to the sub-sectors of the social sector are found to have been disturbed even showing the declining trends and (b) reforms seems to have promoted consumerism, imposed constraints on freedom such as in the context of federal set-up, seem to have increased possibilities of corruption, led to work-loss due to disputes, seem to be associated with rising crime rates etc. (2) Mahendra Dev and Jos Mooij concluded that as a proportion of GDP, the share of social sector expenditure has not increased during the reform period. The shares in 1990s were lower than those of 1980s.[7] (3) Seema Joshi argues that the share of social sector expenditure in the combined expenditures of the central and state governments registered an increase during the reform period. In case of central plan and non-plan expenditure, the social sector spending (as a per cent of aggregate expenditure) increased significantly from 10.59 per cent in the pre-reform period (1986-87 to 1990-91) to 13.87 per cent in the post-reform period (1991-92 to 2002-03). As a proportion of GDP, central government expenditure incurred on the social sector has followed a highly fluctuating trend in both pre-reform and post-reform periods. India is spending a very low percentage of GDP on this particular sector. Even over decade of reforms not much improvement in social sector spending has been made as the share of social sector to GDP remained at a very low of 2.7 per cent in 2000-01 (in 1986-87 it was 2.62 per cent). In the post-reform period (1991-92 to 2000-01) social sector spending (expressed as percentage of GDP and aggregate expenditure) in the states has come down.[8]

Act for the Wage Employment in Rural Areas: To face the growing socio-economic crisis in the process of globalisation and pressure built by the leftist political forces, non-party political organisations[9] and grassroots level Civil Society Organisations, the United Progressive Alliance government at the National level introduced the National Rural Employment Guarantee Act, 2005 and later the prefix Mahatma Gandhi was added. The basic objective of the Act is to enhance livelihood security in rural areas by providing at least 100 days of guaranteed wage employment in a financial year to every household whose adult members volunteer to do unskilled manual work. The Act is also meant to serve other objectives such as generating productive assets, protecting the environment, empowering rural women, reducing rural urban migration and fostering social equity, among others.[10]

Goals of MGNRGEA[11]

- Social protection for the most vulnerable people living in rural India by providing employment opportunities.
- Livelihood security for the poor through creation of durable assets, improved water security, soil conservation and higher land productivity.
- Drought-proofing and flood management in rural India.
- Empowerment of the socially disadvantaged, especially women, Scheduled Castes (SCs) and Scheduled Tribes (STs), through the processes of a rights-based legislation.
- Strengthening decentralised, participatory planning through convergence of various anti-poverty and livelihoods initiatives.
- Deepening democracy at the grass-roots by strengthening Panchayati Raj Institutions.
- Effecting greater transparency and accountability in governance.

Panchayats and MGNREGA: In the implementations of MGNREGA the Panchayati Raj Institution consisting of Gram Sabha/ Ward Sabha, Gram Panchayat, Block Panchayat and Zilla Panchayat has got important role in terms of planning, convergence, transparency, accountability etc.

(a) Gram Sabha: For the direct participation of citizens in decision-making, Gram Sabha, as a Constitutional Body, provides institutional platform. According to Article 243 (b) "Gram Sabha" means a body consisting of persons registered in the electoral rolls relating to a village comprised within the area of Panchayat at the village level. According to Article 243A a Gram Sabha may exercise such powers and perform such functions at the village level as the Legislature of a State may, by law, provide. In the Panchayati Raj set up, the Gram Sabha, the general assembly of villagers has a key role for effective functioning of Panchayats. In the Gram Sabha meeting, the rural poor, the women and the marginalised people would get an opportunity to join in decision-making on matters affecting their lives. Active functioning of the Gram Sabha would ensure a participatory democracy with transparency, accountability and achievement. Gram Sabha is supposed to meet at least in each quarter preferably on Republic Day, *Ambedkar Jayanti*, Independence Day and *Gandhi Jayanti* to decide developmental works to be undertaken by Panchayats based on needs assessment. It also suggests remedial measures for economy and efficiency in the functioning of the Panchayats. Community questions and scrutinise the decisions of Panchayats in the meetings of Gram Sabha. The Gram Sabha also discusses the Annual Financial Statement of Gram Panchayats.

According to MGNREGA guidelines,[12] the Gram Sabha (GS) is the principal forum for wage seekers to raise their voices and make demands. The GS has the following rights and responsibilities under the Act:

- It recommends works to be taken up and is the final authority to determine the order of priority in which works will be initiated under MGNREGA.
- Monitor the execution of works within the GP.
- It is the primary forum for conduct of social audits. It provides a platform to all residents to seek and obtain all relevant information from all the Implementing Agencies including GP in relation to MGNREGA works implemented in the GP area.

The field observations[13] reveals that the Gram Sabha has been vital organ in spreading the awareness about the key elements of MGNREGA through the posters, *Kalajathas,* audio-video cassettes, wall writings etc. The independent studies[14] found that the Gram Sabhas are held in frequently, there is low participation in Gram Sabhas for selection and prioritisation of works, sometimes work selection is not done according to the priorities of Gram Sabha and the proportion of work undertaken by the Gram Panchayat was less than 50 per cent of the total cost of the scheme.[15]

(b) Gram Panchayat: (GP) According to 73rd Constitutional Act, Panchayat means an institution (by whatever name called) of self-government constituted under Article 243B, for the rural areas; "Panchayat area" means the territorial area of a Panchayat.

In MGNREGA, the GP is the pivotal body for planning and implementation. According to the Act, the Programme Officer (PO) is required to allot at least 50 per cent of the works in terms of cost to the GPs for implementation. The GP is responsible for the following activities such as receiving applications for registration, verifying registration applications, registering households, issuing Job Cards (JCs), receiving applications for work, issuing dated receipts for these applications for work, allotting work within fifteen days of submitting the application or from the date when, work is sought in the case of an advance application, whichever is later, irrespective of the implementing agency, conducting periodical surveys to assess demand for work, identification and planning of works, developing shelf of projects including determination of the order of their priority. Forwarding of this list to Programme Officer for scrutiny and preliminary approval, Executing works while meeting the required technical standards and measurements, maintaining records, accounts and providing utilisation certificates in formats prescribed by Central/State Govt., prepare annually a report containing the facts and figures and achievements relating to the implementation of the scheme within its jurisdiction and, copy of the same to be made available to the public on demand and on payment of such fee as may be specified in the scheme, awareness generation and social mobilisation. Convening the GS for planning and social audit, make available all relevant documents including the muster rolls, bills, vouchers, measurement books, copies of sanction orders and other connected books of account and papers to the GS for the purpose of conducting the social audit, monitoring implementation at the village level, pro-actively disclosing information.

The MGNREGA has been assigning the number of responsibilities to the Gram Panchayat.

(c) Block Panchayat: The Block Panchayat operates in between Gram Panchayat and Zilla Panchayat to perform following functions in MGNREGA:

- Approve the Block level Plan for forwarding it to the district Panchayat at the district level for final approval;
- Supervise and monitor the projects taken up at the Gram Panchayat and Block level;
- Carry out such other functions as may be assigned to it by the State Council, from time to time.
- Where Part IX of the Constitution does not apply, local Councils/ authorities as mandated by the State concerned will be invested with these responsibilities.

(d) Zilla Panchayat: The Zilla Panchayat is the apex institution in the three-tier Panchayati Raj system to discharge the following responsibilities in implementation of MGNREGA.

- Consolidation of Annual Block Plans (within the District) into a District Plan;
- Adding any inter-block work that according to them will be a good source of employment;
- Monitoring and supervision of the MGNREG Scheme in the District;
- Carry out such other functions as may be assigned to it by the State Council, from time to time.

The Panchayati Raj Institutions are supposed to be the institutional platform for planning, convergence and transparency and accountability.

(1) Planning: Article 243G which is the operational aspect of the 73rd Amendment to the Constitution says that: "The legislature of a State may, by law, endow the Panchayats with such powers and authority as may be necessary to enable them to function as institution of self-government and such law may contain provisions for the devolution of powers and responsibilities upon Panchayats at the appropriate level, subject to such conditions as may be specified therein, with respect to (a) the preparation of plans for economic development and social justice; and (b) the implementation of schemes for economic development and social justice as may be entrusted to them including those in relation to the matters listed in the Eleventh Schedule." Article 243W of the Constitution contains similar provisions for urban local bodies.

Article 243 ZD of the Constitution says that:

(1) There shall be constituted in every State at the district level a District Planning Committee to consolidate the plans prepared by the Panchayats and Municipalities in the district and to prepare a draft development plan for the district as a whole.

(2) The Legislature of a State may, by law, make provision with respect to:

   (a) The composition of the District Planning Committees;

   (b) The manner in which the seats in such Committees shall be filled. Provided that not less than four-fifth of the total number of members of such Committees shall be elected by, and from amongst the elected members of the Panchayat at the district level and of the municipalities in the district in proportion to the ratio between the population of the rural areas and of the urban areas in the district.

(c) The functions relating to district planning which may be assigned to such Committees.

(d) The manner in which the Chairpersons of such Committees shall be chosen.

(3) Every District Planning Committee shall, in preparing the draft development plan have regard to matters of common interest between the Panchayats and Municipalities including spatial planning, sharing of water and other physical and natural resources, the integrated development of infrastructure and environmental conservation. The extent and type of available resources whether financial or otherwise.

(4) The Chairperson of every District Planning Committee shall forward the development plan, as recommended by such Committee, to the Government of the State.

Above mentioned Constitutional provisions are designed to enable the State Governments to make Panchayats viable institutions so that they can prepare economic and social planning with people's participation at various levels of decentralised governance.

Keeping above in view, it is expected that for the purpose of formulation of the decentralised plan, the first step is that it should be discussed in the Gram Sabha (GS) for onward consideration in the Gram Panchayat. The plans prepared by all GPs falling under the jurisdiction of the Panchayat Samiti are to be assembled at its level with the purpose to have detailed discussion on the plan proposals received by various GPs and any gap or lacunae in the plans prepared by various GPs, should be sorted out. The plans so prepared by all the Panchayat Samitis of the district will be sent to the Zilla Parishad with the purpose for the discussion at its level and if there are gaps they should be sorted out. In this way, plan for the entire rural areas of the district will be prepared by the ZP. In a similar fashion plans of the urban areas will be prepared by the Urban Local Bodies of the District. The plans prepared by the urban local bodies will be integrated by the District Planning Committees. These Committees are expected to prepare the plan for the entire district and will send a draft plan to the State Government.[16]

Planning according to MGNREGA guidelines includes preparing of labour budget, baseline survey to assess quantum and timing of demand for work, preparation of development plan and shelf of projects includes identification of needs, resource envelop, Preparation of Draft Development Plan, Approval of Gram Sabha and Plan finalisation, while following the stages:

- Gram Sabha to approve Gram Panchayat (GP) Annual Plan and submit to Programme Officer (PO);
- PO submits consolidated GP Plans to Block Panchayat;
- Block Panchayat to approve the Block Annual Plan and submit to District Planning Committee (DPC);
- DPC to present District Annual Plan and Labour Budget (LB) to District Panchayat;
- District Panchayat to approve District Annual Plan;
- DPC to ensure that shelf of projects for each GP is ready;
- Labour Budget is submitted to Central Government.

Identification of the Needs: As part of planning for the implementation of MGNREGA across the country following works, broadly, have been identified at the Gram Sabha level through participatory micro level planning and, subsequently, Government of India issued revised guidelines for the permissible works.[17]

- water conservation and water harvesting including contour trenches, contour bunds, boulder checks, gabion structures, underground dykes, earthen dams, stop dams and spring shed development;
- plantation; drought proofing including afforestation and tree irrigation canals including micro and minor irrigation works;
- provision of irrigation facility, dug out farm pond, horticulture, plantation, farm bunding and land development renovation of traditional water bodies including desilting of tanks; land development;
- flood control and protection works including drainage in water logged areas including deepening and repairing of flood channels, chaur renovation, construction of storm water drains for coastal protection; rural connectivity to provide all weather access, including culverts and roads within a village, wherever necessary;
- construction of Bharat Nirman Rajiv Gandhi Sewa Kendra as Knowledge Resource Centre at the Block level and as Gram Panchayat Bhawan at the Gram Panchayat level;
- agriculture related works, such as, NADEP composting, vermi-composting, liquid bio-manures;

- livestock related works, such as, poultry shelter, goat shelter, construction of pucca floor, urine tank and fodder trough for cattle shed, azolla as cattle-feed supplement;
- fisheries related works, such as, fisheries in seasonal water bodies on public land;
- works in coastal areas, such as, fish drying yards, belt vegetation;
- rural drinking water related works, such as, soak pits, recharge pits;
- rural sanitation related works, such as, individual household latrines, school toilet units, anganwadi toilets, solid and liquid waste management; construction of anganwadi centres and
- construction of playfields.

Any other works which can be identified by the Gram Sabha in the process of evolving a participatory micro level planning.

(2) Convergence: For generating employment opportunities, social security measures, providing basic minimum services, building infrastructure and managing land and water resources for sustainable development and to alleviate poverty, the Central and State governments have been spending billions of Rupees. Due to the duplication of resources, non-convergence and non-participatory planning there is a slow progress in the reduction of poverty, unemployment, food insecurity and environmental degradation.

The process of convergence at the institutional, resources and ideas level can achieve the goals such as maximisation of returns from the investment, promotion of Public-Private Community partnerships, left over needs of the community, sustainability in development and effective delivery of services.[18] In order to use resources efficiently and involve the local governments actively, i.e., to apply the principle of subsidiarity in practice, co-existence of horizontal coordination and vertical consolidation are instrumental, where local governments and other planning entities work together and plan development together.

Expected outcomes from convergence initiatives: Convergence is one of the important components of MGNREGA and expecting following outcomes.[19]

- *Increase in Social Capital*: Collective planning and implementation among different stakeholders will enhance social capital. This will improve management and work output.
- *Increase in Physical Capital:* The process will help in creating durable assets and will also improve land productivity.

- *Facilitation of Ecological Synergies:* Natural resource base regeneration through different activities such as afforestation, drought proofing, flood proofing, and watershed will lead to effective use of resources.
- *Mitigating Effects of Climate Change:* NREGA helps in addressing issues such as CO_2 emissions and industrial pollution and stemming.
- *Enhancing Economic Opportunities:* Income opportunities, savings and investments may be generated through activities such as pisciculture.
- *Strengthening Democratic Processes:* Convergence awareness and planning at the grassroots level will lead to greater ownership of projects.
- *Facilitating Sustainable Development:* Convergence efforts through creation of durable assets, rural connectivity, productivity enhancement and capacity development lead to sustainable development.

Framework for Convergence: For the achievement of expected outcomes through convergence of various developmental programmes, the framework which is being given in the following diagram,[20] provides a blueprint for the institutional, resources and ideas convergence.

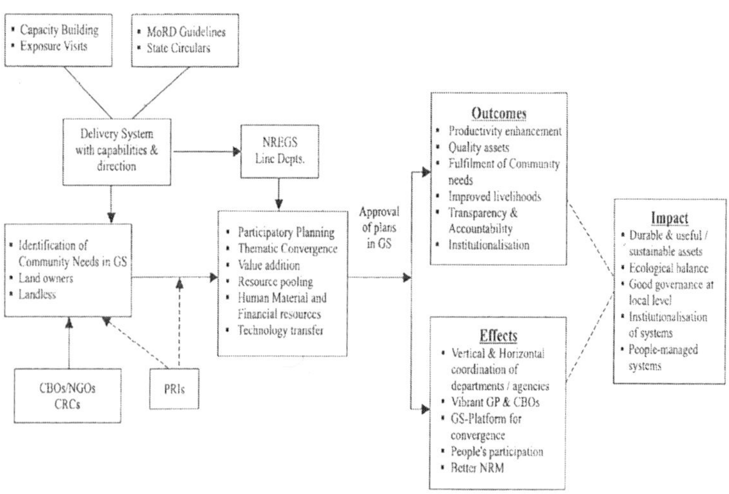

Source: Status Report on Convergence Initiatives of MGNREGA in India (2010), NIRD, p. 9.

Diagram 12.1

Table 12.1: Institutional Arrangements for Convergence[21]

Scheme	*Village level*	*Block level*	*District level*	*State level*	*National level*
NREGS	Gram Sabha Gram Panchayat	Block Panchayat	Zilla Parishad D. P. Coordinator	SEGC	NEGC
BRGF	Gram Panchayat	Block Panchayat	Zilla Parishad D. P. Coordinator	H. P. C	Ministry
RKVY	-	-	Dist. Planning Committee	S. L. Sanctioning Committee (SLSC)	Ministry concerned
SGSY	Gram Sabha	Block SGSY Committee	District SGSY Committee	State SGSY Committee	Central level Coord. committee
NRHM	VH and S committee	PHC Advisory Committee	District Health Mission	Empowered Programme Committee	Mission Steering Group and Empowered Programme Committee
SSA	School Education/ Management Committee	Block Resource Centre	District Mission	State Mission	National Mission Project approval board
Water and Sanitation	Village Level Water and Sanitation Committee	-	Dist. W and S Mission	State W and S Mission	National Drinking Water Mission
IAY	Gram Sabha	-	District Collector	SHC	Ministry concerned
ICDS	-	-	Standing Committee of ZP	-	-

Source: The details are prepared based on the guidelines given by the central ministries.

The Diagram 12.1 provides, some sort of, framework for the convergence, its purpose, process, outcomes effectiveness and impact.

The Table 12.1 is an illustration for the institutional convergence of the centrally sponsored social sector programmes. The institutional convergence from National level to Gram Panchayat level is an effective process for the effective utilisation of the scarce resources, while setting aside the duplication of the works at field level.

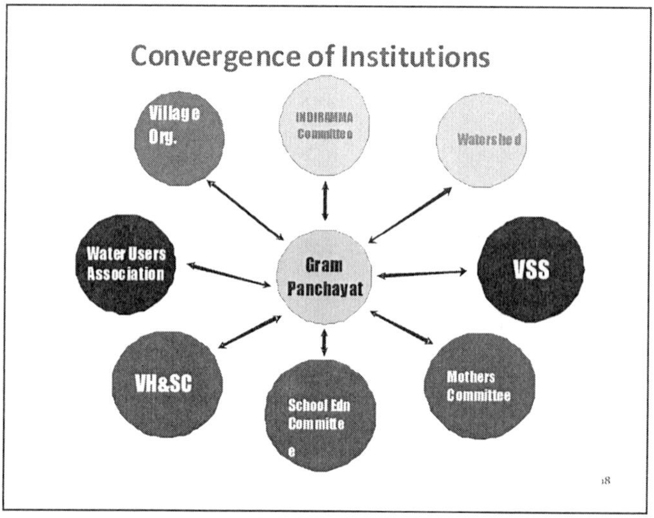

Diagram 12.2: Convergence at Gram Panchayat Level.[22]

Diagram 12.2 is the example for the convergence of multiple institutions/ parallel institutions and programmes with the Gram Panchayat. The process of institutional convergence at the grassroots level is a reciprocal, inter-dependent and cooperative to evolve planning exercise based on the Principle of Subsidiarity. The Table 12.2 reveals that there has been an increase in number of districts from 635 to 645, blocks from 6378 to 6603, but there is no change in number of Gram Panchayats and number of villages. There has been a rapid increase of Gram Panchayats without any expenditure of MGNREGA from 25389 to 47328 during the financial years 2011-12 to 2014-15. During the same period the expenditure on wages, material administration has come down 37072.7 to 22088.5, the number of households which applied for the employment also come down.

Table 12.2: Performance Report of MGNREGA

		FY 2014-2015	*FY 2013-2014*	*FY 2012-2013*	*FY 2011-2012*
Total No. of Districts		645	644	636	635
Total No. of Blocks		6603	6576	6568	6378
Total No. of GPs		247643	247643	247643	247643
Total No. of Villages		778134	778134	778134	778133
Total No. of HH Registered (In Cr)		13.2	13.3	13.2	12.6
Total No. of Workers in Job Card (In Cr)		28.4	29.1	29.3	27.8
Number of GPs with NIL exp		47328	26163	26190	25389
Number of Ongoing Works (In Lakhs)		83.6	69.1	79.1	53.2
Total No. of Works Taken up (New Spill Over) (In lakhs)		90.5	94.5	104.6	80.8
Total Exp (In Cr)	Wages (Rs in Cr.)	16220.3	26556.4	27152.8	24306.2
	Material and skilled Wages (Rs in Cr.)	4845.2	9672.6	10430	10650.5
	Adm Exp:				
	GP Level	54.6	226.6	307.6	301.8
	Block Level	661.5	1342.7	1330.1	1191.7
	District Level	253.2	598.1	482	514.4
	State Level	53.614	201.512	32.936	108.055
	Total Adm Expenditure	1022.9	2369	2152.7	2116
	Total Exp (Rs in Cr.)	22088.5	38598	39735.4	37072.7
	Labour Vs Material (per cent)	77	73.3	72.2	69.5
	Admin Exp (per cent)	4.6	6.1	5.4	5.7
Wage Employment Provided (in lakhs)	Households	330.4	479.2	498.9	506.4
	Individuals	486.6	738.7	797.3	820
	Men	235.5	384.5	422.1	446.6
	Women	251.2	354.2	375.3	373.3
	SCs	109.4	167.8	181.7	185
	STs	89.4	130.8	142.9	147.4
	Persons with Disability	3.5	4.8	4.6	4

(Contd...)

Person days (In Cr)	Total as per LB	227.0	258.6	278.7	199.6
	Person days Generated so far	103.8	220.3	230.5	218.8
	per cent of Total LB	45.7	85.2	82.7	109.6
	per cent as per Proportionate LB	80.3			
	SC person days	23.7	49.8	51.2	48.5
	ST person days	16.8	38.3	41	40.9
Average Wage rate per day per person		137.9	132.7	121.4	114.5
Average days of employment provided per Household		31.4	46	46.2	43.2
Total No. of HHs completed 100 Days of Wage Employment (In Lakhs)		7.2	46.6	51.7	41.7
Per cent payments generated within 15 days		28	45.7	63	57.8
Per cent of payments Disbursed through EFMS (An electronic Fund Management System)		69.7	39.1	12.3	0

Performance since inception: Person days Generated (In Cr.): **1764.49** Total expenditure (Rs in Cr.): **266707.4**
Today 3228845 workers are expected on 197800 worksites (as per e-MustRoll)

Source: http://mnregaweb4. nic. in/netnrega/all_lvl_details_dashboard_new. aspx

The National Sample Survey Organisation 66th Round data for 2009-2010 indicated that for India as a whole, 25 per cent of rural households were provided work under the scheme and around 19 per cent of the total rural households demanded for work but not provided. Some of the poorest States, which required effective social safety nets, such as Bihar (34 per cent), Odisha (29 per cent) and Jharkhand (28 per cent) have low participation rate and high levels of unmet demand. The stated reasons are lower proportion of demand, low institutional capacity to administer the scheme that cannot match with growing demand, lower levels of awareness and empowerment and weak Panchayati Raj Institutions which have a key role to play in the implementation of MGNREGA.[23]

(3) Accountability and Transparency: An innovative feature of the Mahatma Gandhi NREGA is that it has institutionalised 'Social Audit' as a means of continuous public vigilance. Social Audit is a continuous and ongoing process, involving public vigilance and verification of quantity and quality of works at different stages of implementation; and social audit is to be conducted in every Gram Panchayat (GP) at least once in six months. The basic objective of social audit is to ensure public accountability in the implementation of projects, laws and policies. In MGNREGA social audit is incorporated as a inbuilt institutionalised mechanism for an effective means to ensure transparency, participation, consultation and accountability. The process of Social Audit combines people's participation and monitoring with the requirements of the audit discipline. The social audit is supposed to be facilitated by an independent organisation with the participation of people. The Social Audit process is not a fault finding, but a fact finding process.

A social audit is a contingent on participatory auditing which complements financial audit, auditing quality, performance, and strengthens financial audit. The social audit is dependent on people's participation; their participation is dependent on their seeing some tangible outcomes. SA is a Accountability and Development Tool, it is a participatory audit of social goals and performance of the stakeholders and development actors from the point of view of those impacted and other stakeholders. Just as a financial audit can reveal the financial health of an organisation through an official examination of its accounts, a social audit attempts to reveal the 'health' of community development which results from the interplay of public services, housing, employment, the natural and social environment and many other factors.

- Financial Audit = Was the money spent correctly?
- Social Audit = Did the spending make a difference?

Social Audit + Financial Audit = True Picture

Following MGNREGA guidelines social audits have been conducted in Dungarpur district of Rajasthan and Anantapur district of Andhra Pradesh in a massive way in collaboration with the civil society organisations, community based organisations, officials, public representatives etc. The social audit was started with the collection of information pertaining to official records, documents, registers, muster rolls etc., from Gram Panchayat for the confirmation of information with community and visiting the worksite for the physical verification of the work that was done under MGNREGA.

It was found[24] that there was a remarkable degree of administrative preparedness for NREGAS in Dungarpur district, job cards have been issued and works have started on time, muster rolls were available at the worksite, information about the works was available and NREGS has become a high priority for the local administration. Around 1.5 lakh persons were employed in the district, the number represents roughly half of rural households having one member employed under the EGS. Out of 237 Panchayats, 800-odd villages and 1000-odd work sites, where the social audits were conducted, only 15 complaints on corruption involving 185 workers have been brought out. These complaints involved fake names in muster rolls, labourers marked present when they absent and discrepancies between payments shown on the muster rolls and those actually received by labourers. There was a little corruption in the implementation of the EGS (less than 2-3 per cent), at 98.9 per cent of the work sites, muster rolls were available, which is an unheard phenomenon in drought relief works in the past. At the time of conducting social audit, the Gram Sabha used to decide all the works, but the prioritisation was done by the sarpanch, sachiv and few others. A significant finding of the social audit was that 80-90 per cent and sometimes all of the labourers working at the sites were women, People's awareness of entitlements under the act was low.

Another important social audit, which is seen as a model, was took place in Anantapur District, where the Prime Minister Manmohan Singh and UPA Chairman Sonia Gandhi launched the NREGS on 2nd February, 2006 and works were started in the month of April. The state level agency for conducting of the social audit has conducted series of social audits to ensure transparency and accountability in the implementation of the MGNREGA. The experience of the social audit was that where the "social audits" are in progress, there have been several instances of voluntary return of money. In the list are field assistants, technical assistants,

Table 12.3: State-wise Social Audit Report

S.No.	State name	Total District	No. of District Started Social Audit	Total GP	No. of Panchayat Covered	No. of Social Audit	Issue Raised and action taken
1.	ANDHRA PRADESH	22	0	21863	0	0	0
2.	ARUNACHAL PRADESH	16	5	1829	85	104	49
3.	ASSAM	27	27	2644	2561	5500	3772
4.	BIHAR	38	38	8529	8386	16656	8330
5.	CHHATTISGARH	27	27	9915	9367	9381	7412
6.	GOA	2	2	190	115	115	95
7.	GUJARAT	26	26	14315	13921	26225	18278
8.	HARYANA	21	21	6167	4122	5156	3065
9.	HIMACHAL PRADESH	12	11	3243	2523	3395	2341
10.	JAMMU AND KASHMIR	22	17	4143	1353	1457	555
11.	JHARKHAND	24	22	4435	3009	3741	1068
12.	KARNATAKA	30	30	5632	5628	11266	7399
13.	KERALA	14	14	978	862	14423	11314
14.	MADHYA PRADESH	51	27	23013	3167	3355	1592
15.	MAHARASHTRA	33	27	28570	12384	13351	3629
16.	MANIPUR	9	4	3102	281	351	259
17.	MEGHALAYA	11	11	1824	1602	2619	1420
18.	MIZORAM	8	3	828	143	194	113
19.	NAGALAND	11	0	1169	0	0	0
20.	ODISHA	30	30	6232	6196	11742	8283
21.	PUNJAB	22	22	13111	12751	22280	15914
22.	RAJASTHAN	33	33	9177	7678	7820	6271
23.	SIKKIM	4	4	180	90	90	89
24.	TAMIL NADU	31	3	12524	479	1337	0
25.	TELANGANA	0	0	0	0	0	0
26.	TRIPURA	8	8	1135	578	811	511
27.	UTTAR PRADESH	75	67	52035	12800	12924	11110

(Contd...)

28.	UTTARAKHAND	13	12	7661	5625	7210	1864
29.	WEST BENGAL	19	19	3349	2959	5576	2738
30.	ANDAMAN AND NICOBAR	3	1	77	22	42	0
31.	DADRA & NAGAR HAVELI	1	0	11	0	0	0
32.	DAMAN & DIU	2	0	10	0	0	0
33.	CHANDIGARH	1	0	1	0	0	0
34.	LAKSHADWEEP	1	0	10	0	0	0
35.	PUDUCHERRY	2	1	12	5	5	3
	Total	**649**	**512**	**247914**	**118692**	**187126**	**117474**

Source: http://164.100.129.6/netnrega/state_html/social_auditNT.aspx?flag=eng&fin_year=2013-2014)**(Footnotes)**

assistant engineers, branch post masters, sarpanches and a stray MLA's "right hand". These people have embezzled money fraudulently by creating fake muster rolls, inflated bills, exaggerated measurements, and non-existent works, all through bribes and cuts from wage seekers. In amounts ranging from Rs 25 to Rs 3 lakh, in the last five months alone approximately Rs 60 lakh has been returned to the system or to the wage seekers, from whom it has been siphoned off.[25]

Social Audit is a dynamic tool by which people are able to make officials accountable for their performance in the delivery of legally enshrined rights.[26]

Following the broad guidelines and methodology, based on field experiences, issued by the Ministry of Rural Development, Government of India, the social audit process has been started across the country. According to information given in table 12.3, so far 1,87,126 social audits have been conducted all over the country by the independent social audit organisations to find out the effectiveness of the programme.

Conclusion

The attempt to understand the role of Panchayati Raj Institutions in planning, convergence and transparency and accountability reveals that there has been lot of changes in the socio-economic, administrative and governance. With the introduction and implementation of MGNREGA for about one decade has contributed a lot for the improvement of several aspects such as wages of the labour, increase in the income, environment and bio-diversity conservation, security of livelihoods activating the grassroots level institutions and organisations.

(1) As a result of the emphasis on minimum wages in MGNREGA, for the first time across the country a debate has been raised to have uniform minimum wages. Otherwise the question of minimum wages was a subject of the state government. The variations in the minimum wages in different part of the country has emerged as core issue to take up measures to get the legitimate wage rates for the workers who have been sincerely working in the field through introduction of the Time and Motion and Piece Rate System. Apart from the debate for possibility of uniform minimum wages, for the first time at the national level the practice of gender equality has came into existence. The implications from these debates are to make policy initiatives for the regional balances curtail, free riders from the works and ending the gender inequality. The indirect impact of the minimum wages assured in MGNREGA has increased the capacity of agricultural labour to demand more wages for farm work.

(2) Another important change that has been taking place is that establishing the mechanism for the proper payment without middle man and corruption through opening of accounts in the banks, post-offices and providing mobile ATM facility. In fact, in the age of information technology, the post-offices were about to close, because of MGNREGA wage workers payments, the post-offices are being activated.

(3) In order to document the detailed information/data about the implementation process of MGNREGA, the information and tele-communications are being used. Computerisation of applications for Job Cards, applications for work, identification of the works, financial resources and all other aspects, which are involved in the implementation of MGNREGA. The e-documentation process has been facilitating a lot for officials, stake-holders, beneficiaries and for the Civil Society Organisations to verify the transparency and accountability in the implementation of the Act. One of the outstanding achievements of the implementation of MGNREGA is making detail information availability to the public through e-governance mechanism, probably, which is an unprecedented phenomenon in the history of developmental initiatives of India.

(4) The studies on environmental aspects of MGNREGA[27] found that there has been improvement (such as water conservation and harvesting, drought-proofing, irrigation provisioning and improvement works and renovation of traditional water bodies, improved groundwater levels, increased water availability for irrigation, increase area irrigated by ground, surface water sources and finally improved drinking water available for human and livestock).

(5) MGNREGA has contributed a lot for the reduction of vulnerability in the rural areas through generating multiple environmental and socio-economic benefits.[28] The benefits include maintaining or enhancing ground water levels, improving the storage capacity of water bodies, improving irrigation, increasing the SOC content and reducing soil erosion. These benefits have led to improved water availability and soil fertility resulting in increased crop production, increased employment generation reduced migration. Due to the generation of environmental benefits, the adaptive capacities of beneficiary households has increased, reduced their vulnerability risk.

(6) As a result of mandatory provisions of transparency and accountability in MGNREGA, to the maximum extent, despite the existence of several problems, a great deal of information has been generated and it has been accessible to the public in the form of hard and soft copies.

Therefore, the Civil Society Organisations and independent social audit agencies are able to conduct the social audit and bring out the misappropriation, misuse, corruption etc., in the implementation of MGNREGA. In fact, social audit is an innovative community centric auditing mechanism has been producing at least minimum level of expected results. Therefore, the social audit mechanism is being applied in other social sector programmes such as Indira Avas Yojana, Mid-Day Meals etc.

(7) At the time of introduction of MGNREGA, apprehension has been expressed about the capacities of rural local bodies in implementation due to their weak functioning, corruption etc.[29] but when we look at the performance of rural local bodies in the implementation of MGNREGA in the few years has proved that the grassroots level local institutions, which are at the doorstep of the people, are highly effective and efficient in terms of planning, monitoring, convergence, producing documentary evidences and transparency and accountability.

(8) The process of implementation of MGNREGA has become a flexible one in terms of adopting the innovations and learning from the community. In order to reach out the benefits to the deserving people, several hurdles, constraints and gaps are emerging. To overcome the emerging challenges, the MGNREGA has been keep on adopting and updating the latest changes in technology and best practices such as linking of the payments with Adhaar Card, biometric system etc.

It is evident from the above analysis that the MGNREGA has brought about a several changes in the socio-economic, governance and environmental conditions of India. But it is not free from problems and shortfalls such as weak institutional arrangements, low level of awareness, bureaucratic control, and vested political interests which are causing for diverting the programme from achieving its objectives. Therefore, there have been reports of corruption in the implementation of the Act. In this regard, the observation and recommendations made by Controller and Auditor General of India report, for the analysis of corruption in MGNREGA and measures to improve the performance, is highly relevant.[30] Finally, the implementation process of MGNREGA with the partnership of local bodies can be concluded that higher the participation of community and local bodies and greater will be the expected outcome.

Notes

1. See for details, Rural Poverty 2011, http://www.ifad.org/rpr 2011.
2. Singh, Satyajit, Sharma K. Pradeep (ed), *Decentralisation Institutions and Politics in Rural India*, Oxford University Press (2008), p. 7.

3. Panchamukhi, PR, Social Impact of Economic Reforms in India: A Critical Appraisal, *Economic and Political Weekly,* March 4, 2000, p. 836.
4. See for details, Singh, Katar, *Rural Development: Principles, Policies and Management*, SAGE Publications, New Delhi, 2009.
5. See for details, Venkatesu, E, 'The Process of Democratic De-centralization in India: An Analysis in Venkatesu (ed.) *Democratic Decentralisation in India-Experiences, Issues and Challenges* (Under Publication).
6. Panchamukhi, PR, *Ibid*, p. 847.
7. Mahendra Dev, S, Jos Mooij, Social Sector Expenditures in the 1990s Analysis of Central and State Budgets, *Economic and Political Weekly* March 2, 2002, p. 864.
8. Joshi, Seema, Impact of Economic Reforms on Social Sector Expenditure in India, *Economic and Political Weekly*, January 28, 2006, p. 365.
9. Venkatesu, E, Grassroots Politics in India, Serial Publications, 2010, New Delhi.
10. http://nrega.nic.in/Nrega_guidelines.pdf, p. 1.
11. http://nrega.nic.in/netnrega/WriteReaddata/Circulars/Operational_guidelines_4thEdition_eng_2013.pdf, p. 3.
12. *Ibid.*
13. See for details in State Specific Reports of Planning and Implementation og MGNREGA in Different States- A Process Study, http://www.nird.org.in/NIRD_Docs/mgnregs/Orissa_mgnrega.pdf.
14. *Ibid*, MGNREGA SAMEEKSHA.
15. *Ibid*, p. 56.
16. See for details, Manual for Integrated District Planning, (2008) Planning Commission of India.
17. http://nrega.nic.in/netnrega/WriteReaddata/Circulars/Operational_guidelines_4thEdition_eng_2013.pdf, p. 55.
18. First Report of the National Advisory- Cum- Review Committee on Backward Regions Grant Fund, p. 77.
19. Ministry of Rural Development, Government of India and UNDP, Report on Convergence Initiatives in India: An Overview, p. 2.
20. Annexures to First Report of the National Advisory- Cum- Review Committee on Backward Regions Grant Fund, p. 242.
21. First Report of the National Advisory- Cum- Review Committee on Backward Regions Grant Fund, p. 91.
22. *Ibid*, p. 93.
23. MGNREGA SAMEEKSHA, An Anthology of Research Studies on the Mahatma Gandhi National Rural Employment Guarantee Act, 2005, 2006–2012, http://nrega.nic.in/netnrega/writereaddata/Circulars/MGNREGA_SAMEEKSHA.pdf, p. 57.

24. See for detail, Bhatty, Kiran, Employment Guarantee and Child Rights, *Economic and Political Weekly,* May 20, 2006.
25. Karuna Vakati Aakella, Sowmya Kidamb, Social Audits in Andhra Pradesh: A Process in Evolution, *Economic and Political Weekly*, November 24, 2007.
26. Gopal, K. S, NREGA Social Audit: Myths and Reality, *Economic and Political Weekly*, January 17, 2009.
27. See for details, Sebastian, Mathew, K and P.A. Azeez, MGNREGA and Biodiversity Conservation, *Economic and Political Weekly*, March 8, 2014.
28. Tashina Esteves, K V Rao, Bhaskar Sinha, S S Roy, Bhaskar Rao, Shashidhar Kumar Jha, Ajay Bhan Singh, Patil Vishal, Sharma Nitasha, Shashanka Rao, Murthy I K, Rajeev Sharma, Ilona Porsche, Basu K, N H Ravindranath, Agricultural and Livelihood Vulnerability Reduction through the MGNREGA, *Economic and Political Weekly,* December 28, 2013, p. 102-103.
29. Aiyar, Yamini and Salimah Samji, Improving the Effectiveness of National Rural Employment Guarantee Act, *Economic and Political Weekly*, January 28, 2006, p. 323.
30. See for detail, Siddhartha, Anish Vanaik, CAg Report on NREGA: Fact and Fiction, *Economic and Political Weekly*, June 21, 2008.

13

Public Distribution System through e-Governance: A Case Study

—I. Ramabrahmam and Gowd Kiran Kumar

Introduction

The Government of Telangana and Andhra Pradesh seem to be heading to a situation whereby they stand to lose the Central subsidy for Public Distribution System (PDS) for their ineligibility to weed out ineligible sections from the PDS net once again brings to fore the core Governance objective of targeting the needy. Though the two state governments are making efforts to reach the stipulated deadline, the situation appears to be discouraging given the sensitive nature of the task. It affords an opportunity to revisit the basic contours of policy and implementation of policy on right to food.

The World Food Summit of 1996 defined food security as existing "when all people at all times have access to sufficient, safe nutritious food to maintain a healthy and active life." Food availability, food access and food use are the three pillars on which food security is built. Public Distribution System is an important policy intervention that India implemented for the food security in India through Fair Price Shops (FPS) also known as ration shops. The establishment of Food Corporation of India in 1965 is a crucial step for purchasing food commodities (primarily rice, wheat and sugar) and non-food items (mainly oil and kerosene) from farmers and private players and distribute them at subsidised rates through a network of Fair Price Shop (FPS).

Initially, the PDS was universal. All beneficiaries were used to get subsidised foodgrains and kerosene. But it was criticised by the policy experts and scholars especially its impact on finances. Therefore, Government of India changed the nomenclature as Targeted Public Distribution System (TPDS) in 1997. Subsequently, it was restricted to the Below-Poverty-Line (BPL), based on poverty estimates of Planning Commission. TPDS also associated with two major problems: exclusion errors and leakages (Masiero, 2014).[1] Many states address these problems with effective implementation of Information and Communication Technology (ICT) interventions. For example, Chhattisgarh is implementing the project – CORE-PDS covering most of the FPS in the state and use Point of Sale (PoS) devices and smart cards to give portability for the beneficiaries. It appears e-Governance facilitates minimising the diversions and challenges. In 2006, Government of India introduced National e-Governanace Plan (NeGP) for computerisation of Government Departments to ensure citizen centricity, service orientation and transparency. At the macro level National e-Governance Plan (NeGP) attempted to take a holistic view of e-Governance initiatives across the country by integrating them into a collective vision and a shared cause. An attempt was made for creating infrastructure to reach rural areas and an attempt is being made for digitisation of records to enable easy and reliable access over the internet.

With 31 Mission Mode Projects (MMPs), the NeGP focused on various aspects such as banking, land records or commercial taxes etc. Within NeGP, "mission mode" implies that a project has clearly defined objectives, scope, and implementation timelines and milestones, as well as measurable outcomes and service levels. e-PDS is elevated as one of the Mission Mode Project (MMP) and PDS is envisaged as *an end-to-end project covering key functional areas including supply chain management, allocation and utilisation reporting, storage and movement of foodgrains, grievance redressal and transparency portal, digitisation of beneficiary database, automation of Fair Price Shop, etc.*

Over the last decade, relevant literatures are is compiled on the link between PDS and ICTs and are also seen as tools for ensuring efficiency and accountability. The generic term e-governance now has to be seen as "the digital route to good governance" (Heeks, 2001).[2] The use of new technologies enables removal of discretionary power from street-level bureaucrats (Bovens and Zouridis, 2002),[3] resulting in higher transparency of administrative processes (Elbahnasawy, 2014)[4]: these considerations have been widely accepted in India, where the National e-Governance

Plan provides directives to improve governance through ICTs. Recently, new technologies are being put to use by union and state governments to further improve the services.

This study analyses aspects that have a bearing on poverty, hunger, nutrition, food security, Public Distribution System on the one hand and Food Security Act and its political and policy implications, e-governance and e-PDS on the other. The second part of the dissertation concentrates on the implementation of e-PDS system in the new state of Telangana. Technology has been designed and enacted in specific ways, in order to embody the state government's resolve to control leakages and remove 'ghost cards'. Technology, it may be said, may not automatically improve existing implementation of food security goal, current programmes of end-to-end computerisation will help in introducing new means to detect and prevent leakage.

Poverty, Hunger and Food Security

The food security in India has three interlinked aspects i.e., poverty, hunger and nutrition. Notable progress is reported since independence on the situation of poverty as evidenced by macro assessments at the global level as well as at macro levels. Food-based interventions have, to an extent, eliminated starvation deaths and reduced the intensity of hunger. The first Millennium Development Goal identifies poverty and hunger reduction, combining these two targets to emphasise their interrelationship. As Amartya Sen observes, "Hunger is primarily a problem of general poverty, and thus overall economic growth and its distributional pattern cannot but be important in solving the hunger and problem." Hunger reduces poor families' capacity to work and increases their vulnerability to illness and other shocks to their livelihoods. OECD's defines poverty as

> "Poverty encompasses different dimensions of deprivation that relate to human capabilities including consumption and food security, health, education, rights, voice, security, dignity and decent work."[5]

Similarly the definition of poverty line in many countries, including India, is based on the expenditure method. Poverty in India is measured by Planning Commission still recently. Still 2009, poverty is calculated based on Monthly Per-capita Expenditure based on the Suresh Tendulkar Committee report. National Sample Survey Organisation (NSSO) provides information about the expenditure. In 2012, Government of India, appointed a committee under C. Rangarajan to calculate poverty in India. The committee submitted the report in 2014. According to report, there are 37 crore people who are still in below poverty line. In India, large segment of those who are 'very poor' (below 75 per cent of the poverty line) and 'extremely poor' (below 50 per cent of the poverty line) chronically face hunger and malnutrition in various periods of the year. In order for the intensity of hunger to be reduced, the number of poor and specifically those who live in poverty needs to be reduced substantially.

Some analysts opposed the hypothesis stating decrease in poverty leads to the decrease in hunger. It has been studied in the past by many Indian economists and policy analysts like Ray (2005)[6], Patnaik (2007)[7], Subramanyam (2013)[8], Basu and Das (2014)[9] and others. Since Independence, India has made significant progress towards the goal of poverty reduction. Headcount Poverty declined from 55 per cent in 1973-74 to about 20 per cent in 1999-2000. More recent estimates by Planning Commission poverty in India decline to 21.92 per cent in 2011-12 from 29.8 per cent in 2009-10.[10] The data on the prevalence of hunger (or under-nutrition) in India is a matter of concern. The proportion of under-nutrition persons in urban India, i.e., those who are consuming less than 2100 Kcal per day was climbed to 70 per cent in 2009-10 from 58 per cent in 1993-94.[11] In rural areas i.e., those who are consuming less than 2400 Kcal per day, rose from 71 per cent to an astounding 90 per cent during the same period (Basu and Das, 2014). The divergence between the expenditure-based measure of poverty and calorie-based measure of nutrition raise serious questions about the Planning Commission's methodology for estimating the incidents of poverty in India. Basu and Das identified reasons for the under-nutrition: Destruction of rural livelihood, loss of access to common property resources like forests, ponds, grazing lands and river. Second, the structure of occupation has been undergoing rapid changes. Third, and possibly most important, shrinking social expenditure is rendering the urban and rural poor dependent on market prices of non-food essential items, which are typically high.[12]

Figure 13.1, clearly projects that in spite of decrease in the poverty levels, there is increase in malnutrition levels in the country. According to recent available National Family Health Survey (NFHS-3), 40.4 per cent of children under three were underweight, 44.9 per cent of them are stunted, 78.9 per cent of children age 6-35 months were anaemie, 57.9 per cent of pregnant women were anaemic.[13]

India ranked 55 out of 76 countries in Global Food Index for the year 2014. 30.7 per cent children under five are underweight, 17 per cent

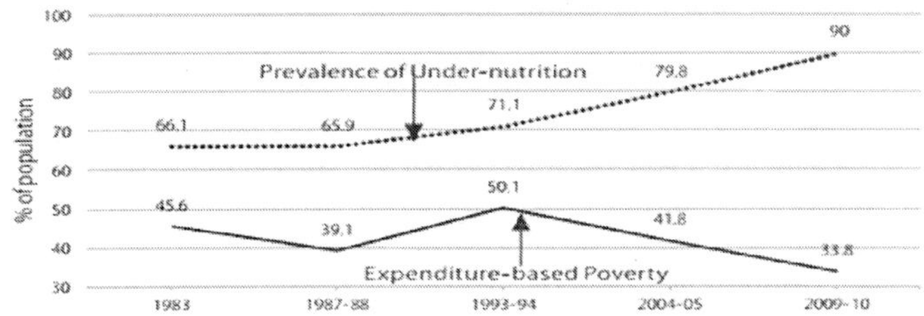

Sources: Deaton and Drèze (2009); GOI (2009), and website of the Planning Commission of India: http://planningcommission.nic.in/news/press_pov1903.pdf

Fig. 13.1: Poverty and Under-nutrition in Rural India since, 1983.

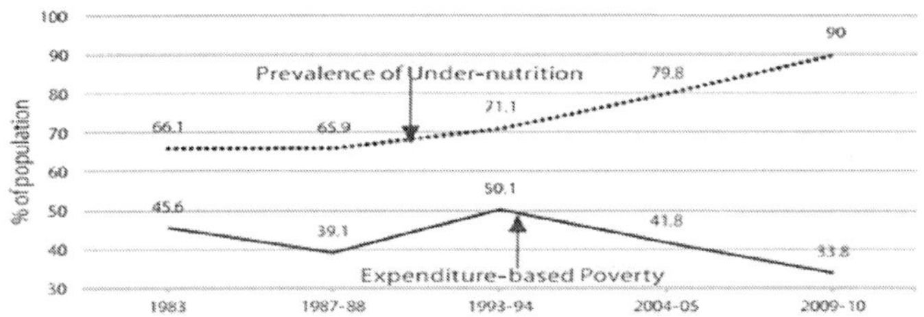

Sources: Deaton and Drèze (2009); GOI (2009), and website of the Planning Commission of India: http://planningcommission.nic.in/news/press_pov1903.pdf

Fig. 13.2: Poverty and Under-nutrition in Urban India since, 1983.

of the total population are underweight.[14] Hence the role of the state is crucial for providing food security and nutritional support for the people.

Food security can be studied from three different viewpoints. These are–(i) availability of food, which depends upon production and distribution; (ii) securing access to food that is guided by purchasing power; and (iii) food absorption. Food absorption implies being able to assimilate the food consumed in order to live a healthy and long life.[15] So, availability, accessibility and absorption are the three components that are needed for the food security in India.

A secured supply of food is necessary for good nutrition, but it does not, by itself, mean that everyone is well nourished. This is because other things such as infections, appetite, the energy concentration of weaning foods, and people's workloads also affect nutrition. 'National food security' means that a country has enough food for everyone. But this does not mean that every family had enough food, because the food may not be evenly distributed. 'Family' or 'household food security' means that every family always has enough to eat. (King and Burgess, 1992). Government promotes national and household food security in different ways. These may include: promoting sustainable methods of food production, improving food distribution and marketing, deciding how much food to import and export, having stores of staple foods that they use to stabilise supplies and prices, and in times of food shortages, controlling and/or subsidising the price of staple foods and other essentials so that poor families can afford enough food, trying to increase incomes of the poorest families by fixing minimum wages, encouraging employment opportunities (King and Burgess, 1992).

Indian Public Distribution System

India's Public Distribution System (PDS) is one of the largest in the world. It supports the foodgrain producers through purchase by the Food Corporation of India at Minimum Support Price (MSP) principally based on the recommendation of an independent body called Commission on Agriculture Cost and Prices (CACP) and allotment of these foodgrains to the states. Allocation is mainly based on the foodgrain produced in the state and the extent of poverty prevailing in that state. The Union Government tries to see that the deficit states get adequate foodgrain to have an inter-regional balance. PDS is an important component of the country's strategy for poverty eradication. Established by Government of India under Ministry of Consumer Affairs, Food and Public Distribution and managed jointly with the state governments. The Central Government, through Food Corporation of India (FCI), has assumed the responsibility for procurement, storage, transportation and bulk allocation of foodgrains to the State Governments. The operational responsibility including allocation within State, identification of eligible families, issue of Ration Cards and supervision of the functioning of Fair Price Shops (FPSs) etc., rest with the State Governments.

Under the PDS, presently the commodities namely, wheat, rice, sugar and kerosene are being allocated to the States/UTs for distribution. Some States/UTs also distribute additional items of mass consumption through the PDS outlets such as pulses, edible oils, iodized salt, spices, etc through Fair Price Shops (FPS). With a network of more than 4.62 lakh fair price shops (FPS) distributing commodities worth more than Rs 30,000 crore annually to about 160 million families, the PDS in India is perhaps the largest distribution network of its kind in the world.[16]

Food Security Act and Political and Policy Implications

According to Jean Dreze, the right to food can be seen in three perspectives. These are: from the perspective of Indian Constitution; from the perspective of International conventions and declarations, for example, the Universal Declaration of Human Right; and considering the right to food as a moral and social right. In his article in EPW, he concentrated more on the first perspective, particularly on the right to food as one of the economic and social rights affirmed in the Directive Principles. The Directive Principles are chiefly due to B R Ambedkar, and they build on his visionary conception of democracy. This vision, in turn, was intimately related to his notion of the good society as a society based on 'liberty, equality and fraternity'. Democracy, as he saw it, was both the end and the means of this ideal. It was the end because he ultimately considered democracy itself as synonymous with the realisation of liberty, equality and fraternity. At the same time, democracy was also the means through which this ideal was to be attained. The Directive Principles are chiefly due to Dr B. R. Ambedkar, and they build on his visionary conception of democracy. This vision, in turn, was intimately related to his notion of the good society as a society based on 'liberty, equality and fraternity'. Democracy, as he saw it, was both the end and the means of this ideal. It was the end because he ultimately considered democracy itself as synonymous with the realisation of liberty, equality and fraternity. At the same time, democracy was also the means through which this ideal was to be attained. Indeed in the Ambedkar's perspective democracy was intrinsically geared to social transformation and human progress (Dreze, 2004). Ambedkar emphasised on linking political democracy with the social and economic democracy. Dreze opines that Sixty-five years down the road, economic democracy has been quietly buried as a principle of public policy, and even political democracy is not exactly in the pink of health (Dreze, 2004).[17] It is in this context that there is an urgent need to revive the concern with economic and social rights expressed in the Directive Principles of the Indian Constitution, including the right to food. After the intensive struggle for the legal right for right to food, in 2011, The National Food Security bill was introduced in the Parliament.

In 2013, the National Food Security Act was passed with the aim to provide food and nutritional security in human life cycle approach, by ensuring access to adequate quantity of quality food at affordable prices to people to live a life with dignity and matters connected therewith or incidental thereto.[18] The National Food Security Act gives statutory backing to the TPDS. It legally entitle 67 per cent of the population (including 75 per cent rural and 50 per cent urban) to get subsidised grains under the Targeted Public Distribution System (TPDS). This legislation marks a shift in the right to food as a legal right rather than a general entitlement. It includes the Midday meal scheme, Integrated Child

Development Services Scheme and the Public Distribution System. Further, the NFSA 2013 recognises maternity entitlement. The Act classifies the population into three categories: excluded (i.e., no entitle-ment), priority (entitlement), and Antyodaya Anna Yojana (AAY; higher entitlement). It establishes responsibilities for the centre and states and creates a grievance redressal mechanism to address non-delivery of entitlements. It is yet to be implemented by some states.

Political and Policy Implications of Food Security Act 2013

Targeted Public Distribution System (TPDS) brought the universal Public Distribution System to targeted population. There are two problems associated with this transformation: first, the huge administrative cost of identifying, issuing and managing the various ration cards – which became a source for political favour and corruption. Another reason was the trimming of a universal PDS to a TPDS created a huge gap between market prices and ration prices. On the one hand this increased the quantum of subsidies by removing the price control function of a Universal PDS system and the erosion of the price control mechanisms of the essential commodities act. On the other hand, the polarisation between the market prices and the ration shop prices also promoted leakages from the PDS system.8[1] Identifying the beneficiaries and issuing ration cards will lead to exclusion of genuine beneficiaries and inclusion of non-beneficiaries.

If we understand the stands of political parties, there are three arguments which come from various political parties. Congress and allies pushed for the passage of bill 2013, by providing food entitlements to 67 per cent of the population. Bharatiya Janata Party (BJP) though supported the bill, but stressed on debate. Left parties totally opposed the bill, stating the bill will lead to more exclusion of beneficiaries and advocated for the Universal Public Distribution System. Recently after the general election, Central Government appointed a High Level Committee (HLC) on reconstruction of Food Corporation of India (FCI) under the chairmanship of Mr Shanta Kumar. HLC recommends that GoI has a second look at NFSA, its commitments and implementation. Given that leakages in PDS range from 40 to 50 per cent, and in some States go as high as 60 to 70 per cent, GoI should defer implementation of NFSA in States that have not done end to end computerisation; have not put the list of beneficiaries online for anyone to verify, and have not set up vigilance committees to check pilferage from PDS.

HLC also recommends to have a relook at the current coverage of 67 per cent of population; priority households getting only 5 kgs/person as allocation; and central issue prices being frozen for three years at Rs 3/2/1/kg for rice/wheat/coarse cereals respectively. HLC's examination of these issue reveals that 67 per cent coverage of population is on much higher side, and should be brought down to around 40 per cent, which will comfortably cover BPL families and some even above that; 5 kg grain per person to priority households is actually making BPL households worse off, who used to get 7 kg/person under the TPDS. So, HLC recommends that they be given 7 kg/person. On central issue prices, HLC recommends while Antyodya households can be given grains at Rs 3/2/1/kg for the time being, but pricing for priority households must be linked to MSP, say 50 per cent of MSP. Else, HLC feels that this NFSA will put undue financial burden on the exchequer, and investments in agriculture and food space may suffer. HLC would recommend greater investments in agriculture in stabilising production and building efficient value chains to help the poor as well as farmers.

HLC recommends that targeted beneficiaries under NFSA or TPDS are given six months ration immediately after the procurement season ends. This will save the consumers from various hassles of monthly arrivals at FPS and also save on the storage costs of agencies. Consumers can be given well designed bins at highly subsidised rates to keep the rations safely in their homes.

HLC recommends gradual introduction of cash transfers in PDS, starting with large cities with more than one million population; extending it to grain surplus states, and then giving option to deficit states to opt for cash or physical grain distribution. This will be much more cost effective way to help the poor, without much distortion in the production basket, and in line with best international practices. HLC's calculations reveal that it can save the exchequer more than Rs 30,000 crores annually, and still giving better deal to consumers. Cash transfers can be indexed with overall price level to protect the amount of real income transfers, given in the name of lady of the house, and routed through Prime Minister's Jan-Dhan Yojana (PMJDY) and dovetailing Aadhaar and Unique Identification (UID) number. This will empower the consumers, plug high leakages in PDS, save resources, and it can be rolled out over the next two to three years.

These recommendations are opposed by various sections of the society. Bringing down the beneficiaries from 67 per cent to 40 per cent will lead to further exclusion and corruption.

Problems of Public Distribution System in India

After analysing various literature available and practical experience, there are problems related to PDS in India. Despite the efforts on the part of the government to make the PDS more effective and efficient, the system continued to be plagued with several inefficiencies:

(i) *Problems of identifying the real beneficiary*: Studies have shown that targeting mechanisms such as TPDS are prone to large inclusion and exclusion errors. This implies that entitled beneficiaries are not getting foodgrains while those that are ineligible are getting undue benefits. An expert group was set up in 2009 to advise the Ministry of Rural Development on the methodology for conducting the BPL census. It estimated that about 61 per cent of the eligible population was excluded from the BPL list while 25 per cent of non-poor households were included in the BPL list.

(ii) *Existence of Ghost Cards:* Another indicator of inaccurate classification of beneficiaries is the existence of ghost cards in several states. Ghost cards are cards made in the name of non-existent people. The existence of ghost cards indicates that grains are diverted from deserving households into the open market. TPDS suffers from large leakages of foodgrains during transportation to and from ration shops.

(iii) *Leakage of foodgrain:* TPDS suffers from large leakages of foodgrains during transportation to and from ration shops into the open market. In an evaluation of TPDS, the Planning Commission found 36 per cent leakage of PDS rice and wheat at the all-India level. The following tables provide data on states with varying leakage of foodgrains.

Table 13.1: Leakage of Foodgrains: State-wise

Low leakage (less than 25 per cent)	Andhra Pradesh, Kerala, Tamil Nadu, Odisha, West
High leakage (25 per cent to 50 per cent)	Bengal, Assam, Gujarat, Himachal Pradesh, Karnataka, Maharashtra, Rajasthan
Very High leakage (50 per cent to 75 per cent)	Haryana, MP, UP
Abnormal leakage (more than 75 per cent)	Bihar, Punjab

Table 13.2: Leakage: Fair Price Shop Level

Very Low Leakage (less than 10 per cent)	Assam, Himachal Pradesh, Madhya Pradesh, Odisha, Tamil Nadu, West Bengal
Moderate Leakage (10 per cent - 25 per cent)	Andhra Pradesh, Gujarat, Karnataka, Kerala, Maharashtra
High Leakage (25 per cent - 50 per cent)	Rajasthan, Uttar Pradesh
Very High Leakage (more than 50 per cent)	Bihar, Haryana, Punjab

Source: Performance Evaluation of Targeted Public Distribution System, Planning Commission, 2005.

And instances of rampant corruption within the supply chain, manual system of maintaining records, inadequate and non-transparent monitoring mechanisms, weak grievance redressal mechanisms and so on.

For this purpose, the Department of Food and Public Distribution launched the e-PDS portal in October, 2012. Designed by the National Informatics Centre (NIC), the portal aims to act as a one stop shop for all PDS related information namely, details about policies, information relating to central and state schemes, prices of PDS commodities, FPS details, ration card information and so on. The portal also provides access to various States PDS websites. By collating all PDS related information, the portal seeks to enhance transparency in the operations of the PDS. Next chapter will be concentrating on the role of e-Governance and how it bringing the effectiveness and efficiency in the PDS by addressing the challenges.

e-Governance and e-PDS

The concept of e-governance means the process of decision-making and the process by which decisions are implemented. The concept of e-governance relates to the quality of relationship between the government and the citizens whom it serves and protects. E-governance could be defined as one in which the concerned authority exercises power, exerts influence and manages the country's social as well as economic resources leading to better development (Deva, 2005). The document of the Asian Development Bank on Governance in Asia: "From Crisis to Opportunity" states the instrumental nature of governance with its four pillars namely , Accountability, Transparency, Predictability and Participation. The universally accepted characteristics of governance include – Participation, Rule of Law, Transparency, Responsiveness, Equality, Inclusiveness, Effectiveness, Efficiency and Accountability (Deva, 2005).

The fundamental motivation for the campaign of e-governance in India and elsewhere is a slogan - to provide SMART government – "SMART" being an acronym for Simple, Moral, Accountable and

Responsive Government (Prabhu, 2004), a laudable ideal, though difficult it may be to achieve in realty. Historically, it was in Chile that a real e-governance initiative was taken up as early as in 1972, when the IT applications were unheard of in government and were limited even in Business. They used techniques of IT not to just make government paper-less or less of paper (as is presently being done) but to perform government work efficiently.

Even though historically it was Chile which implemented real e-governance solution as early as the seventies, the current interest and attention on e-governance applications all over the world has its roots in the "Information Super Highway" concept initiated by the US Vice President Al Gore in early 1990s. The Information Super Highway was defined largely in terms of the information infrastructure at the national level by many countries including the US, UK, Canada, Australia and India. The focus was then largely on development of components of the infrastructure, such as fibre optic networks across the States or Nations. Subsequently, the interest was widened to include socio-economic considerations encapsulated in the concept of Information Society and Knowledge Society, which naturally has to encompass e-governance. During 1980s and 1990s, the governments all over the world lagged behind the commercial world in accepting and implementing Information and Communication Technology (ICT). The commercial world, including the industrial world, had gone for ahead of the governments all over the world in harnessing the potential of ICT in their core and also peripheral activities (Prabhu, 2004). Governments were the last in the bandwagon of institutions attempting to harness ICT in their activities. However, though late, the governments all over the world finally woke up to realise the potential of ICT in all their activities, India is not an exception.

e-PDS

The state governments are also showing inclinations towards e-PDS. Justice Wadhwa's Report and Hon'ble Supreme Court Order - Sept 2010' identified certain issues with the present Public Distribution System (PDS). They are: (1) Problems in accurate targeting and segmentation of APL / BPL beneficiaries. (2) Problem of huge corruption and pilferage of PDS commodities all over the country. (3) Wastage of food grain v/s starvation of masses. (4) Pilferage at every node of supply chain. (5) Problems of Bogus Ration Cards. So, Supreme Court issued orders to computerise TPDS. Based on the judgement, many states followed technology-based reforms to Public Distribution System. Some of the steps are given below.

Table 13.3: Reforms to TPDS: An Overview

Type of Reform	*Benefits of reform*	*States implementing reforms*
Digitisation of ration cards	• Allows for online entry and verification of beneficiary data • Online storing of monthly entitlement of beneficiaries, number of dependants, offtake of food grains by beneficiaries from FPS, etc.	Andhra Pradesh, Chhattishgarh, Tamil Nadu, Madhya Pradesh, Karnataka, Gujarat, Telangana etc. ,
Computerised allocation of FPS	• Computerises FPS allocation, declaration of stock balance, web-based truck challans, etc.	Chhattisgarh, Delhi, Madhra Pradesh, Tamil Nadu.
Issue of smart cards in place of ration cards	• Secure electronic devices used to store beneficiary data • Stores data such as name, address, biometrics, BPL/APL category and monthly entitlement of beneficiaries and family members • Prevents counterfeiting	Haryana, Andhra Pradesh, Odisha
Use of GPS technology	Use of Global Positioning System (GPS) technology to track movement of trucks carrying food grains from state depots to FPS	Chhattisgarh and Tamil Nadu
SMS based monitoring	Allows monitoring by citizens so they can register their mobile numbers and send/receive SMS alerts during dispatch and arrival of TPDS commodities.	
Use of web-based Citizens' portals	Publishes grievance redressal mechanism such as toll free number for call centres to register complaints and suggestions	Chhattisgarh

Source: PRS India. org: Justice Wadhwa Committee Report on Computerisation of PDS operations.

e-PDS helps in computerisation and digitalisation of the existing PDS machinery. The flow chart of the e-PDS process is represented in Fig. 13.3.

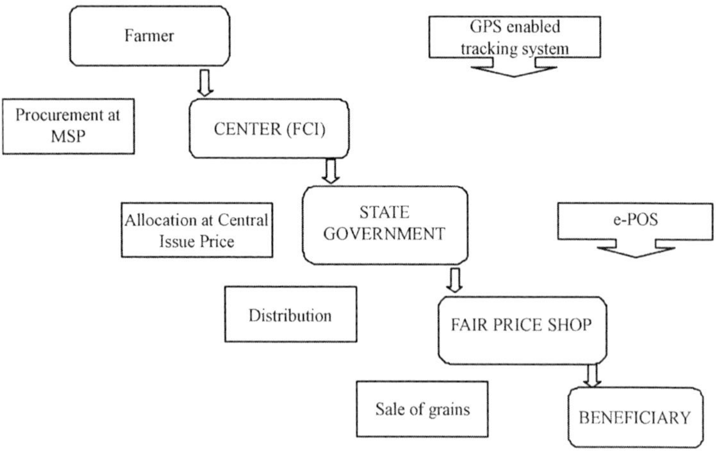

Figure 13.3: e-PDS flow chart.

Chhattisgarh e-PDS Model

Chhattisgarh is a good example of transforming a non-functional PDS into a functioning one with the help of technology and community involvement. The first step was to computerise the whole process to check leakages and diversions. It improved internal management and injected transparency. The state solved the widespread problem of fake ration cards by creating a centralised database which helped eliminate 22.5 lakh fake ration cards. The centralised printing of bar coded ration cards, their distribution in the public gatherings and community monitoring ensured transparency and accountability. In every village/wards, special public functions were held to distribute the ration cards by the representatives. The ration card details were published on the website in Hindi along with details of the holder. This helped confirm authenticity and made the system more transparent and accountable. The second important step was to computerise the movement of the goods. The doorstep delivery system was put in place based on demand and the trucks transported the goods to fair price shops. The actual allocations were fed into the computer system and delivery order was issued. The delivery truck drivers were advised to carry mobile phones with cameras. They were instructed to take pictures of the truck number and the manager whenever the commodity was unloaded. This checked diversion of loaded trucks to unscrupulous people who sold it in the open market. Thus, technology was effectively used to check corruption. The public grievance management system incorporated a call centre with a toll free number functioning for 12 hours. A citizen service website, Jan Bhagidari, was also set up for registering complaints; it worked like RTI. Numerous FIRs were filed and swift actions were taken to punish the fraudulent elements. Besides, there was proactive sharing of information through another portal, nic. in/citizen. Under an interesting initiative, citizens were asked to register their mobile numbers for information on their fair price shops. Whenever grains were dispatched they would automatically receive SMS with details of the truck number and quantity of grains being delivered. Anyone could register for this facility. It made any fraudulent activity by the fair price shop owner or the bureaucracy impossible. Thus, use of technology brought everything under public eyes and eliminated all wrong doing. Total cost of technological intervention was just around 23 crore with three crore as recurring costs. The Chhattisgarh PDS model has won many awards.

Telangana e-PDS System and its Implementation

As discussed in the above chapters, there are some serious issues related to the duplication of cards, ghost cards, corruption and leakages in the Public Distribution System. These issues are common for all the states in the country. Hence newly formed Telangana state is not an exception. This chapter concentrates on understating the role of e-Governance initiatives of Telangana Government for effectively face the challenges. This paper will concentrates on removal of duplication of cards and ghost cards by the State Government e-Governance initiatives but not on the leakages. This is the limitation of the paper.

e-PDS in Government of Telangana

There are about 467 Mandals and 17163 Fair Price Shops (FPS) in Telangana state.16.80 Lakh MT of rice is distributed to the beneficiaries in the state. There are problems like duplication of ration cards, inclusion of non-eligible cards, corruption and leakages with Telangana Public Distribution System. The Civil Supplies Department had been utilising the e-PDS online software developed by NIC in the recent past effectively to digitise the entire ration card data base, to allocate essential commodities to BPL families through fair price shops, for seeding the ration card database with Aadhaar numbers and to eliminate bogus/duplicate cards and units with Aadhaar authentication. After the Supreme Court order, the State of Telangana implemented the end to end computerisation. There are three stages in the computerisation process. They are:

Table 13.4: e-PDS in Telangana

	Component I	*Component II*	*Data Digitisation*
Hon'ble Supreme Court Order – description	Computerisation of complete supply chain up to FPS Availability of information on a Transparency Portal	Electronic authentication of delivery and payments by beneficiary at the fair price shop level	Digitised database of ration cards will be put up in the public domain
Requirements for Computerisation	A. Utilisation reporting and Allocation B. Lifting of commodity from FCI to FPS C. Lifting of commodity from State Godown to FPS	A. Sale of commodity at FPS • Beneficiary authentication • Transaction recording	A. One time beneficiary Data digitisation B. Online management of beneficiary database

Source: NIC, Telangana.

Component I of the Telangana e-PDS concentrates on the computerisation and online tracking of the movement of commodities from the FCI godowns and State godowns to Fair Price Shops. Supply Chain Tracking system is implemented in Hyderabad district on pilot basis. Automation of this component is required for proper tracking of the movement of commodities, as diversions and leakages are common in this part. Component II of the project aims at the computerisation and online tracking of the ration from Fair Price Shops to the real beneficiary. e-Point of Sale (e-POS) machines are used for authentication of beneficiary through biometric data. A SMS will also be delivered to the beneficiary about their entitlements of ration.

By implementing the software, the department was able to deactivate 9.93 lakh bogus ration cards from June to Sept, 2014. The department was able to save 15,779 metric tonnes of rice. The data was provided by the NIC, Telangana. Presently around 15 lakhs cards were removed from the beneficiary list. Following table will provide information regarding ineligible cards elimination.

Table 13.5: e-PDS – Ineligible Cards Elimination

Particulars	*June 2014*	*July 2014*	*August 2014*	*Sept 2014*
No. of BPL Cards	91,64,991	90,22,846	88,83,490	81,71,321
No. of BPL units	3,21,43,953	3,08,42,460	3,06,65,732	2,70,45,270
Rice allocation (MTs)	1,39,037	1,38,006	1,37,107	1,23,258
Savings (cards)		1,42,145	281501	993670
Savings (units)		13,01,493	14,78,221	50,98,683
Savings (Rice in MTs)		1,031	1,930	15,779

Source: NIC, Telangana.

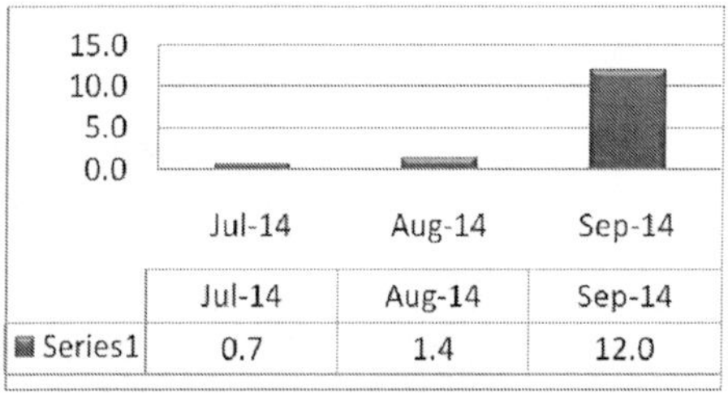

Figure 13.3: Percentage of Rice Saved between Jul-14 to Sep-14.

Aadhar Seeding

Aadhar Seeding is the process of one-to-one mapping of the beneficiary Aadhaar number with his/her record in the scheme database and approval of the same by an appropriate authority. Aadhar Seeding helps in removing duplication and unauthorised beneficiary list. In Telangana, the process of Aadhar seeding is intensively taking up. Following table will provide information related to district-wise Aadhar seeding with Ration Cards.

Table 13.6: Status of Aadhar Seeding: April, 2015

District	*Percentage of Aadhar Seeding with Ration Cards*
Adilabad	93.09
Hyderabad	92.72
Karimnagar	92.41
Mahaboobnagar	92.85
Medak	87.80
Nalgonda	94.333
Nizamabad	93.21
Ranga Reddy	92.58
Warangal	93.03
Total	**90.91**

Source: NIC, Telangana.

New Ration Cards – Exclusions Criteria

All government employees, four wheel owners, all pan card holders/ credit card holders/debit card holders, two wheelers with more than 100 cc, people having landed property more than an extent which may differ from mandal to mandal, People having house with a plinth area with limit to be fixed for corporations/municipalities and rural areas separately.

e-Point of Sale Pilot Project in Hyderabad City

e-POS pilot project was introduced in 45 shops from Oct 2012 to till date. Main purpose of this project is issuing ration after online Aadhaar authentication in a Point of Sale machine by the ration card holder. Food Inspector will authenticate for old and handicapped. Through this project approx upto Rs 45,000 per month per shop will be saved. Main purpose of this project is to deliver the ration to authorised persons only, online verifications of the beneficiary will be facilitated and real time information can be gathered at the State NIC. This project aims at eliminating corruption and facilitates effective decision-making at the state level.

Benefits of e-PDS in Telangana State

1. Grassroots level transparency.
2. Beneficiary empowerment thr;ough the use of coupons, or technology such as smartcards, or even direct cash transfers.
3. Monitoring the movement of goods through the use of technology, such as GPS tracking of trucks.
4. Increased monitoring, supervision, accountability and transparency.
5. A solution that is incentive-compatible for all stakeholders, so that they benefit by participating in the system, rather than trying to benefit through subverting the system.
6. Strengthening the public provision of the State with appropriate use of technology, to bring it on par with best practices in the field.
7. A token-agnostic technology solution that can accept physical coupons, smartcards, electronic coupons, and even facilitate direct cash transfers where different states may choose from different solutions based on their own requirements.

Comparative Study between Chhattisgarh CORE-PDS and Telangana e-PDS

Centralised Online Real-time Electronic PDS (CORE-PDS) is an e-Governance project of Chhattisgarh was designed and implement all over the state. Its main objectives are to capture transactions between Ration Card holder and the FPS, to make the FPS accountable to people (beneficiaries) by offering "Portability" and to eliminate diversion of PDS stocks – by authentication of beneficiary at the FPS before transaction and Regular physical verification of transactions. CORE-PDS project introduced "Annapoorna ATM" Application Software (A3S) which works in online or offline mode and interacts with the PDS server. Many states replicated the CORE-PDS model their respective states and Telangana also implemented certain practices. But Telangana e-PDS is concentrating on the digitalisation of data. Still 10 per cent of Aadhar cards seeding with New Ration Cards have to be done. Authentification through e-POS and tracking of movement of ration are implanted on pilot basis in Hyderabad district.

Table 13.7: Chhattisgarh's CORE-PDS and Telangana's e-PDS : A Comparison

Particulars	*Chhattisgarh*	*Telangana*
New Ration Cards	Smart Ration Cards are issued to all beneficiaries	New Ration Cards are yet to distribute
Digitalisation of Data	100 per cent data Digitalisation	10 per cent of Aadhar seeding has to be done
Online Tracking of Ration	Implemented all over the state with RFID technology	Implemented on pilot basis in Hyderabad circle only
e-POS	"Annapoorna ATMs" are available in all FPS	e-POS project is implemented in 45 FPS in Hyderabad district on pilot basis

Conclusion

Improvements required for the effective and efficient implementation of Telangana e-PDS:

- Exclusion clause for PDS may have to be rigorously implemented. New Ration Cards with smart technology should be distributed to all beneficiaries.
- Online tracking of movement of ration from FCI godowns to beneficiary must be implemented in order to remove the leakages and corruption.

- e-POS system should be leveraged by implementing in all districts of Telangana.
- Awareness about the e-PDS and e-POS in the beneficiaries must be created as a part of change management.
- Grievance Redressal Mechanism is required for addressing the issues of beneficiaries.

There is a clear transition from manual Public Distribution System to e-Public Distribution System for effective and efficient delivery of ration to genuine beneficiary. The focus of e-PDS is to plug out loopholes and problems. By leveraging the Information and Communication Technologies (ICTs), beneficiaries are identified and targeted properly. e-PDS system India can be used effectively to realise the objective of food security. It may reduce corruption and enhance transparency, accountability and efficiency. However, there are some challenges which have to be addressed. The e-PDS of Telangana state reflects the emerging trend of computerisation of social safety nets. If Information and Communication Technologies are to be used to improve existing social schemes, they should address the root causes of the problems into place. e-PDS is an apt example of it. Telangana's e-PDS, has a high potential for improvement. The issue is how effectively and efficiently the e-PDS is implemented with a time-frame. There is a delay in implementing the project across the state. Technology as an enabler has to combat market diversion, corruption and it should ensure reaching of benefits to the genuine beneficiary. But the bureaucratic delays are seen to be affecting the pace and progress of the scheme. The option for Direct Benefit Transfer (DBT) may be tried in one or two assembly constituencies to begin with and an effective monitoring mechanism facilitates whether the Cash Transfers help in enhancing choices of the beneficiaries besides eliminating the multi-layered PDS with attendant consequences. The challenges to DBT like Centre-state coordination, partial coverage of Aadhar, inadequate development of banking channels and challenges in automation of schemes need to be addressed.

Notes

1. Masiero, S., (2014). Redesigning the Indian Food Security System through E-Governance: The Case of Kerala. *World Development*, pp. 126-137.
2. Heeks, R. (2001). *Understanding e-governance for Development*. The University of Manchester, Institute for Development, Policy and Management Information, Systems, Technology and Government: Working Papers Series.

3. Bovens, M., and Zouridis, S. (2002). From street-level to system-level bureaucracies: How information and communication technology is transforming administrative discretion and constitutional control.

   Public Administration Review, pp. 174-184.
4. Elbahnasawy, N. G. (2014). E-government, Internet adoption, and Corruption: An Empirical Investigation. *World Development*, pp. 114-126.
5. OECD Development Action Committee's Guidelines on Poverty Reduction (2001).
6. Ray, R., (2005). Changes in food consumption and implication for food security and Undernourishment: India in the 1990s. *Development and Change*, pp. 321-48.
7. Patnaik, U(2007). Neoliberal and Rural Poverty in India. *Economic and Political Weekly*, pp. 44-7.
8. Subramanian, S (2013). "The Poverty Line". *Oxford India Short Introduction*, New Delhi: Oxford University Press.
9. Basu, D., and Das, D.(2014). Poverty and Hunger Divergence in India. *Economic and Political Weekly*. pp. 22-24.
10. Planning Commission, Poverty Estimates for 2011-12, pp. 6-7.
11. Planning Commission report on Poverty 2009-10.
13. Basu and Das (2014) believed that there is decreasing trend in spending on non-food items in post-reforms period.
14. National Family Health Survey – 3 (2005-06). NFHS-4 is in process.
15. International Food Policy Research publishes National Hunger Index every year.
16. According to A.P.J. Abdul Kalam, who presented a paper in National Food Security Summit, 2004.

    http://www.mssrf.org/sites/default/files/AR2003-2004.pdf
17. Department of Food and Public Distribution website, Government of India.

    http://dfpd.nic.in/
18. Dreze, J., (2004). " Democracy and Right to Food". *Economic and Political Weekly*, pp. 1723-1731.
19. National Food Security Act 2013 states it.
20. Opinion of Vandana Shiva, published in Aljazeera news online version. http://www.aljazeera.com/indepth/opinion/2013/09/20139812222870561 7.html

References

Basu, D., and Das, D., (2014). Poverty and Hunger Divergence in India. *Economic and Political Weekly,* pp. 22-24.

Bhatnagar, S., (2008). *e-Government: From Vision to Implementation: A Practical Guide with Case Studies*. New Delhi: The Sage.

Bovens, M., and Zouridis, S., (2002). From street-level to system-level bureaucracies: How information and communication technology is transforming administrative discretion and constitutional control. *Public Administration Review*, pp. 174-184.

Deva, Vasu, (2005). *e-governance in India: A Reality*. New Delhi: Commonwealth.

Dreze, J., (2004). Democracy and Right to Food. *Economic and Political Weekly*, pp. 1723-1731.

Elbahnasawy, N. G., (2014). E-government, Internet Adoption, and Corruption: An empirical investigation. *World Development*, pp. 114-126.

Gittinger, P. J., Leslie, J., and Hoisington C., (1987). *Food Policy: Integrating Supply, Distribution and Consumption*. Bartimpre: The Johns Hopkins University Press.

Khera, R., (2011). India's public distribution system: Utilisation and impact. *Journal of Development Studies*, pp. 1038-1060.

Heeks, R., (2001). *Understanding e-governance for Development*. The University of Manchester, Institute for Development, Policy and Management Information, Systems, Technology and Government: Working Papers Series.

King, F. S., and Burgeess, A., (1992). *Nutrition for Development Countries*. Somerset: ELBS.

Masiero, S., (2014). Redesigning the Indian Food Security System through E-Governance: The Case of Kerala. *World Development*, pp. 126-137.

Patnaik, U., (2007). Neoliberal and Rural Poverty in India. *Economic and Political Weekly*, pp. 44-7.

Prabhu, C. S. R., (2004). *E-Governance: Concept and Case Studies*. New Delhi: Prentice Hall India.

Ray, R., (2005). Changes in food consumption and implication for food security and Undernourishment: India in the 1990s. *Development and Change*, pp. 321-48.

Subramanian, S., (2013). *The Poverty Line. Oxford India Short Introduction*. New Delhi: Oxford University Press.

Swaminathan, M. S., Medrano, P., Gustafson, J. D., and Pravesh, S., (2004). *National Food Security Summit 2004, Selected papers*. New Delhi: World Food Programme.

14

The Implications of Decentralisation of Health Services: A Case Study of Uttarakhand

—Mehar Puri

Introduction

The decentralisation process in the simplest sense is a dual process wherein a certain governing body faces a deduction in its powers in favour of an increase in the powers of another lower level governing body. It may simply be explained as the parting of one governing body with some of its decision making powers in favour of a lower level governing body. In the Indian case one may understand the process of decentralisation as one where there is the transfer of the decision-making power in favour of Local Self Governance through the institutions of Panchayati Raj System.

This has to do in the broad sense with the central and state governments transferring some of their powers while the local bodies gain higher degrees of control over there administrative process. The system is not restricted just to the administrative process and governance but has flowed over in time, to the dissemination of health services as well, with the help of local bodies. The idea of the system is to involve the local to better be able to meet its specific needs.

The NRHM aims to work through a process of decentralisation, this means involving the Panchayati Raj Institutions at all its levels of functioning. The public health infrastructure will be expected to be managed and have involvement from the Gram Panchayat, Panchayat Samiti (Block), and Zilla Parishad (District).

The Village Health and Sanitation Committee will function under the Gram Sabha; representatives from this committee will also be a part of the Committee that will be responsible for the management of the Sub Health Centre.

The Health System in India

There has been much debate on the percentage of the Gross Domestic Product spent on Public Health, and what that percentage should be raised to as a minimum to achieve health security for the population of India. There is also debate regarding the per capita expenditure on health service, by the government. A major cause of concern has been that a large percentage of the expense on treatment that the citizens of the nation have to pay from their own pocket. In this way economic status becomes an exclusionary factor. Those who can afford to pay for medical treatment are most often the ones that will be able to take advantage of it.

The high cost of treatment is in many cases a cause for the ailing to avoid visits to medical institutions and diagnosis. The alternatives are reliance on home remedies and Quacks. It is in an effort to prevent the persistence of exclusion of certain groups of population from access to healthcare the decentralisation of the health services has been particularly vital.

Another factor that has been exclusionary to a large chunk of the population is the place of residence that is the region that a population lives in. The rural part of the country has been grossly neglected in terms of healthcare services. The urban centres have been better equipped to provide their population with, basic medical services. The rural areas on the other hand has not been as fortunate, there are large groups of population that remained isolated or have very limited access to any sort of infrastructure that could provide quality medical services. Inevitably there have been better facilities in the cities than the rural area.

There has over a period of time emerged an awareness of inequality among the policy-makers and thus led to planning in a way that hopes to overcome these hindrances.

3.1.6 The Eleventh Five Year Plan will provide an opportunity to restructure policies to achieve a New Vision based on faster, broad-based, and inclusive growth. The Plan will facilitate convergence and development of public health systems and services that are responsive to health needs and aspirations of people. Importance will be given to reducing disparities in health across regions and communities by ensuring access to affordable healthcare. (Planning Commission, Government of India, 2008)

The Rural Situation

The rural countryside cannot of course be understood as one undifferentiated whole, the landscape and lifestyles differs across the country; which lead to particular health requirements as well. That apart, there still remains in every region a need for some basic medical facilities and a minimum quality of healthcare. In an attempt to achieve this goal there are programmes that have been envisaged by the Government of India, that have slowly increased the availability of health services in the rural countryside.

Though a multitude of programmes have been implemented nationwide, they have seen success in varying degree across India. As has already been identified it is the rural population that faces more of a challenge in accessing and utilising the healthcare system in comparison to the urban population. The national Health Policy of 2002 recognises the issue of a shortfall of medical practitioners in the country. The document also states that this shortfall is particularly severe for the rural set up. This is one of the reasons that medical facilities in the rural countryside are substandard, since in places where there might even be adequate infrastructure facilities there are not enough qualified medical practitioners to use the facility to provide the population the services they require.

The condition of healthcare also varies across regions and states within the country, while there are some states that are still in a dismal condition, others have been able to achieve a better standard of healthcare for its population. It thus becomes vital to recognise the cause of this difference in status of healthcare across different parts of the country. One such state is Kerala that has been successful in reaching levels of public health that are equivalent to those achieved by numerous developed countries. While on the one hand this is remarkable, on the other it seems only a partial success since this is one of the few states in the nation that is in a position to provide its population basic medical facilities.

The Kerala Situation

This success doesn't mean that issues of the Urban Bias have been wiped out and every member of the population has equitable access to facilities and encounters the same quality of treatment. The important lesson lies in being able to minimise the differences across different populations as far as possible and provide the best services with the given resources. That is also an aspect of decentralisation of health services in the state of Kerala that is believed to make it a model case. The state has achieved these levels of success without being one of the highest per capita spenders in terms of health expenditure.

The decentralised health services of Kerala have historically preceded the decentralisation in the health sector in other states. In fact, in decentralisation in the health sector has been a familiar phenomenon in the area even before Kerala as a state even came into being. It may be traced back to the time of the Maharaja of Travancore. His interest in allopathic medicine is believed to be the reason behind him encouraging it among his subjects and thus making it the responsibility of the state to provide allopathic medicine to them. This supply subsequently led to an increased demand in the province for medical services.

To a great extent it was the supply of health services that led to an increased demand for them, this demand was further encouraged by the increasing rate of education and literacy among the population that made them familiar with issues of health and the available services. Specifically the consistently increasing literacy levels among the women have had very direct and positive results in the overall health situation of the state. Literacy levels in Kerala stand at 93.91 per cent (National Census, 2011). This positive change is the reducing levels of infant and maternal mortality and the increased levels of institutional deliveries as well as benefits of ante-natal care. Kerala's levels in terms of the low levels of infant and maternal mortality beat the nationwide numbers by a very large margin and are comparable to those of developed countries.

In terms of a decentralised health system Kerala has found success in many of the areas where most other states of the country and even the country as a whole has not been able to find success. The areas where maximum success has been achieved have been in the area of maternal and infant health, specifically in reducing the mortality rates of both the mother and the child. The method of achieving this success is even more vital since it has been achieved despite the limited resources available to the state, and the expenditure on health, which is not among the highest in the country. P. G. K. Panikar attributes the success of the decentralised health system to mainly certain processes that occurred simultaneously. Preventive and promotive health measures by which he means better hygiene and sanitation and better curative measures. Immunisation, infant and ante natal care, health education, special education to women in rural areas. Better utilisation of the available healthcare facilities (Panikar, Vol.14, No. 44 (Nov. 3, 1979).

These along with the proper policies and their implementation were the reasons that even the limited resources did not in fact turn into major hurdles in achieving the goals that the state has. Till before the 1970's Kerala spent a larger share of their GDP on providing health services than after that as a result of the deficits it created.

It is post this period that the private sector entered in a big way the chain in the provision of health services. This has both its advantages as well as significant disadvantages. Some believe that the urban bias has in fact been reduced with the coming in of the private sector as health service providers. Yet there are also repercussions of higher cost of medical services and cases of only certain types of services being provided by the private sector despite being concentrated in certain rural areas.

The Private and the Public Sector

Holistically though one cannot overlook the contribution of the public sector to the availability of healthcare. Public Health Centres were often unable to provide services like inpatient care to the patients. For such services it was the private health centres that were depended on. Thus, the lack of availability shifted from that of institutions to that of provision of inpatient care by public institutions.

The Rogi Kaliyan Samiti; understood as the Patients' Welfare Scheme, is a public private partnership. One of the main reasons for the state governments to undertake any Public Private Partnership is as a result of the pressure on resources that leaves them unable to provide quality healthcare to the population. The Rogi Kalyan Samiti is a scheme that functions under the National Rural Health Mission; this is based on the Principles of a Public-Private Partnership. The basis of any such partnership may be define/understood as having some benefits; reducing the financial burden on the government exchequer. The support of the government would help to build on the capacity of the private sector to meet the health needs of the people. The management structures that will be put in place as a result of the new partnership would make the process more efficient, and improve the quality of healthcare. (KUMAR, July 19, 2003)

This PPP doesn't function as a government enterprise but as an NGO and it aims at involving local stakeholders not only in the process of gathering resources and funds but also in the capacity of those individuals that may be involved in the decision-making process. While the government services and assets may be utilised under the scheme in addition to that the funds for the implementation of the scheme may also be raised from other quarters. Another significant feature of this scheme is that the collected funds instead of being deposited in the State treasury are utilised by the Executive Committee put in place by the RKS. This is a programme that has been undertaken by the state of Kerala.

This sort of a system of management has brought local leaders and community members as well as members from the Indian Medical Association. To this there is also the hand of those that are leading donors in the decision-making process along with members from the Panchayati Raj local bodies. There are those that firmly believe that the Private Public Partnership in the form of the RKS has caused more problems than advantages. The problem with this system is believed to be the high dependence on the individuals, which brings in the lack of stability and continuity in the functioning of the system.

There are also results that suggest a failure in terms of decentralisation with regard to the health system, mainly with a look at the primary health centres. One such study states that Panchayats in Kerala were allocating lower proportion of funds to health than was done before the decentralisation process. Active support for the PHC's by the panchayats was only present in some areas, but where it was present; this support had led to positive results (D. Varatharajan, R. Thankappan and Sabeena Jayapalan, 2004).

The Situation in Uttarakhand (A Comparison)

A General Background of the State

The rural society of Uttarakhand is a very traditional society one that has traditionally been isolated from the "outside." It is one that has relied heavily on its traditional methods for governance, it is for this reason that the decentralisation could find success in the state, it to builds on the traditional system of the panchayat and local self-governance. For regions that have had very little exposure to practices and cultures beyond their own it would be wise to build on an already existing system of governance. With the 73rd and the 74th amendment the existing institutions of local self-governance can be improved upon and evolve to prove more successful in meeting the participatory needs of a democratic population. The recommendations of the amendments call for reservations within the panchayats for marginalised groups, with a focus on women and community members belonging to the scheduled tribes and schedule castes categories.

From the field work that the researcher carried out in rural Uttarakhand it came to light that though these considerations were strictly followed with regard to the membership to the various Sabhas and panchyats, the decision-making powers in most cases still lies more strongly with the dominant groups in the community. Most often these are the upper caste male members of the community. This is not to say that the process of decentralisation post the amendments has done nothing to weaken the restrictions that had earlier existed in entering the governing process for many groups.

Just the opportunity to be a part of the institutions of governance and the membership itself of groups for whom membership has been reserved, has been useful in bringing into the ambit issues that concern these people.

The Situation in Terms of Health Care

The situation of healthcare in a state like Kerala is decades ahead of the current situation in some of the other states in India. One of these is Uttarakhand where I have done research in the sphere of the decentralised health system, with the backdrop of the National Rural Health Mission and special focus on maternal and infant mortality.

Uttarakhand, unlike Kerala, has not seen a history of decentralised healthcare in the rural regions; this has very evidently translated into high maternal and infant mortality rates in Uttarakhand. Uttarakhand has one of the highest rates of maternal and infant mortality in the country, and on doing field research it was found that there remains in some villages even now a very high dependence on the Traditional Birth Assistants.

This dependence remains even now despite the availability of Public Health Centres as well as hospitals run by Non-Government Organisations. The traditional way of treatment is still the one that remains the norm. Contrary to belief by policy-makers, monetary as well as material benefits have not been successful in converting the local population in favour of mainstream allopathic medicine and procedures.

The state has been able to achieve an average literacy rate of 79.63 per cent and a female literacy rate of 70.70 per cent among the women, but even these levels of literacy have not, unlike in Kerala had very significant effects in being deciding factors in turning the population towards a greater degree of utilisation of health services.

Traditionally the access to health services has been limited and the quality of the health services has been questionable. Despite an effort under recent government schemes to provide better facilities to more people, there is still a very long way to achieve that goal that have been set as determinants of success for these schemes.

Improving the quality of services is a daunting task because of the large number of vacancies in public health institutions, especially for medical officers, supervisors, and technicians, and poor infrastructure including lack of equipment and inadequate facilities. (Department of Medical Health and Family Welfare Government of Uttaranchal, 2002)

A far cry from the condition of the public health system that have been envisaged by plan documents, the hill state of Uttarakhand boasts of few government run Health centre per administrative Block. Often many villages are found sharing a single health centre, the medical facilities provided there being very limited. There may be more available health centres but the numbers are nowhere nearing the available centres in a state like Kerala. When speaking to the doctor at the Primary Health Centre of Dhari Block in the Nanital District, she mentioned that among the patients that she and the other doctors treated there was a very high incidence of victims of Road Traffic accidents.

She also mentioned that the hospital was not equipped either in terms of facilities or staff to deal with the very serious cases that they often had to treat. As a result, the patients had to be transported to other hospitals that were located at a distance and that was often very detrimental to the health of the patient, and had also in cases resulted in incidents where the patient had succumbed to his injuries.

'*Uttaranchal, given its difficult terrain, has a high incidence of accidents either due to landslides or to rash driving. Emergency services to treat accident cases and to provide trauma care services are grossly inadequate in the state.*' (Department of Medical Health and Family Welfare Government of Uttaranchal, 2002)

The long history of absent health centres have been the cause of the locals being comfortable with and very trusting of traditional methods of medicine, home remedies and cures by quacks. Despite the sudden rise in the hospitals there has been a very limited and slow move towards the use of these services in case of an ailment.

A very immediate issue is the slow progress despite the effort to reduce the rate of maternal and infant mortality in the nation. The National Rural Health Mission offers schemes as well as benefits that would encourage women to opt for institutional deliveries in an effort to turn more deliveries into safe deliveries. These policies are put in place with an effort to achieve the Millennium Development Goals. These goals have set very specific aims for their signatory countries to achieve within a given time span. Goal four and five very specifically focus on reducing child mortality (of which infant mortality is a major component), and improving maternal health.

Though a state like Uttarakhand displays no deficit in terms of the required Primary Health Centres as well as the existing PHC's, yet the state has not been able to achieve the goals set in these sectors.

The Meaning of Decentralisation

Decentralisation in the health system would mean the increase in the decision-making powers of the local community as well as their enhanced involvement. In the State of Uttarakhand there seems to be to begin with, a problem of accessing the existing medical facilities that have been provided. Traditionally as a result of the terrain the access to any form of formal health services was limited, this prevented the local populations not only from accessing health services, but in many cases a health institution was a remote and alien concept.

That sort of an attitude unfortunately persists in many rural parts of the state, and surprisingly even in urban areas. A hospital is still an institution that inspires awe and fear among many, and it is hardly considered a first resort to any medical ailment. There are stereotypes about the institution, the people and practices, even now the doctor and other staff is feared. The biggest fear is that going to a hospital will in most cases result in an operation and a huge financial burden. This belief persists despite efforts to reduce the cost of commuting by providing free transport to the Public Health Centres, and other government hospitals and other efforts to subsidise the cost of treatment.

The Possible Solution

A well implemented decentralisation model in this scenario would greatly reduce the aura of the unknown that surrounds the system of formal allopathic medical system and other government aided health services (recently AYUSH). But for this to be effective there is a need for some prior familiarity with the facilities, and trust in the services. This would then lead the local population to want to be involved in a big way in how the health system created to serve them develops, and create an interest in the decision-making powers and keeping account of the resources at their disposal.

At present the rural scenario is opening up to the facilities very slowly and there is limited utilisation of the available facilities. Based on first hand research, it was found that despite the benefits of the Janani Suraksha Yojna, a scheme aimed at reducing the incidents of maternal and child mortality in the state and many other schemes the utilisation of the health services is very limited. Ironically the women that are eligible under the scheme are willing to accept the material benefits that include the one hundred Iron tablets as well as the food supplements that are provided prior to the birth and post the birth at the ANM centres. Yet they are willing forego the monetary benefits that they would be entitled to if they underwent an institutional delivery at a government hospital, or private hospitals that are eligible for the scheme.

This is a result of the still existing unfamiliarity with the hospital that is not shaking off as fast as is required to improve the health condition in the state. Since historically access was limited the dependence on traditional methods has for decades has been solidified to such an extent that there is high trust, rather blind faith in village Quacks and the "Dai", the Traditional Birth Assistant. It is when these two fail to cure an ailment that as a last resort the doctor might be approached after much deliberation and thought over various aspects, that range from financial cost to transport and most importantly whether there is at all an immediate requirement to be treated.

The problem with such an attitude is that, by the time the ailing visit a hospital for treatment, if at all they do go, it is usually after home remedies and the village quack has failed to treat it. By this time their conditions have greatly deteriorated due to the delay in seeking treatment and often there is very little that the doctors can do to treat the patient. This then has an adverse effect in terms of the trust in the medical system, which is reduced; post such an incident and the negative opinions are reinforced in the minds of the local population. There are information asymmetries that reinforce the existing biases, and only increased participation and involvement of the local communities and greater interaction with the medical system can help get rid of these.

Thus, to best understand the failure of the local population to freely accept and utilise the health services that have been made available to them, one needs to look beyond just factors like the infrastructure, the number of hospital, the economic condition, the distance to the hospital. Though these factors are vital in the decision to utilize services available they don't function in disjunction to sociocultural factors. Traditions are still very deeply rooted in the hearts of the nation's population and the rural population still holds its traditions dear. That is still the reason why women will not demand to be taken to the hospital to deliver their child or breast feed the child for the first twenty- four hours after birth. To want to deliver a child in a hospital unless there is any sort of complication, is considered unnecessary and is looked down upon.

One cannot overlook the dynamics of a society, whether it be the caste class hierarchies that function or the gender biases or the power hierarchies of the community and household. The skewed nature of the utilisation of health services needs to be taken into account and understood. In terms of utilising medical services it is usually the men and the children in the family that are given preference. It is very seldom that the women will be taken to a hospital to be treated for an ailment; the women that are taken are usually the elders in the family.

It is not that the local population is ignorant of and unwilling to accept changes in their situation; there are villages in the region that have qualified for the Nirmal Gram Pruskar. In these cases the people from these villages came together to find solutions to the problems of sanitation and drinking water, facing them and improve their condition. There is a need to create in the minds of the local communities an interest in the particular issue at hand. In terms of the health system there is a need to educate people in the various benefits of formal medical care and rid them of the misconceptions they hold with regard to the expenses, and malpractices. They need to be made aware of the safety and hygiene concerns that cannot be met when treatment is provided at home. There is also a need to create awareness of the danger of accepting remedies provided by quacks as well as the added danger of misdiagnosis of an illness by them.

Through small efforts the locals have attempted at being more involved and improving the situation of the healthcare available to them. During first hand research the researcher found that one village had filed an RTI to find out why it was that the ANM for the village was not present on the days that she was expected at the village ANM centre. They argued that the reason for not converting in a large way towards institutional deliveries was that the distance and cost was a factor, but there are free transport facilities to and from the hospitals for deliveries, the 108 ambulance to the hospital and the 104 from the hospital to the patient's house. The women in the village claimed that they would be more willing to opt for an institutional delivery if the ANM centre could be converted into a hospital.

On the other hand after nearly two decades of intervention by Non-Government organisations and immunisation drives did the population open up to the idea of having their infants immunised. But the misconceptions about women getting the Tetanus toxoid continued to remain long after, there was a belief that the labour pain would reduce and the delivery would as a result become complicated.

In case of schemes like the RKS the Uttarakhand report of 2009 shows that in a survey done to understand the result of the NRHM, from the sample it was found that shockingly only about one per cent of that population knew what the RKS or that VHSE was even functioning in their village. The lack of knowledge translates without a doubt into lack of participation.

The entire purpose of decentralisation and involvement of the local population is lost if one of the main stakeholders is unaware of their rights and duties, and in the particular case of the state most are even unaware of the scheme at all. A larger involvement from the local community in the health service system will help remove many misconceptions.

The ASHA is meant to play this role of the intermediary between the formal medical system and the local population. Her responsibilities are such as to familiarise and over time adapt the local populations to move towards the utilisation of health services and policies as well as government schemes. Hers is a very vital role in ensuring that awareness is disseminated among the local population about the various schemes in the area of maternal and infant health as well the family planning programme.

Not just in the way that the ASHA must work but also in the monitoring of the ASHA is where a true reflection of what was envisaged for the decentralised process at least in the Health scenario can be found. There is constant monitoring of the ASHA workers in each block through a meeting that is held each month and convened by the doctors of the Primary Health Centre. Though as the researcher found when present at these meetings that just the regularity of the meetings and the fact that they are even held at all, and the progress of the ASHA workers is discussed does not hugely reflect in the success rates of the ASHA workers in terms of their efforts and endevours. During these meetings it became very evident that the success rate of an ASHA was hugely dependent on the efforts that she herself made as well as the mindset and the willingness of the local population and their openness towards the efforts and the processes that they advocate.

The monthly meetings are carried out to allow a space for appraisal of the past month's report as well as a comparison to the earlier few months regarding the efforts of the ASHA workers. The meetings are also held in an effort to overcome the hurdles that the ASHA workers might be faced with when attempting to fulfill their assigned duties. At these meetings the ASHA workers could voice their own issues and concerns and interact with each other. Also here those ASHA's that were believed be underperforming were identified and warned that if they did not adequately improve in their duties they would be replaced.

The interest taken by the doctors at the PHC has been significant in allowing the ASHA's to be efficient in their work. It was also seen that the efficient management of the paperwork and funds by the hospitals, encouraged both the ASHA's and the beneficiaries to follow the process and make the effort to come to the hospital for deliveries.

It is not that the system as a whole has failed, yet it could function more efficiently if the beliefs and ideas of the local population were taken into account and the specific concerns of the location. In a state like Uttarakhand the terrain is a major hindrance in accessing medical services and distances are long and tedious to cover. In such a situation to be able to convince the population that holds so dearly onto its traditions (often due to its isolation compared to towns that see more of a mix of people and thought) to trust a virtually alien system of treatment, requires most of all their added involvement in the decision-making process. This will only be possible through providing adequate information and educating the population about both their right to participate in the governance as well as their entitlement in terms of facilities.

In terms of the three tier system of governance, Leela Visaria and Meera Bhatt in their article state the role of the Panchayati Raj Institutions is to behave like a link between the healthcare providers that exist and the people who are in need of their services. Also it is there PRIs that have the ability to make the health services responsive to the specific needs of the local people. Additionally they believe that the process be made participatory and the PRIs be made accountable to the people. The PRIs will be able to priorities the local issues and aim solutions specifically in that direction. (Leela Visaria, 2011, December 3rd).

Though the village Panchayat is known to have a "Swasth sabha/ Panchayat" and there are regular meetings that are held in the village there is hardly ever a discussion on any specific medical concern and the possible suggestion. At the Gram Sabha too there is a need to motivate the people and discuss issues of health. What is of important at the grass root is, more whether these practices are in fact being carried out, whether the PRIs are successful in creating the link between the local people and the healthcare providers and taking advantage of it to benefit the health condition of the community to the extent that they can. There is also a need to link various schemes together to be able to bring about a more holistic change in both attitudes and conditions. The RKS the VHSE and the ASHA programmes together can help involve local populations in a large way and thus ensure a more efficient and fruitful dissemination of the information.

References

D. Varatharajan, R. Thankappan and Sabeena Jayapalan. (2004). Assessing the performance of primary health center under decentralised government in Kerala, India. *Health Policy*, pp. 41-51.

Department of Medical Health and Family Welfare Government of Uttaranchal. (2002). *Health and Population Policy of Uttaranchal.*

Kumar, G. (July 19, 2003). Promoting Public-Private Partnership in Health Services. *Economic and Political Weekly*, pp. 41-45.

Leela Visaria, M. B. (2011, December 3rd). Public Provisioning of Health and Decentralisation in Gujarat. *Economic and Political Weekly*, pp. 59-66.

Panikar, P. (Vol.14, No. 44 (Nov. 3, 1979)). Resources Not the Constraint on Health Improvement: A Case Study of Kerala. *Economic and Political Weekly,* pp. 1803-1809.

Planning Commission Governmen of India. (2008). *Eleventh Five Year Plan, Social Sector Volume.* New Delhi: Oxford University Press.

National Health Policy 2002.

15

Inclusion of Local Community in a Model of Public–Private Partnership for Environment and Climate Governance in India

—Umar Jalees Moniri

Introduction

There are enormous challenges to forest conservation and management of natural resources along with elimination of persisting poverty. Many of these problems are caused due to intensive use of natural resources, governmental policies, and continuing marginalisation of rural and tribal poor who have been managing the natural resources for centuries and administering the forest wealth. But unfortunately, these rural and tribal poor are simply kept out from the administration of forest resources and also they have not been taken on board before launching or initiating any developmental project. There exclusion did serious damage to the environment and this deterioration of the environment had devastating impact on the lives of these individuals affecting the longevity of their life. The destruction of forests leads to the extinction of engendered animal species and also many plant varieties that have immense medicinal values. The degraded soil, depleted aquifers, diminishing forest cover, deteriorating rural environment, and destroyed eco-systems can scarcely support substantive better quality of life in future. This creates an arduous challenge to the government in dealing with this problem, which seems to be not getting solved without the inclusion of all those people who were involved in it before the advent of modern economic development. The government has to develop a model and mechanism with the acknowledgement that poor and tribal are equally efficient and well versed in administering the natural resources. This fact that poor's and tribals are capable of protecting the environment was highlighted in academic writing by Ramachandra Guha and Vandhna Shiva. According to Guha, the environmental movement like Chipko had decisively announced the poor's entry into the domain of environmentalism.

The ecology-related protests come in defense of local rights to forest, fish, and water resources, as well as protests against large dams. The myth that environmentalism is something that can be dealt with by educated elite only is due to the established theory that environmentalism was full-stomach phenomena. The reason behind this notion is that the green movement in the 1960s, which started in West, was widely interpreted as a manifestation of what was called post-materialism. It was thought or rather theorised that a cultivated interest in the protection of nature was possible only when the necessities of life could be taken for granted. From this perspective, the poor were quite simply too poor to be green. Their working hours were spent foraging for food, water, housing, and energy: how could they be concerned with something as elevated as environment.[1] Movement such as Chipko challenged the philosophy and theory that environment is something that can be handled only by the rich, urban-educated middle class. But the environmentalism of subaltern group in India explored new ways of caring for the natural resources through local knowledge of environment and initiatives. There should be a mechanism to ensure efficient, transparent, and reliable administration of environment. There must be participation of those people in decision-making who have direct concern with the natural resources. The local participation should be encouraged as it not only brings in the democratic approach but also ensures reliable protection of the environment. Participative management and technique need to be adopted towards the achievement of inclusive development. If the earth's resources are to be protected from excessive human intervention, there is a need to adopt sound and astringent penal measures. The involvement of local communities, panchayats, cooperative societies, and women is a must toward creating sustainable and self-reliant communities. This approach should be promoted in such a manner that the expressions of the local communities are articulated. The proposed approach of PPP can be incorporated at the community level to monitor and manage the developmental efforts, even though the PPP has a very narrow connotation because it has been something that is understood as participating with a private firm or corporate sector in fulfilling any government task or project. But here, in the proposed paper, it is undertaken in another perspective in which it is emphasised that the "participation of local communities" in the developmental schemes is necessary right from the beginning stage of the development plan through to the execution stage. This is because the culture and livelihoods are dependent on the surrounding natural resources of which they are habitant. PPP approach ensures their place as stakeholders and associates of the developmental course of action and also enables and empowers them to satisfy, plan, sustain, and share the common benefit. The development is essentially a vision of the society; it helps in utilising the knowledge and skills to solve the problems. One of the most important ingredients in participative management is the marginalised group among rural culture, and one of that marginalised groups is women. Environmental change has direct concern on women because it affects them when there is an alteration in the strategies of the utilisation of natural resources, but unfortunately they are least consulted when the development proposals are initiated. Leaving them out or ignoring their presence cannot bring in the desired development output. Their empowerment is imminent as expressed in the National Human Development Report, "The Empowerment of Women." Women have played the role of nurturing their families and the environment. The access to and management of resources through acquisition of land and collection of full fodder, forest produce, and water is crucial for women. PPP at the rural level for governing the environment, which has remarkable impact on development and poverty, could provide a model of governance. It will strengthen the grassroots-level democracy and certainly will help in resolving the conflict between the state agencies and the local poor.

Review of Literature

In view of India's ecological crisis, social protests and movements started emerging from grassroots level. From the early 1970s, the Chipko Movement to protect the mountain forest and the mass campaign against Narmada Dam Project have gained international recognition. These movements are examples of grassroots political opposition gaining momentum. Scholars like Madhav Gadgil and Ramachandra Guha list them as the most prominent examples of environment-related political activities throughout India. India has a long tradition of conflicts over the use of natural resources. Disputes with a clear environmental aspect have occurred at least since the nineteenth century (Gadgil and Guha, 1992;

Arnold and Guha, 1995). Gadgil and Guha (1992) stress that today many environment-related conflicts in India have a sharper social edge than many of the industrialised countries. The livelihood and survival of the poor who are living at subsistence level are normally harmed whenever land use, water access, or urban spaces are in dispute.

Sumi Krishna (1996) points out that for poor people, involved in conflicts viewed as environmental by scholars or journalists, the emphasis is still likely to be on the protection of their immediate livelihood plans. This includes the internationally known Chipko Movement and NBA. In view of these movements, social scientists generally demand a new development model. They claim that the current policies of structural adjustment and world market integration are adding to ecological disaster tendencies (e. g. Shiva, 1991; Gadgil and Guha, 1995). Empowerment of the rural masses is meant to lead to greater environmental protection, particularly as the rural poor depend on the biomass production of their village and surroundings. Development, if it is to result in the generation of wealth with equity and distributive justice, has to be inclusive in terms of spread, access, and sustainability. But unfortunately, the market-driven mode of development with emphasis on production is at the expense of equity and sustainability.

Sumi Krishna (1996) also gave an account of conflict between environment and development, how administrative set up has been manipulated under the politicisation of development and how environmental conflict provided space for research on the environmental movements in India.

Dwivedi and Vajpeyi (1995) analyse the dimensions of development and explore the environmental policies of the developing and third-world countries. They give an account of environment regulations in India and the politics behind these regulations.

Chhatre and Saberwal (2006) in their *Democratizing Nature* try to expose two principal contradictions of the environmental politics in India, i.e. between conservation and large-scale development projects, and between short-term electoral politics and long-term imperatives of environmental protection. Most of these scholars try to highlight the inefficiency in addressing the problem. However, there has been reform in the governing of the developing countries to include local participation in the governance of the people at the local level. PPP is one of the models of governance. The traditional PPP is always concerned about the economics in its operationalisation, which can be seen in the work of de Bettignies and Ross (2004). Keeping the view of economic aspect of PPP, scholar and author Richard K. Ghere has demonstrated the importance of aligning ethics in PPP. This has been described with detail in his work "Aligning the Ethics of Public Private Partnership" (Ghere, 1996). However, the issue of ethics must accompany with welfare motive and the model of PPP in environmental administration has to deal with it in the proposed study.

Conceptual Understanding of PPP

There is no straight forward definition of PPP many form of public-private-partnership cooperation exist and number of definition is available to understand PPP.[2] Loosely defined as cooperative institutional arrangements between public and private sector, but some people agree on what PPP actually is. It is seen by many as a new governance tool that will replace the traditional method of contracting out for public service activities through competitive tendering while other conceive PPP as a new language in public management, designed to cover older established procedures involving private organisation in the delivery of public services.[3] In other view Public–Private-Partnership is an institutional form of cooperation between public and private actors who, on the basis of their own indigenous objectives, work together towards a joint target, in which both parties accept investment risks on the basis of a predefined distribution of revenues and costs.[4]

Scholars have been divided so far in determining how one should think about PPPs. The greatest divides seem to be between those researchers who think PPP as a tool of governance and those who think it is a language game. The belief in the PPPs is that PPPs benefit both the public sector and the private actor. This is so because it is understood that both the public sector and the private partner have specific qualities and if these qualities are combined, then the end result will be better for all. There is also the possibility that the cooperation can result in some new product or services that no one would have thought of if public organisation and private partners come together in sharing their skills, knowledge and competence.[5] In fact, PPPs appear to be the most preferred policy models for providing services in different areas. The public sector organisations getting access to private capitals and construction expertise while private sectors getting new orders and securing new customers.[6] PPPs are also introduced in US in social sector which include human service and welfare service like education, health, administrative and managerial services.[7] PPP is almost omnipresent from developed West to the Developing East in many areas whether it is economic, social or governance. But unfortunately there is not any concrete mechanism of PPP in the area of environment to protect the environmental resources on the one hand and to have sustainable use of the natural resources on the other. The historical evidence of Indian Environmentalism says that local tribals and poor people always preserve the environment and maintain their livelihood without disturbing the ecological balance of the region. But unfortunately up till now there have been exclusion of local communities at the operational level in the management and administration of natural resources.

PPP in the Administration of Environment at the Local Level

With the incoming of neoliberalism, the discourse on governance has taken an interesting turn to further introspection in a changing world. Governance has become a tool to achieve development in most democratic manner perhaps this is what the current neo-liberals philosophy believe and tell us. In spite of such belief there are certain aspects which have been identified as the prerequisite of developmental practices which need some sort of monitoring, control and policy prescription.[8] Improvement and maintaining the status of the environment and environmental concern are one of such area which need some kind of policy framework. It is to be said that natural environment is capable of playing a role of negative externality in the process of economic development. This negative environmental externality emerges from the divergence between private benefit and social benefit as well as between private costs and social costs of an economic project or activity. In a larger context there is hardly any existing specific market mechanism to negotiate between these two kinds of issues. This phenomenon has resulted in an inference that it is beyond the efficiency of the market-clearing model to resolve environmental question in an overall paradigm of development that led to the demand of control, protection and governance mechanism in the administration of Environment. It is emphasised that such control mechanisms need an insight of governance where an authoritative monitoring, policy formulation and implementation as well policies through an administrative structure expected to function, thus the urge to governance the environment continue to arises. Moreover, environmental concern has made an entry into both the discourse of administration and development in an interconnected manner. The objective of the environmental administration is to achieve sustainability and development together keeping the environment in focus. In a country like India its environmental administration is more than mere exercising sustainable use natural resources. In India, the use is not only protection of biodiversity and ecological stability but also the protection of the right to access to natural resources for the marginalised local poor to sustain their livelihood. For these marginalised poor who include tribals, women and other rural people, nature is not only a reserve of resources but a boon of endowment.

This aspect of the importance of natural resources as source to livelihood put the local people in conflict with the state or rather with the state led developmental project. Such the conflict took the shape of environmental movement which got worldwide recognition and at the same time it marks the entry of the poor into the domain of environmental protection. Technically these movements highlighted the capability, skill, knowledge and responsiveness of the poor people in managing and administering the natural resources at the local level. These protests compel the government to frame some formal institutional arrangements regarding environmental management in India.

One of the major breakthroughs came in empowering the local indigenous people for the management and administration of environmental resources was the 73rd Constitutional amendments which added schedule XI of the constitution which has assigned eight entries (2, 3, 6, 7, 12, 15 and 29) linked with environmental protection and conservation , like soil conservation, water management, social and farm forestry, drinking water, fuel and fodder, non-conventional energy sources and maintenance of community assets to panchayats. However, such measures were more legislative in nature and less administrative in character. It did give political space to the local community at the political decision level but hardly anything has been done from the administrative perspective to incorporate the local skill, ability, in a market language which can be called local entrepreneurship to govern the environment at the local level by the local people. This absence of institutions in a formal structure can be filled up by the institutional model of Public-Private-Partnership. In this PPP model public agencies will establish a partnership with the local individuals who have experiences and skills to manage the natural resources for hundreds of years. These private individuals will have no corporate background of private companies running experiences but still they will be acting as private partners in the administration of environment at local level.

Conclusion

The public-private-partnership in environmental administration at local level could lead to the accommodation of local talent, skill and entrepreneurship in the utilisation of local resources. Moreover, as the traditional PPP model speaks that in PPP all partners are equal in sharing responsibility and accountability as well as benefit, thus it will relieve the local partners from the dominatiort of bureaucratic adventurism because the PPP is not in this operation will act like traditional bureaucratic model but rather in market mechanism.

Notes

1. Guha, R. (2002). 'Environmentalist of the poor,' *Economic and Political Weekly*,Vol. 37, No. 3, pp. 204–207.
2. Spiering, Mirjam Bult and Geert Dewulf (2006). *Public-Private-Partnership: An International Perspective*, London, Blackwell Publishing.
3. Hodge, Fraeme and Carsten Greve (2005). *The Challenges of Public-Private Partnership: Learning from International Experiences,* Cheltenham, Edward Elgar Publishing Limited, p. 1.
4. Spiering, Mirjam Bult and Geert Dewulf (2006). *Public-Private-Partnership: An International Perspective*, London, Blackwell Publishing.
5. Hodge, Fraeme and Carsten Greve (2005). *The Challenges of Public-Private Partnership: Learning from International Experiences*, Cheltenham, Edward Elgar Publishing Limited.
6. *Ibid.*
7. Rom, M.C. (1999). 'From welfare state to opportunity inc. Public Private – Partnership in Welfare Reform', *The American Behavioral Scientist,* Vol. 43 No. 1.
8. Badajna, Sutirtha (2012). 'Between Ecology and Economy: Environmental Governance in India' in Ranbbbir Samaddar and Suhitk Sen '*New Subject and New Governance in* India', New Delhi. Rutledge Taylor & Francis, p. 155.

References

Bandyopadhyay, J., and Shiva, V. (1984). *Ecological Audit of Eucalyptus Cultivation*, Dehra Dun: Natraj.

Bandyopadhyay, J., and Shiva, V. (1988). 'Political Economy of Ecology Movements,' *Economic and Political Weekly*, Vol. 23, No. 24, pp. 1223-1232.

Baviskar, A. (1995). *In the Belly of the'River: Tribal Conflicts over Development in the Narmada Valley*, New Delhi: Oxford University Press.

Chhatre, A., and Saberwal, V. K. (2006). *Democratizing Nature: Politics, Conservation, and Development in India*. New Delhi: Oxford University Press.

de Bettignies, J. -E., and Ross, T. W. (2004). 'The Economics of Public Private Partnership,' *Canadian Public Policy*, Vol. 30, No. 2, pp.135-154.

Dembowski, H. (2001). *Taking the State to Court: Public Interest Litigation and the Public Sphere in Metropolitan India*, Essen: Asia House.

Dwivedi, O. P., and Vajpeyi, D. K., eds. (1995). *Environmental Policies in the Third World.* Westpoint: Greenwood Press.

Gadgil, M., and Guha, R. (1992). *This Fissured Land: An Ecological History of India*, New Delhi: Oxford University Press.

Gadgil, M., and Guha, R. (1995). *Ecology and Equity: The Use and Abuse of Nature in Contemporary India*, London: Routledge.

Ghere, R. K. (1996). 'Aligning the Ethics of Public Private Partnership: The Issue of Local Economic Development,' *Journal of Public Administration Research and Theory*, Vol. 6, No. 4, pp. 599-621.

Guha, R. (1988). 'Ideological Trends in Indian Environmentalism,' *Economic and Political Weekly*, Vol. 23, No. 49, pp. 2578-2581.

Guha, R. (1989). *The Unquiet Woods: Ecological Change and Peasant Resistance in the Himalaya*, New Delhi: Oxford University Press.

Guha, R., and Martinez-Alier, J. (1999). 'Political Ecology, the Environmentalism of the Poor and the Global Movement for Environmental Justice,' *Kurswechsel*, Vol. 3, pp. 27-40.

Karan, P. P. (1994), 'Environmental Movements in India,' *Geographical Review*, Vol. 84, No.1, pp. 32-41.

Krishna, S. (1996). *Environmental Politics: People's Lives and Development Choices*. New Delhi: Sage.

Parameshwaran, M. P. (1979). 'Significance of Silent Valley,' *Economic and Political Weekly*, Vol.14, No. 27, pp. 1117-1119.

Reddy, V. R. (1997). *Environmental Movements in India: Some Reflections*. Discussion Paper 64. Heidelberg: Research Centre for International Economic and Agricultural Development Association.

Shah, G. (2004). *Social Movements in India: A Review of Literature*, New Delhi: Sage.

Shiva, V. (1991). *Ecology and the Politics of Survival: Conflicts over Natural Resources in India*, New Delhi: Sage.

Shiva, V., and Bandyopadhyay, J. (1986a). 'Environmental Conflicts and Public Interest Science' *Economic and Political Weekly*, Vol. 21, No. 2, pp. 84-90.

Shiva, V., and Bandyopadhyay, J. (1986b). 'The Evolution, Structure and Impact of the Chipko Movement,' *Mountain Research and Development*, Vol. 6, No. 2, pp. 133-142.

Stuligross, D. (1999). 'The Political Economy of Environmental Regulation in India,' *Pacific Affairs*, Vol. 72, No. 3, pp. 392-406.

Swain, A. (1997). 'Democratic consolidation? Environmental Movements in India,' *Asian Survey*, Vol. 37, No. 9, pp. 818-832.

TISS. (2009). *Performance and Development Effectiveness of the Sardar Sarovar Project*, Mumbai: Tata Institute of Social Sciences.

Vyas, V. S., and Reddy, V. R. (1998). 'Assessment of Environmental Policies and Policy Implementation in India,' *Economic and Political Weekly*, Vol. 33, No.1/2, pp. 48-54.

16

Implementation of MGNREGA: Top down Design without Accountability

—Murali Karnam

A lot of things are claimed by the rulers in the name of Mahatma Gandhi National Rural Employment Guarantee Act (MGNREGA) They claim that bottom up approach is followed, community assets are created and it became a viable source of income and corrupt practices are held accountable. While some of these are half-truths, the last claim borders the myth.

Lands and Commons

Existing unequal control of agricultural lands and commons has huge impact on the effectiveness of the NREGA. It should be realised that development of fallow lands of weaker sections and 'commons' through NREGA is a way of redistribution of sources of income in village community. This redraws the boundaries of relationships between the poor and the powerful as the former at present are dependent in many ways on the later beyond agriculture. This is bound to impact almost permanently at least the existing agricultural relationships. Those who loose general control over poor and their labour see that this does not happen. Hence NREGA as a standalone programme will have only a limited impact if implemented without trying to address these issues. Implementation of NREGA without addressing the problems of land records and control of commons by powerful may even widen the inequalities even if the poor get their due of wages. All these problems and their implications naturally create no sense of owning among the community of labourers. Hence creation of assets is not proportionate to the amount of money spent. So there is a huge need to simultaneously involve the revenue administration, while planning the works under NREGA.

Involving Revenue Administration to Settle Land Records Straight

Only those lands, which are completely under the control of the poor, should be undertaken for development under NREGA. Otherwise the lands of the poor in revenue records but under the control of landlords are being developed in the name of small and marginal farmers. This defeats the objectives of the Act.

(a) Clearing the land records of the poor of disputes by involving revenue administration and establishing the clear cut possession in **record as well as in person** of lands by the poor in public should be the first step before planning the NREGA in the villages.

(b) Those who have clear possession of land legitimately but without land records should be given *pattas* for the purpose of development under NREGA. Since majority of tribals have no official records for lands, their lands are not covered under NREGA especially in Agency Areas. At least in cases of tribal lands the state should restrain from acting as compulsive litigant and following the 'let the court decide' approach. Wherever possible, the state should settle these issues quickly.

Setting the Priorities Right and Sticking to that

(a) The priorities of any programme have a great deal to say about the way they are understood and executed. After establishing clear cut possessions of lands, a strict order of priorities of works to be executed in the villages should be drawn and that should never be crossed in the name of achieving the 100 days. Only the lands of the poorest in the order of priority should be undertaken to provide work for the labourers. Since individual stakes are stronger than the collective stakes, only works related to individuals should be taken on a priority basis and then the collective or common works. In addition to providing the wages, the works undertaken should have the social meaning of working for the poorest or last person. This should be a fundamental pre-condition for anyone seeking the work. The upper caste families forming a group of labourers refuse to work in the lands of scheduled castes and scheduled tribes, who got land development scheme under NREGA. There are many instances where labourers from upper castes worked in their own land, got the wage and shown the work meant for dalit was executed. At present the NREGA is not generating the social value or meaning as it is reduced to providing wages by any means. The individualised wage seeking at the cost of individual as well as community asset creation should be dispensed with.

(b) At present in the name of community works, all sorts of works are undertaken though they may not have any benefit to the community. For instance, de-silting of tanks are taken up though all the sources of water to them are closed or de-linked. These kinds of works provide just wages, while wasting the human resource of labour and create no asset. The achieving indicators of comprehensive outcomes of each work undertaken should be the criteria for community works.

Bottom up Approach

The law of NREGA says that the Gram Sabha will identify, plan and execute the works. If the bottom up approach is followed seriously, the poor should have absolute say in identifying the priorities and executing them. The claim of bottom up approach, instead of top down approach, being followed at present is more a well-meaning rhetoric than a reality. At present it is lower level bureaucracy at Mandal level, under heavy influence of the powerful politicians and landlords, that plans the works to be taken up under NREGA. The bureaucracy which does not have sense of priority and direction but focuses on meeting targets and making money. Neither does the bureaucracy have the human resource capacity to plan meticulously and prioritise keeping in view of the objectives and comprehensive outcome of the programme. The poorly paid and trained and insecure staff of rural development is more interested in making quick bucks than giving heart and mind to achieve the objectives of the Act. If the government is really interested in the daunting task of eradicating the poverty and creating community assets, it cannot afford to staff the programme with such poor human resource.

Human Resource with Quality

Young professionals of highly motivated and trained in community work required to be deployed with a five-year term of contract. They should have deep understanding into the complexities of rural social and economic life and be able to find creative solutions taking the community into confidence. The village community should be able to own the plans and priorities of MGNREGS. They should be able to minimise the conflict of interests between different social groups in the execution of works. Creating an imagination of poverty-free and developed community among the villagers is a much more serious challenge than creating software-based wage scheme.

Technology and Middlemen

The technology in NREGA is more intended to prevent the corruption in the bureaucracy but it made the programme's designs and priorities inaccessible to the unskilled labourers. So the community of labourers has no say over the programme. Despite deployment of heavy digital technology in states like AP, still there are too many middlemen involved at the cutting edge of distribution of wages: banks/ post offices, service providers, distributors of money from SHGs etc. The organised employees of NREGA are able to influence these meddling groups and the result is spillage in the wage delivery.

At least in areas where ATMs are accessible in small towns and villages, wages can be made directly to the labourers. This attempt would reduce the spillage to a large extent. This can be a practical reality in states like Andhra Pradesh where there are large number of ATMs in small towns and big villages.

Too little to own the Programme

What is offered is too little for the community of labourers to own the programme. The number of days and actual wages offered is too little to the labourers to give long-term commitment for a particular work, which requires for creation of assets. Sixty days of work on an average annually and Rs 60 to 70 per day are hardly meaningful source of income for giving any commitment by labourers. This is the reason that NREGA became only an additional source of income rather than a sustainable and reliable one. The meagerness of the income forces the labourers to look for multiples sources of earning and is still forcing them to migrate. If regular salaries of employees have to be linked to inflation, why not the wages of those who are devastated by inflation? The unconscionable policy of paying less than minimum wages cannot make the NREGA a success. It should be made a reliable and meaningful source of income for the poor, if the government really wants the community to own the programme and create durable assets.

Social Auditing with Accountability

Section 17 of the Mahatma Gandhi National Rural Employment Guarantee Act 2005 provides for organising social audit of the scheme designed and implemented. The focus of social audit is generally more on the entitlements of individual labourers. The attention on the priorities of EGS works, creation of commons, and the process, without which the objectives of programme will derail is almost wanting. The social component of the audit is largely missing. The undemocratic decision-making process followed in Gram Sabha by the dominant is watched helplessly as the support of community to social audit is missing. As a result the fullest meaning of the monetary deviations captured is not coming to the fore in the open forums.

Finding irregularities in the records constitute major part of the social auditing but clever manipulations in the implementation of the scheme are rarely found out. Roll call mode of social audit is easier than the macro view of the EGS, which can give insights into the irregularities beyond the written records. The meaning and mode of social accountability are not deeply ingrained in the understanding of the social auditors as the emphasis is more on checking the formats and rules already designed by the government. The importance of culture of accountability and transparency in governance as democratic process are yet to become point of reference for social audit.

Serious irregularities, which defeat the objectives of the programme are brushed aside by the officials terming them as procedural lapses. Without scrupulous commitment to procedures, the ends of programmes cannot be achieved. In general the bureaucrats cite the procedures to thwart the citizens from accessing the programme. There is need to make the social auditors to realise the importance of procedures while auditing. It is a great spectacle to see the well fed politicians and bureaucrats anxiously waiting in the open forum to answer the social auditors, while the villagers sitting cool and relaxed. Whatever the final outcome of the social audit, the spectacle of the public debate demystifies the aura of authority and perhaps eroding the legitimacy of authority. This may have some impact on the poor in the long run but it emboldens the bureaucracy in the short run.

Trust Deficit

Gram Sabha: Gram Sabha is very important political space where the poor can point out the lacunas in the implementation of NREGA.

The dynamics in the village usually prevent the poor from expressing their grievances. The fear of consequences often prevents them from complaining. The consequences range from denial of work under NREGA and by farmers during regular cultivation. The NREGA removes only a part of livelihood dependency of poor and other forms of dependency continue to have hold on them. Mobilising the poor as a conscious collective is necessary to withstand the pressures from the powerful in the villages. The economic activity without concomitant social mobilisation cannot take the leverage created by the NREGA to stretch the boundaries of other (social) forms of dependency. It can stir the waters of social dynamics in the village from without and loosen the social clutch a bit.

The importance of Gram Sabha is that it is their ground but rules of the regime is defined by the dominant. The poor have to win the battle in their own ground. How far EGS can stir the quiet social waters may depend on the number of factors including mobilising the poor to speak up in the Gram Sabha.

Corruption has no Consequences

Since the inception of the NREGA in 2006, around Rs 25000 crores have been spent in the state. As per the survey by Government of India, the percentage of works of community assets completed range from 10 to 30 per cent. This is an indicator of level of meaninglessness of implementation of the NREGA and the level of corruption. The social audit alone unearthed the corruption to the tune of 450 crores with clear evidences. Except dismissing the lowest employees at the village level, the government could not do anything to the corrupt bureaucrats. More the corruption, more are they organised. Actually the public exposure of the corruption without consequences has actually emboldened the bureaucracy to harass the labourers more.

Realising the consequences of the non-action, the government legislated AP Promotion of Social Audit and Prevention Corrupt Practices Act 2012. The bureaucracy is able to collectively resists the implementation of the Act. This is further aided by the slumbar of High Court to set up adequate mobile magistrate courts. Moreover, the lowest level employees are sent to prison under the Act. The legal attempt to make the NREGA work more for poor is a non-starter.

Expertise vs Primacy of Statement of the Poor

The process of delivery of public services to the poor is very political and very often the poor are made to believe that what they got is what they are entitled to. Where the unwritten political rules of the power and corruption are in operation, the poor are in effect given the signal that what they got or did not get is what they deserve. This is more so when the poor mobilise themselves collectively and protest the violation of the accepted rule of the delivery of the wages. In either case, the negative effect is palpable but their redressal mechanism is not comprehensible. All that they know is that their entitlements did not reach them. They are not sure how it reaches them or what the stages at which it spills. The complex system of chain of command and responsibility in the bureaucracy is beyond the comprehension of the poor. In additon to this technologisation of the implementation of MGNREGS made the process more complicated as human accountability is replaced with technological deficiency.

The social auditors are primarily drawn from the first generation literates of the poor families, who are the stakeholders of the EGS. The experience of the poor and their young generation with the officialdom is anything but cordial, equal and positive. Their social experience always lingers in the backdrop like a shadow while they deal with the officials. Their ability to take on officials is much less than required and it can only be marginally improved through trainings unless it is destructively political. They are more trained in the regulatory regime of rules, which are more important for establishment rather than in underlying political thread that inform the rules.

The social auditors are drawn from the community of poor, which is politically in itself rather than for itself. Their own experience as part of government is far from liberating themselves from the feudal social relations but reinforcing them, ignoring the rational legal basis of authority. These social and legal backgrounds of social auditors condition their approach in handling the condescending and corrupt bureaucracy. The assymetrical social and economic relations between the bureaucracy and social auditors largely determine the process of social audit in practice.

What is the meaning and mode of making organic leaders of community powerful? This is not to exercise power without concomitant accountability. The social audit is made essential by the age old trend of exercising the power without accountability. Obviously the social auditors should not mimic the bureaucracy they audit. They should derive their power from their understanding of precise but complex process by which the EGS or any other programme is delivered at every stage and points of spillage.

They should be able to capture the points of spillage at their invisibility. Their ability to unearth the hidden facts in the process makes the exercise powerful and meaningful. This is because the complex process itself is a means of scuttling the ends of welfare measures. The complexity appears to be intrinsic to the process. Therefore the social auditors should be experts to substantiate the simple truth expressed by the primary stake holders. But these experts should have fundamental faith in the entitlements of the poor and their ability to perceive what is just and unjust. This expertise is not to scuttle the process but make it work the way it ought to be.

17

Transparency and Accountability Mechanism in Panchayats and Autonomous Councils: A Comparative Study in Assam

—*Harsha, S*

The present chapter ventures into the most cardinal issue in local governance which is accountability and transparency. In the light of theories of decentralisation, it takes up a comparative study of transparency and accountability mechanisms of Panchayats and Autonomous Council of Assam. Based on the comparative study, the paper comes up with recommendations to streamline transparency and accountability mechanism and reinvigorate local governance.

Decentralisation (devolution) offers significant opportunities to improve government accountability. It creates the possibility of exerting stronger pressures on government performance both from below (the demand side) and from above (the supply side). Decentralisation reshapes power relations among the local residents, local governments, producers of local government services, and higher levels of government (including central government). It sets new rules of the political game, helping new local leaders to emerge in the political competition. It thus redefines the interactions between local leaders and their constituencies. Similarly, as a result of new regulatory and financial powers over procurement and service delivery, the decisions and actions of local governments have a greater impact on local economies. Decentralisation thus leads to new interactions and contractual relationships between local governments, between small and big private firms, and between providers and producers of services, and communities and nongovernmental organisations.

In India, decentralisation envisages substantive devolution of powers to rural and urban local bodies. As Planning and rural development by Panchayats assumes significance in the context of Article 243 'G' which states that subject to the provisions of the Constitution, the legislature of a State may endow the Panchayats with such powers and authority as may be necessary to enable them to function as institutions of Self-Government. In the light of this, the Amendment also gives powers to Panchayats to formulate plans and implement them for economic development and social justice, taking into account the matters listed in the Eleventh Schedule.

In the light of extensive transfer of powers, functions and functionaries to the panchayats subsequent to 73rd Constitutional Amendment in the country, it is imperative to review the accountability and transparency mechanisms of the panchayats. In India, subsequent to 73rd Constitutional Amendment several states have introduced innovative transparency and accountability mechanisms in the panchayats of their states. For instance, Madhya Pradesh introduced a concept of direct democracy through Gaon Sabha's which had powers to recall the elected representatives of the panchayats, Kerala state introduced Local Government Ombudsman and Karnataka initiated Panchayat Jamabandhi programme. An assessment of the extant transparency and accountability mechanisms would reveal the efficacy of diverse accountability and transparency mechanisms. An attempt has been made below to define the concepts of accountability and transparency.

Accountability is critical to representative democracy. The legitimacy and stability of the democratic system is dependent on the extent to which the electorate believes that government and other public officials are operating in public interest. However, in many democracies there is a pervasive lack of accountability within government and the public departments. This happens in spite of increased emphasis on the importance of constitutional safeguards, electoral mechanism and other checks and balances. The intransigence of politicians and lack of will to demand on the part of affected population are said to be the reasons for such substandard outcomes.

Joy. M. Moncrieffe (2001) proposed two types of accountability as follows:

1. Ex-post accountability
2. Ex-ante /Positive accountability

Ex-post Accountability

It refers to holding public officials accountable through the law, other monitoring and sanctioning mechanisms and ultimately through elections. It is being liable to sanction if, in the perception of citizens, the responsibilities of the office have been executed inappropriately and unsatisfactorily.

Ex-ante /Positive Accountability

This accountability suggests that in order to act effectively in the citizen's interest, the representatives must know what these interests are. Further, the representatives must allow for deliberation and consultation, not only with members of governing body but also with the opposition, affected parties and experts so that policies may be corrected where appropriate. This allows for checks and balances during policy formulation and acts as a safeguard against dictatorial styles of leadership. It further suggests that the representatives keep the public apprised of policy choices and provide explanations and opportunities for public response, particularly where it is not obvious that actions are in accordance with public's expressed interests. Finally the representatives should provide mechanisms and act in such a way that citizens are able to assess the quality of their representation. Thus, ex-ante accountability allows for continual checks on policies, enhances the responsiveness of the people and in turn improves the quality of representation.

A noted scholar Samuel Paul (1992) referred to accountability as the process of holding individuals and organisations responsible for performance as objectively as possible. He felt that though most of the traditional mechanisms of accountability, both vertical and horizontal, are present in India, all is not well with public accountability in India.

According to scholars Yilmaz and others (2010), "As decentralisation reforms become widespread across the world, they often try to increase the autonomy and discretion of local governments without thinking through the accountability incentive structures that are crucial to obtain more responsible and accountable governments." The authors opine that decentralised local self-governments automatically doesn't bring about accountability and transparency, but there is a need to establish accountability mechanisms which makes local self-governments more accountable to their constituents.

Transparency and Accountability Mechanism in the Panchayat

Transparency and Accountability mechanisms existing in the

Panchayats also has a bearing on the effective implementation of programme. Transparency mechanisms that have been introduced in the Panchayats in Assam are being analysed as follows.

Audit of Accounts

The audit of accounts maintained by Village Panchayat is done by Director of Local Fund Audit. In respect of Anchalik Panchayats, the audit is done by Local Fund Audit Department.

There is no separate Public Accounts Committees (PACs) for reviewing audit of Panchayats. There is no separate Fiscal Responsibility Act for elected local authorities. Panchayat accounts are maintained by the Panchayat Secretaries. There are a few instances of such responsibilities being outsourced.

Social Audit

Social Audit is another important mechanism of transparency and accountability in the panchayats. In Assam Social Audit of Panchayat through Gaon Sabha has been introduced in view of the guidelines of central government schemes which mandates the conduct of social audit. As per the guidelines the Village Panchayat shall make available all relevant documents including the muster rolls, bills, vouchers, measurement books, copies of sanction orders, photos before, during and after the execution of the work and other connected books of account and papers to the Gaon Sabha. Notwithstanding these guidelines, social audit through Gram Sabha is a lacklustre affair in Assam. At present social audit in Assam is conducted only under Mahatma Gandhi National Rural Employment Guarantee scheme (MGNREGA). In sharp contrast to conduct of social audit in Panchayats, in Autonomous Council areas the guidelines are silent about the institution which should conduct the social audit. Usually the District Collector is entrusted with the task of conducting social audit in the autonomous council areas. However, the social audit is a mere formality in the autonomous council areas.

Activity Mapping

In Government of Assam Activity mapping of 29 departments have been finalised and government notification has already been issued to this effect on 26th of July, 2002. However, activity mapping in the sense of transfering of powers of line departments to panchayats is yet to materialise in PRIs of Assam. The elected representatives of Cachar ZP revealed that activity mapping is not a reality in Assam because they are not able to monitor and control 29 departments.

Right to Information

Right to Information (RTI) Act 2005 of India has received accolades throughout the country. Being public entities, both panchayats and autonomous councils come under the purview of RTI Act. The experience of people filing RTIs in panchayats of Cachar district shows that illiteracy and ignorance has constrained the citizens from taking recourse to RTI for obtaining information and scrutinising documents and records. In comparison to Panchayats of Cachar district, Karbi Anglong autonomous council is relatively better in the sense people are assertive in demanding information through RTIs.

Gaon Sabha

Gram Sabha include all the adult citizens of the village. According to Assam Panchayat Act, 1994 functions of Gaon Sabha should consider the following matters and may make recommendations and suggestions to the Gaon Panchayats.

- The report in respect of development programme of the Gaon Panchayat relating to the preceding year and development programme proposed to be undertaken during the current year;
- The promotion of unity and harmony among all sections of society in the villages; Such other matters as may be prescribed.

Functions of Gaon Sabha

According to the act the functions of the Gaon Sabha are as follows:

- Mobilising voluntary labour and contribution in kind and cash for the community welfare programmes.
- Identification of beneficiaries for the implementation of development schemes pertaining to the villages.
- Gaon Sabha shall meet from time to time but a period of three months shall not intervene between any two meetings.

Thus, Assam Panchayati Raj Act has envisaged holding of Gaon Sabha's at least four times in a year and it has conceived the Gaon Sabha as a social audit mechanism. Moreover, the Ministry of Rural Development guidelines has made Gaon Sabha mandatory for preparing the action plans and for performing the social audit of some of the schemes. A visit to some Gaon Sabha's in the selected panchayats revealed that Sabha's are not well attended by people of the constituency. The women representatives rarely participate in the Gaon Sabha and the other several do not participate, instead their husband or other male counterparts are participated in their name. If participated they generally keep mum in the meetings. Moreover, people's attitude towards the Gaon Sabha is cynical. Common perception of people towards the concept of Gaon Sabha is something like "*platform of battle for the representatives.*"

KAAC and the Issues of Transparency and Accountability

It is well known fact that the Mikir Hills District section was renamed as Karbi Anglong in 1976. The Karbi Anglong Autonomous Council become much more powerful than their counterparts in other states of the region after a MoU was signed between State government and Autonomous State Demand Committee in the presence of Union Home Ministry officials. Consequently, the funds allotted to the council have also risen; the State Government have also lessened their control over the KAAC and now the KAAC have almost 30 departments under its jurisdiction and only the Home and Law and Order is in the hands of State Government. Besides implementing several plans, projects and schemes of the central government like MGNREGA, NSAP, IYA, PMGSY etc. like the Panchayati Raj Institutions in other Plain district of the state, the KAAC have also been initiating several schemes initiated by them. Thus, the KAAC day by increasingly involving in more and more monetary transaction. Hence, the issues pertaining to transparency and accountability become more significant. However, audit of account of KAAC by the state and central audit team is mandatory like any other decentralised governance. However, the existing transparency and accountability mechanism have failed to curb corruption and revitalise local governance in council areas. Therefore, there is a urgent need to understand the transparency and accountability mechanisms and their shortcomings in order to strengthen transparency and accountability in council areas. Some mechanisms prevailing in KAAC are discuss as follows.

Audit and Account

The Council has separate bank accounts and separate PD Accounts in the treasury for their own funds, from where cheques are issued to each Head of Department. Non-plan allocations are also credited to the account of the Council. Bills on expenditure are retained and then sent to the AG for audit.

Social Audit

Social Audit is another important mechanism of transparency and accountability. Still the KAAC by their own do not initiate to conduct social audit however Mahatma Gandhi National Rural Employment

Guarantee Act 2005 (MGNREGA) have been implementing under the support of the KAAC hence it is mandatory for them to conduct the social audit particularly for MGNREGA. But, the such noble task generally conduct in the papers only and in reality social audit still remain as unheard term for those poor beneficiaries.

RTI

Another most important mechanism called Right to Information (RTI) Act 2005 has been praised by many people across the country. Such mechanism is also applicable in KAAC too but filing a RTI in KAAC office is something unthinkable. For instance, in order to prevent you from getting the information, the public information officer may charge huge amount of money as a cost of photocopy and printing of the documents.

VDC

VDC is grassroot institution of KAAC but it is not a democratic or popular institution. Generally, members of the VDC are nominated by Executive Committee and local MAC is the Ex-officio chairman of VDC if he or she belongs to ruling party. If MAC of a constituency is from opposition then CEM nominate person from his party. In some cases if the local MAC have many responsibilities (e.g. If become EM entrusted with two three department or CEM) than he/she given the responsibilities of VDC to a person belong to party or very close to him/her. However, these VDC in the village level are also not elected body and hence, the opposition leaders like to call it as illegal body. Because, in most of the time the party whoever in power in the council nominate their party members to these VDCs and these bodies have been playing a significant role in selecting beneficiary of various government schemes in the villages. According to the reports they never conduct any public meetings like the Gaon Sabha conducted by the Panchayats where the people can participate in the decision-making process. However, executive members talked of public meetings in the villages, when such questions have posed but cross-checking such questions with public it comes to know that some meeting are conducted by VDCs where agendas pertaining to selection of beneficiaries is discussed but mostly in these meetings only their party members are invited.

In the decision-making process, CEM and EMs have more power than any other member. In determining location of the project, selection of beneficiaries and in awarding contracts, the members of ruling group play a significant role and the members of opposition have very nominal role. The opposition and nominated members also not have any role in VDC and selection of beneficiary. The members of non-ruling party are not also have any role to play in the VDC therefore they rarely able to select any beneficiary. Therefore, one MAC of opposition said that VDC is the illegal body because in a democratic system VDC is fully tyrannically formed by ruling party. However, according to the sources the central government continoues to request KAAC regarding the formation of democractic body in the village level. But still such mechanisms in the village level yet to realised.

Confidential Report

Most of the officials in KAAC are deputed by the state government however it is executive committee of KAAC who can write confidential report and their performance report to the government and also have the power to take several types of disciplinary action against the officials. Hence, the officials are always accountable to the executive committee of KAAC.

E-Governance

Website, Display Board, Monitoring Committee, Community Information Centre (CIC) are functioning in Karbi Anglong. Again, there is a provision to disseminate various information regarding various programmes, receipts and expenditure, name of the beneficiaries etc. through the website and electronic media. However, these websites are not accessible to majority of the populace who are usually uneducated and live in rural areas. During the focus group discussions people levelled several charges against official and elected representatives and reported that transparency mechanisms have become weak in Karbi Anglong. For instance, the cases of corruption in Public Distribution System at Tokhadi in Karbi Anglong and the newspaper reports on misappropriation of MNREGA funds in Karbi Anglong points to the need for reinforcing of transparency and accountability mechanisms in the KAAC.

People's Perceptions of Transparency in Panchayats and Autonomous Councils

In the present section an attempt has been made to collate the perceptions of the citizens of the panchayats and autonomous councils with regard to some of the indicators of transparency in local governance. Based on the comparative assessment of their perceptions, similarities and differences in the transparency mechanisms of both institutions have been highlighted. This section begins with conceptual definitions of each of these indicators.

Gram Sabha (Village Assembly) is most significant institution of accountability and transparency in India. Realising its significance, Ministry of Rural Development has made social audit through Gaon Sabha mandatory for flagship rural development programmes such as MGNREGA. Next important mechanism of transparency is display of schemes/programme details in panchayat notice board or in panchayat website. States like Karnataka have provided exclusive website for Panchayats. Publicity given to financial allocation to the panchayat, empowers the people with the information to hold panchayats accountable.

One of the most important innovations of the Rajasthan-based NGO MKSS has been the method of Jan Sunwais or Public Hearings where detailed documents derived from official expenditure records were read aloud to the people of the villages or constituents. Jan Sunwais are organised independent of the government but government officials are invited to attend. In the form of a hearing, people are invited to give their testimonies which often reveal differences between official records and people's experiences. Before the existence of the RTI Act, it was very difficult to access official records and not many Jan Sunwais could be organised. Many states in India have made it compulsory for panchayats to hold public hearings.

Social Audits are now widely accepted as an important mechanism that allows people to enforce accountability and transparency in government service delivery. It provides the end users an opportunity to scrutinise the procedures and benefits of development initiative. The states such as Kerala and Karnataka have developed some social audit mechanisms.

Electronic Media such as TV, Radio and Print Media such as vernacular newspapers could play an important role highlighting the omissions and commissions of Local government institutions as well as creating awareness among the people.

The researcher has made an attempt below to collect the perceptions of the people/constituents of both the local government institutions with regard to their assessment or usefulness of these mechanisms of transparency and accountability.

Table 17.1: Citizens Perception of Effectiveness of Transparency Mechanisms in Panchayats of Cachar district

	Not effective	*Moderately effective*	*Effective*	*Total*
Gaon Sabha		25 *(83)*	5 *(17)*	30 *(100)*
Display of Various programmes at the Panchayat office or in the website	20 *(67)*	7 *(23)*	3 *(10)*	30 *(100)*
Publication of the details of the allocation and expenditure of various programmes	25 *(83)*	5 *(17)*		30 *(100)*
Publication and Dissemination of prospective beneficiary list	21 *(70)*	9 *(30)*		30 *(100)*
Media, Newspapers, TV, newsletters	10 *(33)*	15 *(50)*	5 *(17)*	30 *(100)*
Social Audit	6 *(20)*	20 *(67)*	4 *(13)*	30 *(100)*

Source: Based on the field work in Panchayats. Figures in italics are in percentage.

Majority of the residents of panchayats are aware of the institution of Gaon Sabha. However, the people differ with regard to the effectiveness of this institution. Some people told that it is very rarely held and others opined that it is held as a ritual only to announce beneficiaries and as a mandatory requirement under MGNREGA. From the above table, it is clear that 83 per cent of the people reported that Gaon Sabha is moderately effective in their constituencies whereas only 17 per cent reported that it is effective. Thus, it is clear that majority of the people deem Gaon Sabha as an important institution. However, only 17 per cent perceive that it is effective because Sabha's are held without giving any publicity or its meetings are less than four times in a year. Moreover, all the decisions were taken in the panchayat meetings prior to holding Gaon Sabha's and Gaon Sabha meetings were held only to ratify these decisions. Hence, majority of the citizens evinced least interest in attending these meetings.

The display of various programmes at the panchayat office or in the website has been rated as not effective by 67 per cent of the people, 23 per cent reported moderately effective and only 10 per cent reported as effective. It was found by the researcher that only few panchayats had displayed details regarding different programmes in their display board and in Assam Gaon Panchayats and Anchalik Panchayats do not have their websites.

With regard to display of financial details 83 per cent revealed that it is not effective and only 17 per cent revealed that it is moderately effective. The researcher found that majority of the panchayats did not display details regarding financial allocations in the panchayat office but worksites displayed the source of funding and the allocation of money.

Dissemination of or publicity for prospective beneficiary list is a good practice adopted by Panchayats in states like Kerala. The wide publicity given to the prospective beneficiary list either in Gaon Sabha or elsewhere provides an opportunity for the people to scrutinise the list and to raise their objections. However, such a practice is rare in the panchayats of Cachar district.

Print Media and Electronic Media has penetrated the Barak valley. However, the media is not very active in highlighting the omissions and commissions of Panchayats or in exposing the reluctance of Assam state government in transferring more powers to panchayat raj institutions. Notwithstanding this, 17 per cent of the people said Media is effective and 50 per cent reported that it is moderately effective.

Social Audit mechanisms such as Jamabandhi in Karnataka and Local Government Ombudsman in Kerala are conspicuous by their absence in Cachar district of Assam. However, 13 per cent of the people felt that social audit through Gaon Sabha is very effective and 67 per cent felt that it is moderately effective.

Table 17.2: Citizens Perception of Effectiveness of Transparency Mechanisms in KAAC

	Not effective	*Moderately effective*	*Effective*	*Total*
Village Development Committee (VDC)	29*(63.04)*	17 *(36.96)*	———	46 *(100)*
Display of KAAC programmes at the office or in the website	10*(21.73)*	20 *(43.48)*	16*(34.78)*	46 *(100)*
Publication of the details of the allocation and expenditure of various programmes	5 *(10.87)*	26 *(56.52)*	15 *(36.61)*	46 *(100)*
Publication and Dissemination of prospective beneficiary list	———	20 *(43.48)*	26 *(56.52)*	46 *(100)*
Media, Newspapers, TV, newsletters	———	13*(28.26)*	33*(71.74)*	46 *(100)*
Social Audit	36*(78.26)*	10*(21.74)*	———	46 *(100)*

Source: Based on the field work in Karbi Anglong. Figures in italics are in percentage.

Gaon Sabha are conspicuous by their absence in Karbi Anglong district which is a sixth schedule area. VDC is a nominal body which exists to select beneficiaries and prioritise developmental works. However, there is no unanimity among the people with regard to composition, role and mandate of VDCs. It needs to be acknowledge here that in Tripura and Mizoram autonomous councils have popularly elected bodies at the grassroots level. Such a popularly elected bodies known as Village Committees and Village Councils respectively are supposed to be more accountable in comparison to autonomous councils of Assam which are yet to establish elected bodies at the grassroot level. In this regard the expert committee (Report of the Expert Committee, 2006) appointed to review the working of six schedule councils recommended that sixth schedule councils should replicate the democratic institutions established in Tripura and Mizoram in order to make these institutions more accountable and transparent.

The display of various programmes at the autonomous council office or in the website has been rated as effective by 37 per cent of the people and 57 per cent reported moderately effective. However, the zonal offices of Karbi Anglong autonomous council did not display any information. Hence, people living in far-flung regions were deprived of information with regard to government schemes.

With regard to display of financial details 35 per cent revealed that it is effective and only 44 per cent revealed that it is moderately effective, however, the remaining 22 per cent revealed that it is not effective. The researcher found that majority of the sub-zonal offices did not display details regarding financial allocations to their regions/areas. But worksites displayed the source of funding and the allocation of money.

Dissemination of or publicity for prospective beneficiary list has not been followed in Karbi Anglong district. However, 57 per cent said that if VDCs publicise beneficiary list it could be effective and the remaining 43 per cent opined that it might not be effective in council areas.

Karbi Anglong has a good presence of Print Media and Electronic Media. However, the media is not very active in highlighting the omissions and commissions of the council. Notwithstanding this, 72 per cent of the people said Media is effective and 28 per cent reported that it is moderately effective.

Social Audit mechanisms are completely absent in Karbi Anglong. Ministry of Rural Development scheme guidelines such as MGNREGA are silent with regard to social audit mechanism which needs to be adopted in sixth schedule areas where District Collector implements these schemes. The results show that 96 per cent of the people reported that social audit is absent in the council areas and four per cent revealed that social audit performed by VDCs is moderately effective.

Observations

(1) Gaon Sabha is an institution of social audit and public deliberation. However, the panchayats of Cachar district presents a very bleak picture. In majority of the panchayats Gaon Sabha's are not held minimum four times in a year and even if it is held its task is confined to announcing beneficiaries or works already decided in panchayat meetings. However, in comparison to Autonomous Councils Panchayats are in better position by having a deliberative body called Gaon Sabha. In order to strengthen social audit and accountability, there is urgent need to establish Panchayats or elected bodies at the grassroot level in the autonomous council areas.

(2) With regard to display of schemes and financial details, Autonomous council areas are better than Panchayats. But both the institutions of local governance lack in opacity when it comes to far-flung areas or sub-zonal offices.

(3) According to people, media is playing an important role in Karbi Anglong council areas in comparison to Cachar district Media perceptions of people. However, in both the places media is not very active in exposing graft and corruption.

(4) Although activity mapping has been officially promulgated in Assam, it has not been implemented in reality. Line Departments continue to dominate and panchayats do not have supervisory powers.

(5) Both Karbi Anglong Council and Cachar district panchayats are bereft of Social Audit mechanisms.

(6) It has been claimed by both KAAC and PRI representatives in Cachar as well as Karbi Anglong that the RTI is very powerful mechanism to bring transparency in the region. However, the majority of the citizens are not aware of RTI and those who file RTI are generally discouraged by officials by charging a huge amount in the name of photocopy and print.

(7) Both the Cachar Zilla Parishad and the KAAC have their official websites but they are hardly updated with topical and

important information such as financial statements, audited accounts and the names of the beneficiaries selected in particular scheme etc.

References

Gassah, L. S. (ed.) 1997. *'The Autonomous District Councils'*, New Delhi: Omson Publications.

Ghosh, B. K. (ed.) 2011. *'The Assam Panchayat Act with Rules'*, Guwahati: Assam Law House.

Hansaria, B. L. (revised by Vijay Hansaria), 2005. *Sixth Schedule to the Constitution.* New Delhi: Universal Law Publishing Co.

Moncrieffe Joy. M.2001. Accountability: Idea, Ideals and Constraints. *Democratisation*, Vol. 8, No. 3, pp. 26-50.

Paul, Samuel.1992. Accountability in Public Services. *World Development,* Vol. 20, No.7, pp. 1047-1060.

Report of the Expert Committee (2006). 'Planning for the Sixth Schedule Areas,' Ministry of Panchayat Raj, Government of India, New Delhi.

18

Panchayati Raj Institutions in Goa and Emerging Constraints for the Participation of People in Post 73rd Amendment Era

—*Aditi M. Rane*

"Our democracy cannot become strong unless the democracy at the village is strong. A broad consensus, cutting across party lines, has emerged over the past few years and it was realised that genuine development of rural areas can take place only through a process of decentralised planning and implementation fully involving the local people. To achieve this goal, we stand committed to the task of devolution of powers and financial resources to the Panchayati Raj Institutions enabling fullest participation of people in the process of nation building and development. "[1]

—*P. V. Narasimha Rao*

The quote speaks of the importance attached to the Panchayati Raj Institutions (PRIs) by the Congress government at the centre at the time of the 73rd Amendment to the Constitution of India in 1992. It also highlights the need for the local self-government to work as institutions for planning and development at the grassroots level. Much of the devolution of powers and resources had not taken place pre-73rd amendment era, though various state governments tried to fulfil the provisions made under Art. 40 of the Directive Principles and the recommendations of Balwantrai Mehta Committee as well as Asoka Mehta Committee which were appointed by the Central Government to investigate into the devolution of powers. Thus, the 73rd amendment was needed to constitutionalise the institutions of Panchayati Raj. The sole aim of this amendment was to achieve the evolution of powers by devolving funds, functionaries and finances to these local bodies in order to make them vibrant, self-reliant and functional.

As conformity legislation to the 73rd Amendment Act, the Goa Panchayati Raj Act was passed in 1994. The Act provides for the two-tier of Panchayati Raj Institutions; one at the village level and the second at the District level. Though the Congress government under Chief Ministership of Francisco Sardinha amended the Goa Panchayati Raj Act in 1999 to insert the provisions for the Taluka Panchayats[2], they have still not been constituted in Goa.[3] The paper will mainly focus on the Panchayati Raj Institutions in Goa after the 73rd amendment to the Constitution in 1992 by taking up a subaltern perspective. Subaltern approach makes us to listen and understand the voices of the people from below or at grassroots level. Since Panchayati Raj Institutions have to work at the grassroots level and the people at this level are affected by it, what these people feel about its working becomes more significant. Mere transfer of power (usually remain on the paper) to these local bodies is not sufficient what is actually required that these local bodies should be able to possess those powers and exercise them. Therefore, Subaltern perspective studies such voices of the people.

If one examines the Goa Panchayati Raj Act, 1994 and the provisions therein, one would look upon Goa as a torch-bearer state to the other states in India. However, the actual practice differs from the precept. In the initial amendments to the Goa Panchayati Raj Act, the secretary of the Panchayat, who is a paid clerk was given more powers than that of a Sarpanch, who is a representative of people.[4]

Goa, till date, has had four elections to the Village Panchayats and three elections to the Zilla Panchayats, under the Goa Panchayati Raj Act, 1994. Though Art. 243 K of part IX in the Constitution speaks of appointing a State Election Commission, Goa State Election Commission was constituted in 1999 i.e. five years after the passage of Goa Panchayati Raj Act and two years after the constitution of the first Village Panchayat in 1997.

Though the 73rd Amendment Act provides for free and fair elections to the PRIs, the constitution of the Election Commission for this purpose was entirely the state duty, with the powers for superintendence, direction and control of elections and preparation of electoral roll and the conduct of all Panchayat elections. Even today the State government's interference in the work of the State Election Commission is noticed at every Panchayat election in Goa. Goa still does not have an election authority with its own permanent staff, independent of the state government. Therefore, right from the first election in 1997 till today, the elections have not been conducted in a free and fair manner. The state government seems to be reluctant to address to controversies raised by the Goans at the time of elections and to find some suitable solutions to these problems. Every time, the elections to the Panchayats are held, the issue of faulty delimitation as well as the reservation of seats for women and reservation for ST and SC come to the fore. To quote Roland Martins, an activist and convenor of an NGO, GOACAN, "the major issue that is raised at every Panchayat election is that of delimitation. People living in an area which is not contiguous to the geographical area of the ward in question have been found to have been listed as the voters in another ward and vice-versa."[5]

The 73rd Amendment Act 1992, provides for the reservation of SC and ST candidates to these bodies at all the three levels in proportion to their population. This means that the wards reserved for SC and ST candidates may have very less population and this problem is exclusive in Goa. Durgadas Gaonkar, a teacher and activist from Corlim village Panchayat (Tiswadi Taluka, North Goa District) notes that "STs are then forced to contest elections from non-ST population ward or wards with negligible ST population and do not have the familiarity with the immediate ward concerns and this paves the way for MLAs men to get elected, even if it be an ST."[6] He points out that he has noticed this trend in Old Goa, Corlim, Carambolim and Cumharjua. (All in Tiswadi Taluka, North Goa District)

Even with regard to the reservation of seats for women, at the two levels of PRIs in Goa, are manipulated by some of the Sarpanchas (or even MLAs) who are close to the Ministers to change the number of wards so that those wards which are reserved for women can be changed in a particular manner as to be favourable to them.[7]

The elections to the Panchayat bodies in Goa have always come under criticism from the people of Goa due to the role played by Political Parties. Though, elections are not held on party basis and it is the individuals, who contest on their own strength, the BJP as well as the Congress have always claimed victories for their respective parties even before the counting of votes could end in the Panchayat elections in 2002.[8] Though, there had been a debate over the official involvement of Political Parties in the elections to the Panchayat bodies in India, West Bengal witnessed this phenomenon in the local elections of 4th June 1978, in which Communist Party of India-Marxist (CPI-M) and its allies preferred the official recognition of parties in the Panchayat elections. They believed that the direct involvement of Political Parties in the Panchayat institutions would make its leadership more disciplined and responsible in managing these institutions of rural democracy.[9]

Janata party in Karnataka also opined that if Political Parties are indispensable for Parliamentary democracy, is it not important that they must take root in the villages through the elections to the village bodies which are the nurseries of democracy.[10] Therefore, in the Panchayat elections of 2002 in Goa, BJP considered as an opportunity for the party to strengthen the organisation at the grassroots level. Further, it was also noticed that the panels owning allegiance to MLAs who were in the BJP have won. This trend has been seen in all the elections to the Panchayats in Goa. The party in power would always claim its victory in the elections be it Village Panchayats or Zilla Panchayats. For instance, in the elections to the Zilla Panchayats in 2005, the Congress Party which was in power announced that it got a majority in the North and South Goa Panchayats and was in a position to get its nominees elected to the post of Chairpersons. The Congress party opined that in the South Goa district, it bagged 16 of the 20 seats.[11] It is also believed that the local self-government system is more of a political base for the assembly elections than a functioning government and for the sake of development, it is ruling party's favoured candidate that ultimately assumes the office of Sarpanch.[12] Moving beyond the 73rd Constitutional Amendment framework, Panchayats have to be transformed from representative Political Institutions to Community Institutions.[13]

A kind of an elite rule is also seen in the elections to these panchayat bodies giving rise to a system of 'family Raj' (and not Panchayat Raj). When a particular ward was reserved for a woman, the man representing that ward earlier normally fielded his wife and if not married his sister or a relative. The idea in doing so was to keep control of the ward within the family.[14] Further, the geographical size of the villages and the Panchayats have given a rise to a trend that family members have been elected to the same Panchayats. Husband and wife teams have won in few, siblings in others and parents and children in others. For instance, in Santa Cruz Panchayat, (Bardez Taluka in North Goa District) there were four from a family that were elected which is considered as a record.[15] This, I believe, is a flagrant violation of the letter and spirit of 73rd amendment 1992 in Goa.

The 73rd Amendment Act to the Constitution in 1992 gives major responsibility to the states as the states have to decide what further powers and functions should be devolved to the Village Panchayats and other local authorities. It is stipulated in Art. 243 I of the 73rd Amendment that within one year from 25th April 1993 i.e. the date on which the Constitution 73rd Amendment Act came into force and afterwards every five years the State government shall appoint a Finance Commission to review the financial position of the Panchayats..., the first State Commission in Goa was constituted in February 1999, i.e. two years after the constitution of first Village Panchayats and one year prior to the constitution of Zilla Panchayats. Though the State Finance Commissions recommendations are not fully binding, there is an expectation of evolution of a convention to expeditiously accept and implement them as has been already developed for central finance commission for sharing and distribution of resources between the Centre and the States.[16]

In the case of Goa, the report submitted by the both State Finance Commissions in 1999 and 2007 for devolving finances to the Panchayat bodies have been sidelined and till the date no funds are devolved directly to the Village Panchayats. There is no political will for the transfer of finances to the PRIs and funds are transferred in structured ways, in the form of grants from the state governments[17] as well as special grants to weak Panchayats.[18]

The Political Parties in Goa promises devolution of power only in their manifesto at the time of state legislative elections but the actual devolution has not yet occurred. Similar is the case with the Powers and the Functions of Zilla Panchayats. When these bodies were constituted in 2000, these elected representatives were almost unaware of their powers and responsibilities as the organs of local self-government. Be it any party in power at the state level, political leadership was reluctant to share powers to these village Panchayats. In fact, Village Panchayats in Goa have very limited powers and no powers are given to the Zilla Panchayats. When asked about the powers of the elected representatives to the first Zilla Panchayats, the then Chief Minister of Goa, Francisco Sardinha said that the way an MLA has power to speak in the assembly, these representatives too have the same power to speak at their meetings.[19]

It was believed that after the constitution of Zilla Panchayats in Goa, State government will shed some of its duties to the two district assemblies allowing the MLAs more time to concentrate on legislative matters. But some of the MLAs felt that once the Zilla Panchayats are in place, legislative assembly will have very less work left to do and hence will lose importance. Therefore, instead of constituting Zilla Panchayats along with the Village Panchayats in 1997, they were indefinitely postponed. They were constituted in 2000 when the Goa Bench of Bombay High Court compelled the government to hold these elections.

The confusion over the powers and functions of Zilla Panchayats occurred due to the introduction of Taluka Panchayat by an amendment in 1999 as some of these powers belong to the Taluka Panchayats. To devolve powers to the local bodies, powers have to be shared by the Ministers of education, agriculture, health, public works department, village industries and a number of other departments which could be properly co-ordinated only by the Chief Minister.[20]

However, the devolution of powers and functions too is not limited to the XI Schedule which has an indicative list of 29 items and subjects for transfer to PRIs. The financial resources given to the Panchayats need not be limited to the devolution recommended by a State Finance Commission.[21] We cannot speak of devolution of more powers to these bodies in Goa, as what actually belongs to them are not devolved yet. The importance of the 73rd Amendment Act lies in the fact that the village Panchayats could play an important role in social transformation and implementation of development programmes could not be ignored easily.

It is provided in the Goa Panchayati Raj Act, 1994, that the decision taken by the Gram Sabha shall be binding on the Panchayat provided it is not contrary to the rules and regulations framed under this act or any other law for the time being in force and it shall be the duty of the Sarpanch to execute the same as early as possible. It also provides for the four regular meetings of Gram Sabha on any Sunday of January, April, July and October to be convened by the Sarpanch besides the Special Gram Sabha meetings to be convened on 26th January, 15th August, 2nd October and 19th December in Goa. In the initial years of the constitution of village panchayats in Goa, the percentage of attendance for the gram sabha meetings were comparatively less and there were many instances of meetings being adjourned for want of a quorum.

However, it is noticed now there have been rising voices in the Gram Sabha meetings against the corrupt practices of some of the Sarpanchas and Panchayat members. Especially in 2007-08, in every Gram Sabha conducted there were protest and dissents voiced by the citizens.

This is only because Panchayat administration is not transparent and is seen to be more pro-builders and pro-industrialists instead of being pro-people.[22]

As tourism industry started taking roots in Goa, construction of hotels, motels, guest-houses and huge building complexes started mushrooming in the villages. Builders and developers who needed construction licenses, occupancy certificates and other certificates started giving gifts in kind as well as in cash to Sarpanchas and Panchas in order to avoid delays in getting the licenses and certificates. Once this trend set in, then some Sarpanchas and Panchas started delaying the issuing of certificates or licenses purposely. The builders and developers had no option but to grease the palms of the Panchayat authorities to get their work done fast.

There were even the newspaper reports stating that now the Gram Sabhas are becoming 'Garam' (Hot) Sabhas as the people have started demanding the transparency and accountability in the Panchayat administration. For instance, on 26th January, 2007 at all Special Gram Sabha meetings in various Panchayats across Goa, resolutions were passed demanding the scrapping of Regional Plan 2011, Gram Sabhas showed a determined will to stop mega projects in Goa to save the environment of their villages and also the Goan identity. Similar was the case with Special Economic Zones. Because of strong Goan voice through the Gram Sabhas against SEZs, Goa Government had to bow down before the sentiments of the people and now SEZ are kept on hold.[23]

There have been a lot of problems faced by some of the village Panchayats in Goa. Declining water resources for drinking, domestic use and for farming and pollution of water bodies, garbage accumulation, sewage seepage, lack of proper electricity and now recently has been the issue of illegal mining. Further, the mega projects that have been established in some of the villages in Goa put pressure on the basic necessities and the Goans living nearby these projects get affected. For instance, the case of Colva Panchayat (Salcette Taluka, South Goa District) where 5000 more water connections have been given in the last five years.[24]

Different criterias are used to sanction some projects and not sanction others and also there is no Panchayat accountability in this regard. There have also been efforts with vested interest including some of MLAs not to hold regular Gram Sabha meetings. The topography of villages in Goa is changing towards construction and rapid urbanisation, thus resulting in garbage and sewage issues. There are hotels on the beaches in flagrant violation of CRZ regulations.

There have been some cases in Goa which has convincingly shown that when the government 'imposes' projects on the villages, it only arouses the hostility and resentment. Whether it was Nylon 6, 6 plant, the metatrips project, the Zuari Agro-chemicals or the allocation of river side areas for ship building yards, the local people have been aroused, even to the extent of becoming violent in their protest. The current agitations revolve around the wholesale sell out of land to land sharks in the name of I.T. Parks, Info-tech habitats or Special Economic Zones. It speaks very poorly of Government (Congress or BJP) when it 'imposes' development on the people without their consent or participation.[25]

With regard to the composition of Zilla Panchayats in Goa, Alexandre Barbosa is of the opinion that Goa with an area of 3702 sq. km and a population of less than 1.5 million with two modest districts does not require an institution such as the Zilla Panchayats. The entire state is like a city and creation of these new institutions is merely a burden on the exchequer.[26] This is actually true in case of Goa. Goa is over represented with two MPs to the Lok Sabha, one MP to the Rajya Sabha and with forty MLAs elected to the state assembly. Thus, there is no need of this tier to the small state like Goa.

The very purpose for which the 73rd Amendment Act 1992 to the constitution was carried out has not been fulfilled in Goa and not efficiently executed under the Goa Panchayati Raj Act. There are many challenges before these institutions in Goa in terms of devolution of powers and funds, the agenda that is taken up at the meetings of Gram Sabha meetings is also questionable, as sometimes personal rivalries are taken up as social issues, there is no accountability and transparency in the Panchayat administration and above all corruption is rampant. This has all led to the belief that these institutions of Panchayati Raj in Goa have become redundant.

Notes

1. Inagural address of the then PM, Shri P.V. Narasimha Rao, at the conference of Ministers and Secretaries in Charge of Panchayats of States and Union Territories on the Constitution (73rd Amendment Act), 1992, New Delhi, July 03, 1993.
2. See Goa Panchayati Raj Act, 1994 with the amendments in 1999.
3. This is mainly because population of Goa is about 15 lakhs and the constitution of Taluka Panchayats are optional for the states having less than 20 lakh population.
4. Goa Today, January 1997.

5. Almeida, Albertina, "*Quo Vadis Panchayat Raj*" in Goa Today, May, 2012.
6. *Ibid.*
7. Goa Today, January 1997.
8. Barbosa, Alexandre, "*Panchayat Polls 2002, Booster for BJP?*" in Goa Today, February 2002.
9. Palanithurai, G. (Ed) (2000), *Dynamics of New Panchayat Raj in India,* Concept Publishing Co. New Delhi, p. 18.
10 *Ibid*, p. 19.
11. Goa Today, April 2005.
12. Barbosa, Alexandre, "*Panchayat Polls 2002, Booster for BJP?*" in Goa Today, February 2002.
13. Fernandes, Aureliano (2008), *Panchayatantra: Empowering Local Governance Through Role Definition*, University Book House, Jaipur, p. 3.
14. Cardoza, Tomazina, "Mapping Out Goa's Panchayati Raj" in Goa Today, June 2012.
15. Barbosa, Alexandre, "*Panchayat Polls 2002, Booster for BJP*?" in Goa Today, February 2002.
16. Buch, Nirmala, *Let the Sun Shine on the Grassroots Too: 73rd Constitutional Amendment, Story of Implementation and Deviations*, in Bandopadyay, D and Mukherjee, A (2004), *New Issues in Panchayati Raj*, Concept Publishing Company, New Delhi, p. 97.
17. During the year 2002-03, an amount of Rs. 615 lakh was released to 123 Panchayats @ Rs. 5 lakh per Panchayat Grants for payment of salaries and allowances to sarpanch, Dy. Sarpanch and other members of Panchayats.
18. For example, in 2002-03, special grants were released by state government to village panchayats having an annual income of less than 3 lakh. See Economic Survey, 2003-04, Directorate of Planning, statistics and Evaluation, Government of Goa.
19. Barbosa, Alexandre, "*Stalemate After The Polls*" in Goa Today, March 2000.
20. Palanithurai, G. (Ed) (2000), *Dynamics of New Panchayat Raj in India*, Vol. II Select States, Concept Publishing Co. New Delhi, p. 24.
21. Buch, Nirmala, *Let the Sun Shine on the Grassroots Too: 73rd Constitutional Amendment, Story of Implementation and Deviations*, in Bandopadyay, D and Mukherjee, A (2004), *New Issues in Panchayati Raj*, Concept Publishing Company, New Delhi, p. 97.
22. Cardozo, Tomazinho, "*Goa, Then and Now*" in Goa Today, November 2011.
23. Cardozo, Tomazinho, "*Peoples' Power is Supremein A Democracy*" in Goa Today, July 2008
24. Almeida, Albertina, "*Quo Vadis Panchayat Raj*" in Goa Today, May 2012.
25. Cardozo, Tomazinho, "*Peoples' Power is Supreme in A Democracy*" in Goa Today, July 2008.
26. Barbosa, Alexandre L, "*Stalemate After The Polls*" in Goa Today, March 2000.

19

Two Decades of Democratic Decentralisation in India: Issues and Challenges

—Ch. Bala Ramulu

Introduction

Democratic decentralisation has been a matter of great concern in India both at the conceptual and implementation levels despite the passage of more than five decades of Panhayatti Raj Institutions (PRIs). The foremost concern of these institutions is that they have to operate in conformity with the constitutional mandate and in the broader societal context. They have to address the major challenges of Indian society such as elimination of poverty, unemployment, inequalities, etc to establish an egalitarian society. Another concern of decentralised institutions is impact of the globalised economy on the developmental policies and institutions of governance. The public policies, concepts, norms and institutions, technology, capital, resources, of late, are globalised. The Indian state has little freedom to modify the norms of the policies/projects as most of them are financially and technically supported by the International Governmental Organisations (IGOs). In a way it amounts to 'globalisation of democratic power' (formulation of policies) which ought to rest with the people. In this context, democratic decentralisation process appears to be a 'myth'.

The 73rd Constitutional Amendment Act (CAA), 1992, which came into operation from 1993, is considered an important landmark in the democratic decentralisation process as it accorded Constitutional status to rural local institutions. The implicit intention of the amendment is that the rural local institutions should have a functional domain of their own and such domain has to be constructed by transferring some functions of the state government (29 subjects mentioned in the Eleventh and Twelfth Schedules) to the rural local institutions and the latter should have full autonomy to discharge those functions. But the experience of with 73rd CAA, 1992, during the past two decades indicates that many state governments have not enforced the true spirit of the Act. It is time to examine the causes and consequences of the implementation of the Act and suggest way forward for making the decentralised institutions worthy for development.

The present study is presented in four sections. Section I deals with the update on PRIs which would give us insight on the subject. The context of enacting 73rd CAA, 1992 and core issues of democratic decentralisation process is presented in Section II and III, respectively. Section IV sets the conclusions of the study.

Section - 1

Update on PRIs

The Indian Constitution envisages the decentralisation process to be a State subject, while the Central government devolves powers and finance to the state governments and if necessary amend the Constitution to make local governments more self-reliant. The Central government, during the last six and a half decades, initiated measures to devolve powers to the State governments and in turn to the local institutions. The Former Prime Minister Jawaharlal Nehru visualised that moving decisively towards participatory development as distinct from bureaucratically-delivered, development is important for reducing poverty and inequalities. At the inauguration of Panchayati Raj in Nagpur on 2 October 1959, Nehru said,

"To uplift lakhs of villages is not an ordinary task...The reason for the slow progress is our dependence on official machinery. An officer is probably necessary because he is an expert. But this work can be done only if the people take up the responsibility in their own hands...The people are not merely to be consulted. Effective power has to be entrusted to them...Real change comes, of course, from within the village, from the very people living in the village, and is not imposed from outside", (Quoted by Keshva Dev Gaur, 1992).

Since the Congress party ruled many States Nehru's voice prevailed in decision-making circles all the governments fell smartly into line with the directive that they make appropriate legal provisions for Panchayati Raj. With a lot of enthusiasm and fanfare, democratic elections on the basis of universal adult suffrage and one person-one vote principle, led to the establishment of PRIs across rural India. Thus, without altering a comma in the Constitution, Panchayati Raj was decreed all over the country. During the decade of 1957–67 the polity of the nation as a whole was brought into conformity with the regime of Panchayati Raj (Manishaka Iyar, 2011). In many states, PRIs enjoyed autonomy in managing their surroundings, as many of the subjects like agriculture and its allied subjects and functionaries for discharging these subjects were placed under PRIs. They, in fact, to a greater extent, influenced the national and state level politics, as the PRIs were controlled by Upper Castes and landed gentry, especially landlords. The persons, who were contesting the positions of Members of Legislative Assembly or Members of Parliament, were dependent on the support of the then panchayat leadership and the latter support or non-support to the former made all the difference. But from 1990s' onwards this situation has reversed. As the OBCs and weaker sections entered these institutions through reservation or open competition many State governments either curtailed or withdrew the powers, funds and functionaries of PRIs. The MLAs/MPs are controlling the day-to-day functioning of PRIs and it is described as MLA RAJ not PANCHAYAT RAJ. (Bala Ramulu, Ch, and Ravinder, D, 2012).

A glance at the role of the Panchayati Raj Institutions (PRIs) in addressing the core issues of development, especially during the last two decades of Post 73rd Constitutional Amendment Act, 1992, reveals mixed opinion. The government reports and advocates of PRIs applaud their contribution for the emergence of new leadership especially among marginalised communities at the grassroots levels, enhancement of their management skills, participation in the decision-making and implementation of policies, creation of infrastructure for development and delivery of services to the people etc. But the critics of PRIs argue that infrastructure and services constitute only a means for development but they can not be indicators of inclusive growth reducing inequalities. In an unequal socio-economic system as in rural India, these facilities will be cornered-off by the relatively better off sections of the society and the poor would be neglected in the development process (Hara Gopal, G and Bala Ramulu, Ch.1988, 1989, and 2012). Further the critics maintain that the working of PRIs is in no way different from that of government departments, as they act as the field agencies of the central and state governments in implementing the schemes. These tendencies indicate that the very purpose of creation of PRIs is defeated.

One can not, however, undermine the role of PRIs in resolving the problems of rural people. The pointers like improvement in legislation or institutional design, attitudinal changes treating PRIs as their equal partners in governance of the country, active participation of people, especially the marginalised sections in decision-making, etc, would progressively enhance the governance of PRIs. The proper way to understand CAA, 1992 is to comprehend and analyse the context and socio-economic and political compulsions that obligated the policy granting of constitutional status to the PRIs and its consequences for development.

Section - II

The Context of Constitutional Amendment Act (CAA), 1992

The circumstances that compelled the Indian state to consider granting constitutional status to PRIs were: (i) failure of public policies to address the issue of elimination of poverty and inequalities in the society, especially in hinterland; (ii) instability of National polity and centralisation of power; (iii) emergence of regional political parties and demand for greater autonomy from the centre; (iv) the emergence of new middle class, contractors, pyraveekars and their aspirations to have a share in the power at the state level and grass-roots level; (v) legitimising the power structure of ruling class; (vii) influence of IGOs in the formulation of policies and governance and (vi) New Economic Reforms which led to globalisation of capital, technology and resources.

Public Policies

The Democratic Decentralisation has to be understood in the broader context of nature of development policies. The public policies are two types: One, the policies which can touch the structure; and policies which are of incremental character. The policies like land reforms, if enforced effectively, can affect the ownership of means of production and lead to certain structural changes. The policies like- Pensions to old-aged people, widows, physically challenged persons; scholarships to the students, fee-reimbursement to the students; foodgrain distribution at subsidised rate; subsidy based anti-poverty programmes etc, lead to incrementalism and provide some immediate relief to the deprived sections without affecting the basic socio-economic structure of the society. Today, Indian State is undermining the structural change policies and opting for incremental policies. Therefore, even if the 29 subjects are transferred to PRIs, their role would be limited as the policies are incremental. The reduction of poverty and inequalities through incremental approach either by national, state governments or PRIs would only serve limited purpose.

Though the strategies of Growth with Trickle Down and Green Revolution launched during 1950s and 1960s contributed to increase the agricultural production, they also resulted in widening the inequalities between the rich and the poor and different regions. These strategies also helped the Indian monopoly houses, particularly those collaborating with the Multinational Corporations. Instead of bringing structural changes, the State initiated incremental policies and created Special Agencies/ institutions such as Small Farmer Development Agencies and Marginal Farmers and Agricultural Labour Development Agencies (1969), to cover about eighty per cent of rural population. But these institutions were kept outside umbrella of PRIs. This was a serious lapse on the part of the Central and State Governments for not placing the special agencies under the purview of PRIs (Bala Ramulu, Ch, 1984).

Instability of National Polity

The Fourth General Elections in early 1967 saw a dramatic transformation in the national polity with the emergence of non-Congress governments resulting in great instability within the leadership of the Indian National Congress. Indira Gandhi consolidated her position within her Party and the country at large by a process of concentration of political and administrative power that inevitably meant more centralisation than more decentralisation. During the subsequent two decades (1970-1990), PRIs in India went through a phase of crisis. This phase was described as "whimsical Panchayati Raj. " Elections were conducted as per the whims and fancies of the government. Elected local self-government institutions were not allowed to take office or dismissed soon after their oath of office or indefinitely extended, to suit the political compulsions of the State governments concerned. Similarly, powers were endowed, withdrawn or ignored to suit the higher political echelon.

Emergence of Regional Political Parties

The growth process also contributed for emergence of Regional Political Parties in different states. State governments raised the voice against the centralisation of power and demanded for more autonomy and powers to the state governments. For instance, Sri N. T. Rama Rao Former Chief Minister of Andhra Pradesh and President of Telugu Desam Party went to the extent of describing the Central Government as a 'myth' and the State Government as a 'reality' for development. The Indian National Congress, which was known as 'dominant mass political party' since the Independence of the country for about two decades, could not stomach the situation and tried to establish direct rapport with the district administration and local organisations ignoring/bypassing the state governments.

As a part of the strategy, the Central Government made the District Collector/ Project Officers in-charge of the special agencies or developmental programmes and also transferred the budget directly to the district administration to regain the rapport with the rural masses. Former Prime Minister of India Late Sri Rajiv Gandhi directly addressed a letter to all the political executives of rural local bodies about the need for their active role in the implementation of the schemes. But the State governments, particularly ruled by opposition parties protested against this act and directed the district authorities not to distribute the letter to the political executives of the PRIs. This conflict has affected the functioning of PRIs.

Emergence of New Middle Class

The development process of the country also resulted in the emergence of new middle class- contractors, pyraveekars and raised the aspirations of these groups to have a share in the power at the state level and grass-roots level across the states. The national and regional political parties which are controlled by the powerful social groups and landed gentry, during 1970's and 1980's, made efforts to co-opt the middle and lower middle classes and social groups for their political support. Instead of focusing on the issues of poverty, unemployment and inequalities, the higher level governments resorted to accommodating the relatively better-off among the poor by creating new institutions/positions at the grass-roots level and thereby curtailing the unrest among the poor. For instance, the TDP Government introduced reforms to the PR Act in 1986 which created new levels (four tier systems) and expansion of position/units of PRI. The Government has created 1104 Mandal Parishads – an inter-mediate unit – by abolishing 330 Panchayat Samities in the state. It also created new positions like Members of Mandal Parishad Territorial Constituencies and Members of Zilla Parishad Territorial Constituencies (Bala Ramulu, Ch, Ravinder, D, 2008). But these positions turned out to be ornamental because of establishment of four-tier body called "District Planning and Development Review Council" consisting of Minister, MLAs, and District Collector and District Officials, and was entrusted with powers to advise and review the developmental actives of PRIs.

New Economic Reforms

The economic and political situation/crises, within and outside the country, during late 1980's weakened the autonomy of the Indian State at all levels of governance, including that of self-governing institutions. The severe economic crises, demand for reservation to Other Backward Classes (OBCs) in the Central Government, the effects of Gulf War on world economy, the collapse of Communism in USSR and East Europe, and imposition of Washington consensus etc compelled the Government of Indian to accept World Bank, International Monetary Fund directed structural adjustment programme – New Economic Reforms (NER). The reforms (1991) laid emphasis on globalisation of the economy through a process of abolition of import control over all items, privatisation of public sector and adoption of a better market economy to determine the pattern of investment and output. The reforms consisted of two broad aspects i.e., one, Macro-economic reforms and two, non-economic reforms. The latter emphasised the protection of human rights, social safety measures and democratic decentralisation. As a part of this package, the 73rd CAA 1992, National Human Rights Commission, 1993 and Voluntary Retirement Scheme etc, came into existence or operation (Bala Ramulu, Ch, and Narashima Rao, 2011). Therefore, the enactment of 73rd CAA 1992 also has to be understood in the context of the package of NERs.

The experience with the NERs reveals that the state is withdrawing its socio-economic responsibilities and assigning them to the private sector, or operating through public-private partnership. Its main intention is to earn profit rather serve the people. The subjects, which are assigned to the PRIs through CAA, 1992, are also privatized. This has limited the role of PRIs in the development process.

Section - III

The Issues and Challenges of PRIs

The experience with the functioning of PRIs reveals that basic problems elude solutions even to date. The institutions are becoming weakened mostly due to the following issues.

Devolution of Powers and Functions

Many State Governments has not delegated powers and functions to the PRIs in the true spirit of 73rd CAA, 1992. Even if the functions have been delegated, the required powers to execute the said functions are not with the PRIs. As a result, the delegation of powers and function has taken place on paper the PRIs actually are not in a position to perform the expected role. The major reasons for this state of affairs are: increasing suspicion of the state level leadership about the PRIs and their functionaries; the overall tendency of centralisation of power in

Indian Polity; growing socio-economic crises resulting in political instability at national level and inability of the central government to direct the state governments to devolve powers and functions to the PRIs; general reluctance on the part of bureaucracy to share their existing powers and authority with the newly elected PRIs; formation of SHGs to accommodate them at the local level; privatisation of public services like health, education, drinking water supply by PRIs; non-release of grants by the State and also inadequate financial resources to the PRIs; absence of conscious political support to the local leadership to bring pressure on the state government to devolve powers, etc. All these individually and collectively made the PRIs make ornamental bodies (Bala Ramulu, Ch, Ravinder, D, 2012).

Devolution of Financial Powers

The legislature of a State may by law-(a) empower panchayats (Article 243H) to levy several taxes, subject to the approval of state government; (b) provide for making such grants-in-aid to the panchayats from the Consolidated Fund of the State; (c) constitute State Finance Commission (SFC) to review the financial position of the PRIs and make recommendations for granting money to the PRIs. It is believed that these measures would make the PRIs financially independent and self-reliant and monitor expenditure to fulfill the locally-felt needs.

In addition to the above, many of the State Governments have agreed to give PRIs a specific percentage of share in some of the state taxes like land revenue and cess on it, additional stamp duty, entertainment tax, royalties on minerals and mines, forest revenue and market fee. But these taxes are less buoyant in nature and have no relation to the powers and functions to be devolved across panchayats. More buoyant taxes like sales tax and excise are kept outside the PRIs. Moreover, the SFC reports have paid less attention to the issues of autonomy, financial management and auditing procedures. The main deficiency of reports lies in the fact that the recommendations are not based on a clear statement of spending responsibilities of local bodies. Indeed the absence of attention to the elementary principle that expenditure assignment must precede any tax or revenue assignment has made most of the SFC's recommendations suspect. In certain states, the State Governments are not constituting SFC's immediately after the expiry of the term of SFC (Oommen, MA (2010); Gopinath Reddy, M, 2013).

The major problem with the state government is non-release of grants in time to the PRIs or and assigning inadequate financial resources to the

PRIs. It is pertinent to mention here the comment made by the Former Home Minister. "We may create organisations, delegate powers and functions to the lower levels of the organisation, but in the absence of providing adequate finance to lower level bodies, it is something like decorating dead man." This comment is equally applicable in the case of PRIs as they do not have adequate finance to perform its duties and responsibilities. In Andhra Pradesh, there are several instances where the local leadership threatened to resign their positions for not keeping their promises to the people due to lack of sufficient financial powers. The local leadership, particularly Gram Sarpanches remarked that 'Paisalu Lenidi Padavulu Enduku', which means 'what is the use of holding positions without money for discharging their duties', thus making the panchayat leadership 'decorated statues', ornamental bodies of the government.

Devolution of Functionaries

Even after the two decades of 73rd CAA, 1992, the State Governments continues to dominate PRIs through the district bureaucracy. At the district level the District Collector/Deputy Commissioner remains a key person for governing and administering the subjects mentioned in Eleventh Schedule and also the activities of Centrally Sponsored Schemes (CSSs). The common response from most of the top officials at the state and district levels is that the present role given to the PRIs is more than adequate and there is no need for devolving any further powers to them. There has been resistance from the Government across many states for transferring functionaries to PRIs. In some cases states have even reversed such transfers. This is more so since 1990's onwards, the period of new economic reforms. The state governments gradually withdrew the services of officials, who were working on deputation in PRIs defeating the very spirit of Act (Bala Ramulu, Ch, and Ravinder, D, 2008).

On the other hand, the State governments are not allowing/granting powers to the PRIs to recruit the functionaries of their own. Today, the PRIs have skeleton staff and that too appointed through outsourcing method or contract basis. These functionaries do not have proper human resource policy and thus lack the commitment to carry out the activities. It is pertinent to mention here that, in the initial stages of PRIs i.e., from 1959 to 1989 all the functionaries of development sectors working at the intermediary panchayat levels and below, except the law and order and revenue departments, were placed under the supervision and control of the PRIs. This was the period when landed gentry of the villages occupied the positions of PRIs. (Bala Ramulu, Ch, and Ravinder, D, 2012).

Peoples' Participation

The basic philosophy of democratic decentralisation is to ensure peoples participation. Here participation has two dimensions i.e. passive participation and active participation of people. The passive participation includes: involving people in actions that have been thought out, designed and controlled by government or higher level bureaucracy. The government generally makes use of governing elite (the party in power), administrative structures, mass media and non-governmental organisations (NGOs) as techniques for ensuring participation of people in the developmental process. The state uses these techniques to a limited extent and that too to serve their interests. It is true at all levels of government, including PRIs.

But the real democratic decentralisation is possible only when there is active participation of people in identification of the problems, fixing the priorities in the planning, decision-making, implementation, evaluation and sharing of benefits or managing the local organisation. There are several instances where the government undermined the people's active participation, especially when the poor organise themselves and identify the issues, priorities of the people and try to manage their surroundings (Bala Ramulu, Ch, 2002).

Management of Natural Resources

One of the major activities of PRIs is to manage the natural resources/ capital judicially and equitably. But the experience indicates that many gram panchayat pradhans or up-pradhans and rural elite are becoming powerful with the support of musclemen by grabbing land and resources meant for the welfare of the people they represent. This phenomenon is more frequent in the state-led development projects involving the PRIs. Inevitably, a tussle begins for a share in the contracts linked with these projects. The pressure brought on by greed to control resources is leading to ugly and violent clashes in all parts of the country. It has been observed by the scholars that state-led democracy and violence are deeply interlinked (Badri Narayana, 2013).

The Special Economic Zone (SEZ) Policy of the State is exploiting the natural resources- land, water, forest- of the villages and PRIs are losing its power over managing natural resources. The corporate sector with the support of the police, bureaucracy and politicians are managing the PRIs' leaders either by bribing and threatening or by financing the local leaders to contest the elections.

Centrally Sponsored Schemes

The Centrally Sponsored Programme (CSS) are conceived by the Government of India under the provision of Article 282 of the Indian Constitution, with a view to making the grants available to the states to tackle the problems of national importance. The CSSs, which emerged initially to look at the issues of national importance and inter-state nature, subsequently have been extended to cover wide range of issues across the sectors and social groups, especially from the introduction of Economic Reforms. These programmes were mostly promoted with the technical and financial support of International Organisations (IGOs). Though the support of donor agencies/IGOs to the development projects/CSS is based on human and ethical grounds, it has implications to the democratic decentralisation in the country. The guidelines for implementation of CSS are formulated by Central government as per the directions of IGOs or donor agencies and the state governments and local bodies/PRIs have little or no autonomy to modify the guidelines, even if they are not feasible at the ground level (Garg, SC, 2006). The major issues that are associated with CSS are: ever increasing number of CSSs and fund allocation to them seen as potent threat Indian Federalism; sanction and release of conditional grants of CSS by the Central Government to the state governments undermining their role; the method of direct release of funds under many of the CSSs to district authorities or special agencies, which are managed by bureaucracy, amounting to bypassing the state governments and PRIs; overlapping of the programmes undertaken under CSSs subjects allotted to PRIs under Eleventh Schedule; the top-down approach in the planning of CSS is contradictory to the plans prepared by District Planning Committees/undermining Powers of PRIs to emerge as institutions of self-government especially to prepare and implement plans for economic development and social justice (IRMA, 2008).

The Eleventh Plan highlighted that several of CSSs have not generated the results commensurate with allocations. The plan attributes the poor results attained by the schemes to factors like their inadequate convergence, rigid and inconsistent design and approach, and weak professional support. In a similar tone, the expert group on grassroots planning argued that the CSSs are even coming in the way of real emergence of decentralised planning (GOI, 2006). In the process, the panchayats have been compelled to act merely as agents for channelising the funds of CSSs rather than emergence as empowered institutions for development planning. The Eleventh Plan calls for radically altering the guidelines and structure of

CSSs by giving a pivotal role to PRIs in their planning and implementation of CSSs (GoI, 2008).

Parallel Institutions

Along with the PRIs, the parallel bodies/agencies such as special agencies and self-help groups (SHGs) are considered an important strategy for ensuring peoples' participation in the development process at the grass-roots level since 1995. This approach is also coined as participatory approach to development, advocated by the World Bank. The World Bank report on the "State in the Changing World" reveals that development is not just about getting the right or appropriate economic and technical inputs but also creation of effective institutional environment.

As part of the participatory approach to development, the governments have been assigning the developmental programmes or CSS including the subjects mentioned in IXth Schedule to the parallel institutions, especially women SHGs, ignoring the PRIs. Though the achievements of SHGs, to some extent, are laudable in certain states like Andhra Pradesh, the overall assessment of formation of SHGs indicates that it is in no way different to that of any government department/s. The major problems are: guided and controlled by the government SHGs do not have autonomy in preparing the plans and implementation of the programmes; the political parties are using SHGs to accommodate the persons, who are politically unemployed, and also using them as field agents in securing votes in the elections; the persons, who have no knowledge about the activities of SHGs, are becoming the chairmen/members of the groups; prevalence of corruption in executing the schemes; the real beneficiaries are the political party workers, contractors, pyraveekars, instead of the members of the group. (Balaramulu Ch, 2002 and 2003).

Planning

As per Article 243G of CAA, 1992, the PRIs are entrusted with the responsibility of preparing micro-plans for economic development in their respective jurisdiction, beginning at panchayat level. These institutions are also responsible for implementation of the schemes aimed at socio-economic development and exercise of powers delegated in respect of 29 subjects as prescribed in IXth Schedule of the Constitution. The flow of funds for economic development would be based on the plans prepared by the respective bodies of PRIs. For about a decade, many state governments have not paid adequate attention to constitute District Planning Committees (DPC) to consolidate the rural and urban local organisations' plans and prepare the Integrated District Plan. Looking at this scenario the Government of India insisted on the state governments to constitute the DPC, failing which the rural/urban bodies would forego the financial assistance from Central Government to the development projects, such as Backward Regions Grant Fund.

However, the major problems of the DPCs are: lack of reliable information and lack of technical personnel to prepare the district plan. The DPC consists mostly of non-officials who do not have the technical knowledge even to scrutinise the plans prepared by the experts; and in many cases, the DPC meets only to fulfill the norm of getting funds from the central government.

Inclusive Governance for Inclusive Growth

The imperative of Inclusive Growth has been grasped both in 11th and 12th Five Year Plans, but the imperative of Inclusive Governance has been barely incorporated into the conception and implementation of programmes for inclusion, equity and social justice. The Deputy Chairman of the Planning Commission (on the eve of finalisation of approach to the Twelfth Five-Year Plan (2012-17) underlined the point that while the economy had performed spectacularly on GDP growth rates, the single biggest failure of the Eleventh Plan (2007-12) had been the failure to secure "inclusive growth" notwithstanding the exponential increase in Central government funds made available to States under some 139 CSS. He attributed the failure of translating dramatically augmented outlays into commensurate outcomes to "management failures" on the part of the States. The critical systemic fault originates in the present practice of policy formulation and implementation at the state, district and Panchyat levels. Over a hundred social sector and poverty alleviation Centrally Sponsored Schemes (CSS) are implemented by separate agencies for each scheme operating through parallel bodies or line departments set up by the Central and State government bureaucracy in collaboration with civil society organisations. In consequence, the beneficiaries remain hapless recipients of government/NGO largesse instead of actively participating in designing the schemes, adapting them to local community priorities and being effectively in charge of supervision, guidance and disciplinary action. In these circumstances, it is hardly surprising that Gram Sabhas (village assemblies) are reduced to hapless spectators and rubber-stamps instead of providing "advice and consent" to the elected panchayat executive as is the democratic requirement when the executive is held responsible to the people (Manishankar Iyar, 2012).

The Way Forward

Even if we presume that the 73rd CAA, 1992 has the capacity to tackle the problems at the grassroots level, there is a need to address the following issues and challenges at the implementation level. They are: the demand for implementation of 73rd CAA in its true spirit; ensuring people's active participation in decision-making, protection of natural resources and use them for sustainable development, strengthening the planning process, adopting inclusive governance for inclusive development, appointment of competent functionaries, modification of guidelines of CSS suitable to local conditions, elimination of poverty and inequalities, etc.

Enforcement of Act in its letter and spirit would resolve some of these issues and ensure desired changes in the socio-economic structure of rural India. Therefore, the primary responsibility of the Central and State Governments is to rise to its constitutional responsibilities under Parts IX and IXA of the Constitution to devolve powers, functions, funds, functionaries to PRIs and make them as the centrality in planning and implementation of developmental programmes and CSSs. A bare mention of modifying guidelines in the plan documents is not enough. What is required is political will and the investment of political capital to alter/ change the existing inequalities. A pro-active role by the Central and State governments could make a significant difference to the more efficient and effective delivery of public goods and services to the poor and vulnerable to provide for a measure of equity in the face of inescapable widening of inequalities in income and wealth promoted by the present high-growth model.

The holistic approach for implementing in letter and spirit of the provisions of the CAA, 1992 in any given State, is to put into practice Inclusive Governance for inclusive growth- primary education, primary health, including nutrition, the provision of potable drinking water, total sanitation, housing for all, food security, minor irrigation, village infrastructure and several other subjects listed in the Eleventh Schedule. In the absence of Inclusive Governance, the intended beneficiaries of poverty alleviation programmes are left abjectly dependent on a bureaucratic delivery mechanism over which they have no effective control. It is appropriate to paraphrase the argument that "Panchayat Raj has failed; Panchayat Raj must succeed."

References

Badrinarayana (2013): 'Democracy and Violence', *Economic and Political Weekly*, Vol. XLVIII, No.14, April 6, p. 14.

Bala Ramulu, Ch. (2004): *'Development Policy and Governance in India from 1947 to 2003'*, Indian Journal of Public Administration, New Delhi, Vol. L, January-March, No. 1.

———(2003): *'Water Resource Management: Reforms in Andhra Pradesh'*, Indian Journal of Public Administration, New Delhi, Vol. LIX, July-Dec, No. 3.

———(2002): *'Participatory Development: The Experience of Andhra Pradesh'*, Indian Journal of Public Administration, New Delhi, Vol. XLVIII, Oct-Dec, No. 4.

———(1991): *'Public Policies: An Evaluation of Integrated Rural Development Programme'*, Ajantha Publications, New Delhi.

———(1984): *'Administration on Anti-Poverty Programme (A study of SFDA)'*, Kakatiya School of Public Administration, Warangal.

Balaramulu, Ch, Ravinder, D (2012): *'Five Decades of Democratic Decentralisation Process in Andhra Pradesh'* Social Change, Vol. 42, No. 2, Journal of CSD, Sage Publications.

———(2008): *Governance of Panchyats in Andhra Pradesh: The Need for Revitalisation:* Indian Journal of Public Administration, New Delhi, Vol. LIV, No.1, January-March.

Cited in Keshav Dev Gaur (1992): 'Dynamics of Rural Development', Chapter 7, Panchayat Raj Institutions for Democracy and Development, Mittal Publications, New Delhi, p. 100.

Government of India (2006): 'Planning at the Grass-roots level: An Action Programme for the Eleventh Five Year Plan', *Report of the Export Group*, New Delhi; Ministry of Panchayat Raj.

———(2008): 'Eleventh Five Year Plan, 2007-12', Volume 1, *Inclusive Growth*, New Delhi, Planning Commission.

Garg, SC, (2006): 'Transformation of Central Grants to States: Growing Conditionality and bypassing State Budgets', *Economic and Political Weekly*, 41 (48, pp. 4977-84).

Gopinath Reddy, M. (2012): 'Fiscal Transfer to Local Bodies-Andhra Pradesh Experience', paper presented at the National Seminar, on *Centre-State Relations in Indian Fiscal Context*, held on 5-6th November, 2012.

Hara Gopal, G and Bala Ramulu,Ch (1989): *'Poverty Alleviation Programmes: IRDP in Andhra Pradesh District'*, Economic and Political Weekly, Vol. XXIV, Nos. 35 and 36.

———(1988): *'Structural Changes'*, *Journal of Seminar*, 347, July.

Institute of Rural Management Anand (2008-09): 'State of Panchayats Report', Volume-I Centrally Sponsored Schemes and Panchayats: Issues and Evidence, Sponsored by Ministry of Panchayat Raj, Govt. of India, p. 13.

Manishankar Aiyar (2011): 'Inclusive Governance for Inclusive Development: The History, Politics and Economics of Panchayat Raj', unpublished paper.

Oommen, M A (2010): 'Have the State Finance Commissions Fulfilled Their Constitutional Mandates?' *Economic & Political Weekly*, 30, July pp. 24-3.

Index